Deleuze *on Music, Painting, and the Arts*

Deleuze *on Music, Painting, and the Arts*

RONALD BOGUE

Routledge
New York and London

Published in 2003 by
Routledge
29 West 35th Street
New York, NY 10001
routledge-ny.com

Published in Great Britain by
Routledge
11 New Fetter Lane
London EC4P 4EE
routledge.co.uk

10 9 8 7 6 5 4
Cataloging-in-Publication Data is available from the Library of Congress

ISBN 0-415-96607-8 (hb)
ISBN 0-415-96608-6 (pb)

For my son
Curtis

Contents

Abbreviations

All translations from Deleuze, Guattari, and Deleuze-Guattari are my own. For works that have appeared in English translation, citations include page numbers of the original French edition followed by the page numbers of the corresponding passages in the English translation.

AO   Deleuze and Guattari. *L'Anti-Oedipe: Capitalisme et schizophrénie I.* Paris: Minuit, 1972. Trans. Robert Hurley, Mark Seem, and Helen R. Lane under the title *Anti-Oedipus* (Minneapolis: University of Minnesota Press, 1977).

CC   Deleuze. *Critique et clinique.* Paris: Minuit, 1993. Trans. Daniel W. Smith and Michael A. Greco under the title *Essays Critical and Clinical* (Minneapolis: University of Minnesota Press, 1997).

CH   Guattari. *Chaosmose.* Paris: Galilée, 1992. Trans. Paul Bains and Julian Pefanis under the title *Chaosmosis* (Bloomington: Indiana University Press, 1995).

DR   Deleuze, *Différence et répétition.* Paris: Presses Universitaires de France, 1968. Trans. Paul Patton under the title *Difference and Repetition* (New York: Columbia University Press, 1994).

FB   Deleuze. *Francis Bacon: Logique de la sensation.* Vol 1. Paris: Editions de la différence, 1981.

IM   Deleuze. *Cinéma 1: L'Image-mouvement.* Paris: Minuit, 1983.
       Trans. Hugh Tomlinson and Barbara Habberjam under the title
       Cinema 1: The Movement-Image (Minneapolis: University of
       Minnesota Press, 1986).

IT   Deleuze. *Cinéma 2: L'Image-temps.* Paris, Minuit, 1985. Trans.
       Hugh Tomlinson and Robert Galeta under the title *Cinema 2:
       The Time-Image* (Minneapolis: University of Minnesota Press,
       1989).

LP   Deleuze. *Le Pli: Leibniz et le baroque.* Paris: Minuit, 1988. Trans.
       Tom Conley under the title *The Fold: Leibniz and the Baroque*
       (Minneapolis: University of Minnesota Press, 1993).

LS   Deleuze. *Logique du sens.* Paris: Minuit, 1969. Trans. Mark Lester,
       with Charles Stivale, ed. Constantin V. Boundas under the title
       The Logic of Sense (New York: Columbia University Press, 1990).

MP   Deleuze and Guattari. *Mille plateaux: Capitalisme et schizophrénie, II.*
       Paris: Minuit, 1980. Trans. Brian Massumi under the title *A
       Thousand Plateaus* (Minneapolis: University of Minnesota Press,
       1987).

PP   Deleuze. *Pourparlers.* Paris: Minuit, 1990. Trans. Martin Joughin
       under the title *Negotiations* (New York: Columbia University
       Press, 1995).

PT   Guattari. *Psychoanalyse et transversalité.* Paris: Maspero, 1972.

QP   Deleuze and Guattari. *Qu'est-ce que la philosophie?* Paris: Minuit,
       1991. Trans. Hugh Tomlinson and Graham Burchell under the
       title *What Is Philosophy?* (New York: Columbia University Press,
       1994).

S   Deleuze. *Spinoza: Philosophie pratique.* 2nd ed. Paris: Minuit, 1981.
       Trans. Robert Hurley under the title *Spinoza: Practical Philosophy*
       (San Francisco: City Lights, 1988).

TE   Guattari. *Les trois écologies.* Paris: Galilée, 1989. Trans. Ian Pindar
       and Paul Sutton under the title *Three Ecologies* (London:
       Athlone, 2000).

Introduction

In some twenty-five books written between 1953 and 1993, the French philosopher Gilles Deleuze enunciated a body of thought that touched on a dizzying number of subjects, ranging from embryology, ethology, mathematics, and physics to economics, anthropology, linguistics, and metallurgy. Among the areas to which he most frequently turned were the arts, especially in the fifteen years preceding his death in 1995. He wrote books on Proust (1964, revised and expanded in 1970 and 1976), on the nineteenth-century novelist Leopold Sacher-Masoch (1967), and on Kafka (1975), as well as a final collection of literary essays titled *Essays Critical and Clinical* (1993), and references to literature abound in *The Logic of Sense* (1969), *Difference and Repetition* (1969), *Anti-Oedipus* (1972), and *A Thousand Plateaus* (1980). In *Cinema 1: The Movement-Image* (1983) and *Cinema 2: The Time-Image* (1985), he developed an elaborate taxonomy of cinematic images and signs that drew examples from hundreds of films representative of all eras and major tendencies of world cinema. The arts of music and painting he addressed in *A Thousand Plateaus*, and in *Francis Bacon: The Logic of Sensation* (1981) he sketched the outlines of a general theory and history of painting in the course of a close examination of Bacon's art.

Although literature and cinema are the arts of which Deleuze speaks at greatest length, music and painting hold a special place in his thought. When commenting on the differing domains of the various arts, he often focuses on music and painting, and he frequently characterizes the capacities and limitations of music and painting by contrasting the two arts. When he considers the relationship among philosophy, science, and the arts in the concluding chapters of *What Is Philosophy?* (1991), the discussion is dominated by concepts and examples specific to music and painting. In music Deleuze finds the key to an understanding of art's relation to the natural world. Through reflection on the elements connecting human music and birdsong, he develops a general theory of animal behavior and evolutionary biology as forms of thematic rhythmic patterning, ultimately extending the musical model to describe the interactions of the natural world as an extended symphony of contrapuntal refrains. Deleuze regards painting as the paradigmatic art of sensation, and hence as the medium that most fully discloses the inner dimension of aesthetic experience. The most carnal of the arts, painting engages the body in a "becoming-other," while disembodying sensation and reincarnating it in a world of apersonal affects and percepts. In *What Is Philosophy?* Deleuze delimits the realm of the arts primarily through the concepts of sensation and the refrain, and in large part his general theory of the arts may be seen as a logical development of his theories of painting and music, painting suggesting art's function as a force that transforms inner and outer experience, and music revealing art's position within the creative processes of the natural world. My primary aim in this book, therefore, is to elucidate Deleuze's thought on music and painting and situate it within his account of the aesthetic enterprise as a whole.

Although Deleuze refers to his work at one point as a "constructionism" (PP 201; 147) and at another as a kind of "vitalism" (PP 196; 143), his thought is perhaps best characterized as a philosophy of creation. Deleuze often describes philosophy as the invention of concepts, an activity he parallels to the creative activity of the artist. As the painter works with color or the composer with sounds, so the philosopher invents in the medium of concepts. In this sense Deleuze's philosophy is a "constructionism," a process of constructing in concepts. But philosophical construction is related as well to spheres of creation much broader even than the arts themselves. In *What Is Philosophy?*, the sciences, the arts and philosophy are all said to constitute "forms of thought or creation" (QP 196; 208), and those creative modes of thought are regarded as inseparable from the creative processes of the natural world. As molecules bond, embryos divide, or birds grow and sing, so painters paint, philosophers conceptualize, and scientists postulate, experiment, and theorize. Genuine conceptual thought engages a "power of non-organic life" (PP 196; 143) that passes through all things, and in this sense Deleuze's philosophy is a kind of "vitalism" as well as a kind of "constructionism." It is not surprising, then, that aesthetic concerns inevitably lead Deleuze to discuss political, social, and physico-biological questions, since the formation of artworks is but a dimension of human creation in general, which in turn is indissociable from the ongoing creative processes of the natural world. Nor is it surprising that whenever Deleuze examines any one of the arts, he invariably does so from the vantage of the artist rather than the audience. Each art he defines by its problems, by the challenges faced by the creator in the task of making something new; questions of reception remain for him of secondary concern. His guides to the arts are the artists themselves, more so than the critics, and his effort is always to confront the artworks, heed the words the creators use to talk about their creations, and then invent concepts adequate to, yet distinct from, the art under consideration.

Deleuze approaches the arts in a systematic fashion, but he does not propose a unified "system of the arts," for each art has its own problems and potential for development. Deleuze identifies music's object as the "deterritorialization of the refrain," and part I of this book is devoted to an exploration of that proposition. Roughly put, Deleuze's contention is that the refrain is any rhythmic motif that may help structure an organism's milieu, territory, or social field, and that composers encounter and transform refrains when they create music. Chapter 1 details the workings of refrains in nature, especially as they relate to territorial animals such as birds, and then examines the compositional practices of Olivier Messiaen, who perhaps more than any other composer makes a systematic use of birdsong in his music. Messiaen's exploitations of birdsong are shown to be paradigmatic instances of the process of "becoming-animal" whereby composers deterritorialize refrains. What Messiaen calls "rhythmic characters," "added values," and "nonretrogradable rhythms" are then considered as exemplary techniques of temporal deterritorialization, techniques that function as musical analogues of the unorthodox, nonchronometric time that Deleuze associates with becoming and the event.

Chapter 2 extends this analysis to consider other composers, as well as Deleuze's conception of the history of Western art music from Classicism to the present. Messiaen's appropriation of birdsong is unusual among composers, but Deleuze sees in this practice a general process of "becoming-other" that all musicians enter into when they create something genuinely new. "Becoming-other" may take the form of a "becoming-animal," but also a "becoming-woman," a "becoming-child," or a "becoming-molecular," and in certain vocal practices from the Renaissance to the twentieth century Deleuze discovers a general deterritorialization of the voice that engages all these becomings. Becoming-other always provides a "transverse" connection between conventional musical components, and the history of music for Deleuze is a history of such transverse becomings. In delineating the broad periods of Classical, Romantic, and Modern music, Deleuze relates specifically musical developments of form to three dimensions of the territorial refrain, showing how each may be regarded as a transverse becoming-other. The Classical attention to closed structures he associates with the emergence of biological milieus; the Romantic interest in organic form he relates to the conversion of milieus into territories; and the Modern concern for open structures he links to the opening of territories to a cosmic line of flight.

In chapter 3, the relation between nature and music is again examined, in this instance from the perspective of what might be called a musical ethology, biology, and ecology. If music may be seen as a natural activity, Deleuze argues, nature may be regarded as a kind of cosmic music. The behavior of animals is structured by rhythmic patterns, each of which functions as a motif that combines with other motifs to constitute a milieu, a territory, or a social domain. This behavioral network of motifs is inseparable from the biological formation of individual organisms, and the genesis of organisms itself may be treated as the unfolding of a motif. The birth, growth, maturation, and eventual death of each organism is a continuous process, and that ongoing process of self-formation is best conceived of as the expression in time of a kind of developmental melody. Each organism's inner developmental melody unfolds in interaction with the motifs of its environment, and when viewed from the perspective of evolutionary biology, the emergence of organisms and environments may be taken as the creative coevolution of melodies and motifs over an extended period of time. Nature, finally, proves to be a composer whose grand composition is itself, and the human art of music emerges within this composition as but a highly specialized expression of a *natura musicans*.

In part II, I turn from the problems and objectives of music to those of the art of painting. If music's problem is to deterritorialize the refrain, painting's is to deterritorialize the "face-landscape" and "harness forces." The "face-landscape" forms part of a visual "gridding" that Deleuze labels "faciality"; chapter 4 is dedicated to an explication of this elusive concept. The human face Deleuze sees as an important constituent of every social configuration of language practices and power relations, and as composers deterritorialize refrains, so painters deterritorialize the facialized "grids" whereby bodies and landscapes are structured by the gaze. In every society, discursive and nondiscursive power relations are organized according to a "regime of signs," within which the face functions as an active visual component. A general "visibility," or mode of organizing the visible, emerges from each regime of signs, extending from the face to bodies and finally to the world at large. When painters engage the visible world, they confront an already facialized realm of conventional facial expressions, gestures, postures, and landscapes, all of which reinforce dominant power relations. The task of painters is to disrupt the patterns of faciality and disengage the forces that are regulated and controlled by the prevailing regime of signs. When painters succeed in this task, they capture and render visible the invisible metamorphic forces that play through faces, bodies, and landscapes, thereby inducing transverse becomings that allow the emergence of something new.

Chapters 5 and 6 examine this capture of forces as Deleuze details it in his study of Francis Bacon. Deleuze makes extensive use of Henri Maldiney's analyses of rhythm and color in Cézanne, and in *Francis Bacon: The Logic of Sensation* Deleuze develops something like an asubjective phenomenology of painting, first charting the rhythmic interplay of forces in the figures, contours, and fields of Bacon's canvases, then showing how color functions as the generative element of all his paintings. Bacon says that he tries to render the "brutality of fact" in his art by painting images that bypass the brain and work directly on the nerves. Deleuze sees in this project an effort to escape visual clichés and engage the domain of "sensation," in which metamorphic forces of becoming blur distinctions between inside and outside and create zones of indiscernibility between external entities. Bacon paints recognizable figures and objects, but he deforms the "good forms" of conventional representation by first introducing random chaotic strokes, smudges, and blotches into his works, and then using those marks as a diagram for the development of his compositions. Through these deformations he manages to engage the forces of becoming that escape commonsense perception and conventional representation. The contorted faces, malleable limbs, and mottled flesh of his human figures register internal forces of mutation and external forces of compression. Forces of coupling pass between pairs of figures, and a force of separation issues from the monochrome field in which the figures float. And in the midst of this complex play of forces, a strange "body without organs" emerges, one whose surfaces form an affective topological space and whose rhythms are those of an intensive, nonpulsed time.

Every painter repeats the history of painting, Deleuze claims, and in Bacon's deployment of "shallow depth," metamorphic figures, vibrating color fields, and "tactile" broken tones Deleuze sees traces of a history of space-color relations that extends from Egyptian art through Graeco-Roman and Byzantine art to the colorism of Cézanne and van Gogh. This history of color, as manifest in Bacon, forms the subject of the final chapter of part II. Adopting Alois Riegl's distinction between optic and haptic (or tactile) space, Deleuze approaches painting in terms of the relationship between the hand and the eye. In much of Western art, the hand is subordinate to the eye, seeing and touching reinforcing one another in constructing a rational, perspectival space. In Egyptian art, the emphasis is reversed, the hand dominating the eye, the flattened space and planar figures revealing a sort of "seeing by touching." But in both traditions, eye and hand have only a relative autonomy. In Byzantine art, by contrast, the eye is liberated from the hand, the figures and ground both emerging from the diastolic and systolic rhythms of color and light. Another means of liberating eye and hand is evident in Gothic art, the zigzag line of Gothic ornamentation revealing a haptic force that escapes the control of the eye. The contrast of optic Byzantine color and haptic Gothic line might suggest that eye and hand are opposed as color to line, but Deleuze finds an alternative to the Byzantine use of color in certain haptic practices of colorists like Delacroix, Cézanne, and van Gogh. Color need not be a purely optical element, Deleuze claims, but may be rendered a tactile medium through an exploitation of hue over value. And in Bacon's use of broken tones and complementary hues Deleuze finds a haptic colorism, one that puts the hand in the eye and renders color the generative medium of a tactile space of sensation.

At several points in his work Deleuze makes passing observations about the relationship of the arts to one another and to philosophy, but only in *What Is Philosophy?* does he address this topic directly. In chapter 7 I offer a speculative reading of the difficult closing sections of *What Is Philosophy?*, as well as an assessment of what Deleuze sees as the relative powers of the individual arts and their affinities with philosophy. The key to Deleuze's theory of the arts I find in the biological model of the embryo, whose generative unfolding traces a musical refrain within a painterly domain of sensation. Philosophy and the arts arise within the natural world, and each engages a creative virtual force that informs all processes of connection and growth. Philosophy extracts that virtual force from bodies, whereas the arts embody it in matter that renders palpable the "being of sensation." In painting, the materiality of art is most easily discerned. In music, art's continuity with the processes of natural creation is most clearly revealed. But in both, artistic invention is fundamentally an engagement with the apersonal becoming-other of sensation.

Deleuze is a profound and original analyst of the arts, I believe, but there are formidable obstacles to a ready assimilation of his thought. He is an inveterate neologizer and inventor of concepts, whose works at times read like one extended definition of terms. His arguments are often dense, and they always entail a thought that proceeds by means of paradox. Although carefully structured and gracefully crafted, his chapters frequently challenge readers' abilities to follow the arabesques of the general line of reasoning. He is scrupulous in his citation of sources, but his texts often require a thorough familiarity with the cited works in order to be completely intelligible. He offers copious analogies and examples to illustrate his points, yet seldom does he engage in prolonged discussions of any one analogy or example. Finally, he advocates and practices an unorthodox "nomadic thought," whereby concepts are at times modified and transformed from work to work, and even from section to section of the same work.

To help overcome these obstacles, I have attempted a *reading* of Deleuze, in several senses of the term. First, I have focused much of my analysis on the explication of difficult passages. Broad overviews are useful, but moving from the general to the specific can be especially perilous in interpreting Deleuze. He is most fascinating and most demanding in the subtle twists and turns of his arguments, and often the most resistant sentence or paragraph proves the key to understanding an entire section of a work. As part of this explication of difficult passages, I have ventured as well to trace the filaments that interconnect dense textual nodes and articulate the logic that informs the development of individual concepts. I have also attempted a "reading along with" Deleuze, investigating his sources and indicating the ways in which he appropriates other writers' terms, analyses, and illustrations for his own purposes. Often Deleuze's seemingly arcane remarks are simply highly allusive, and once one is familiar with his sources, his arguments become relatively straightforward. My reading of Deleuze has required as well an effort to tease out the implications of the analogies and examples he offers to explain various abstract concepts. Some of the most exhilarating and intriguing moments in Deleuze's writings begin with the phrase "it's as if . . . ," and with careful elaboration of the hints supplied in his passing illustrations many opaque notions become considerably more transparent. Finally, I have proposed a reading of Deleuzian concepts that discriminates shifts in usage from context to context and suggests the possible rationale behind those shifts.

Deleuze is first and foremost a philosopher, and he repeatedly insists that philosophy has its own problems and methods that must be distinguished from those of other disciplines and practices. Yet he also asserts that philosophy has need of a "nonphilosophical comprehension of philosophy itself" (PP 223; 164), and that nonphilosophical comprehension he associates with the arts. For this reason I have felt justified in addressing several audiences in this book, not merely philosophers but also practitioners and students of the various arts. I have tried to clarify without simplifying the complexities of Deleuze's philosophical arguments, but so as to make them comprehensible to nonphilosophers. I have also endeavored to ask what practical consequences Deleuze's various concepts might have for the analysis of actual works of art. Finally, although Deleuze views each art as relatively autonomous, his treatments of music and painting are mutually illuminating, and there is much that a painter might gain from the musical concept of the refrain, or a composer from the notion of faciality. I therefore have tried to make discussions of each of the arts accessible to nonspecialists. I hope that readers will bear these facts in mind and have patience when rudimentary concepts from their area of expertise are glossed or when familiar debates are rehearsed.

This book is the third of a trilogy on Deleuze and the arts, the others being *Deleuze on Literature* and *Deleuze on Cinema*. Though each is designed as a separate work, they form a single project. In all three I have addressed myself to as broad an audience as possible, with the aim of making Deleuze's thought accessible to anyone interested in the relationship between philosophy and the arts. Deleuze's writings on the arts are mutually enriching and illuminating, and readers interested in his studies of music and painting should find his works on literature and cinema equally rewarding. Should this book prove useful, readers may wish to consult the other two volumes of this project as well.

Many excellent studies of Deleuze have appeared both in French and in English over the last several years. I have learned a great deal from many of them, but I have foregone extended commentary on any of these works, citing only those texts that help clarify a particular point in Deleuze's arguments. I have found especially useful the important essays of Bensmaïa, Boundas, and Smith, as well as the books of Alliez, Ansell Pearson, Buchanan, Buydens, Colebrook, Colombat, Goodchild, Hardt, Holland, Kennedy, Lambert, Massumi, May, Olkowski, Patton, Rajchman, Rodowick, Stivale, and Zourabichvili. All these works will be of great assistance to anyone negotiating the difficulties of Deleuze's texts.

I must add one final methodological comment. Anyone who writes on Deleuze faces a peculiar problem for which there is no simple solution. Four of his most important works were written in collaboration with Félix Guattari, a major theorist in his own right whose contributions to their cowritten works are significant. The Deleuze-Guattari texts have a style of their own that is unlike anything written by Deleuze or Guattari alone. Yet determining which idea is Deleuze's and which Guattari's is impossible, so thoroughly are their thoughts and styles combined. When they resume their individual projects after a given collaborative venture, each treats the coauthored work as his own, freely expanding on that work's concepts and extending them into new areas of investigation. I see no choice but to treat Deleuze's books and the Deleuze-Guattari volumes as constituents of a single body of work. Were I to focus my attention on Guattari, I would likewise regard his works and the Deleuze-Guattari books as components of a single Guattari oeuvre. Hence, though I frequently speak of "Deleuze's thought" while citing Deleuze-Guattari texts, by no means am I discounting the essential role Guattari has played in the creation of those works, nor am I ignoring the important influence Guattari has clearly exercised on the formation of Deleuze's philosophy.

Many have assisted me in this project, which has extended over a number of years. The University of Georgia Research Foundation and the University of Georgia Center for Humanities and Arts provided generous support through grants that allowed time for research and writing.[1] Ian Buchanan, Constantin Boundas, Paul Patton, and Charles Stivale offered welcome encouragement at various stages of the process. I am especially grateful to Jerry Herron and Mihai Spariosu for their friendship and support, and to Florin Berindeanu for his helpful comments on the manuscript. I have gained a great deal from students in my Deleuze seminars over the years, especially Michael Baltasi, Ravinder Kaur Banerjee, Andrew Brown, Balance Chow, Hyung-chul Chung, Letitia Guran, Paulo Oneto, Wei Qin, Astra Taylor, and Maria Chungmin Tu. But my greatest debt is to my family, for their encouragement, understanding, and support throughout the process.

1. An abridged version of chapter 1 appeared as "Rhizomusicosmology," in *SubStance* 66 (1991): 85–101 © 1991 University of Wisconsin Press. An abridged version of chapter 3 appeared under the title "Art and Territory" in *South Atlantic Quarterly*, v. 96, n. 3 (Summer 1997): 465–82 © 1997 Duke University Press. I am grateful to the University of Wisconsin Press and the Duke University Press for permission to reprint these essays.

Part I

MUSIC

Chapter One

MUSICA NATURANS:
DETERRITORIALIZING THE REFRAIN

In an afterword to the English translation of Jacques Attali's *Noise,* Susan McClary aptly notes that

> it is quite clear to most listeners that music moves them, that they respond deeply to music in a variety of ways, even though in our society they are told that they cannot know anything about music without having absorbed the whole theoretical apparatus necessary for music specialization. But to learn this apparatus is to learn to renounce one's responses, to discover that the musical phenomenon is to be understood mechanistically, mathematically. Thus non-trained listeners are prevented from talking about social and expressive dimensions of music (for they lack the vocabulary to refer to its parts) and so are trained musicians (for they have been taught, in learning the proper vocabulary, that music is strictly self-contained structure). (McClary 150)

The issue McClary articulates, that of the contradiction between listeners' personal experience of music and the professional theorization of music, points to a fundamental question: Is music strictly self-contained structure, or does it have some relation to that which is outside itself—to the emotions of human listeners, but also to their lives, their activities, and the myriad dynamic processes going on in the world around them? In *A Thousand Plateaus*, especially in plateau 11, "The Refrain" ("*De la ritournelle*"), Deleuze and Guattari argue that music is an open structure that permeates and is permeated by the world. They offer a reading of the relationship between the cosmos and music not as mechanical and mathematical but as machinic and rhythmical. Their point of departure is birdsong, a topic that might initially seem tangential to the business at hand. But this topic allows them to situate music within the general context of sonic and rhythmic patterning in nature and to suggest a continuity among human and nonhuman species in their modes of occupying space and establishing interspecific and conspecific relationships. It also allows them to develop the implications of some of the concepts and practices of the composer Olivier Messiaen, whose approach to rhythm and birdsong in his musical compositions and theoretical writings opens the way toward a conception of music as an engagement of cosmic forces. The object of this chapter is to outline the basic features of Deleuze and Guattari's musical cosmology, and then to show through Messiaen's work how this general theory may be related to musical composition per se. The next chapter concerns Deleuze and Guattari's remarks on music history and their approach to periodization, and the third addresses the question of the relationship between music and nature, this time exploring the biological implications of Deleuze and Guattari's musical cosmology.

MUSIC AND COSMOS IN ANTIQUITY

If contemporary music theorists generally treat music as a self-referential system divorced from psychological, social, and natural considerations, their Western predecessors from classical antiquity through the Renaissance tend to regard music as intimately tied to the order of microcosm and macrocosm. The disciplines of arithmetic, geometry, astronomy, and music, which make up the medieval *quadrivium*, are already closely allied in much ancient thought, and the concept of the "harmony of the spheres," which explicitly links music and cosmology, is regularly invoked throughout antiquity, the Middle Ages and the Renaissance.[1] What is important to note is the extent to which these ideas are informed by many of the fundamental themes of Platonism.

Pythagoras is said to have been the first in the West systematically to establish the connection between musical and cosmic order.[2] Pythagoras and his followers noted that the relation between musical pitches may be expressed in terms of numerical ratios—the octave as 2:1, the fifth, 3:2, the fourth, 4:3, the whole tone, 9:8—and that similar proportional relations govern the structure of the created world. The Pythagoreans regarded number as the generative force of all geometric and physical forms, and they found both musical and numerical consonance in the movement of the planets, which, they claimed, emitted a celestial music as each sphere followed its perfectly proportioned course. For the Pythagoreans, the world is characterized by the two principles of *peras*, or limit, and *kosmos*, a word "which unites, as perhaps only the Greek spirit could, the notion of order, arrangement or structural perfection with that of beauty" (Guthrie 206).[3] In the Pythagorean cosmogony, *apeiron*, or the unlimited, is the formless, boundless, and chaotic flux which precedes the cosmos, and which, by being submitted to the force of limit (*peras*), is transformed into a universe that possesses form, order, proportion, and wholeness. *Apeiron*, we might note, is also the source of time, but an unmeasured time that limit converts into *chronos*, or time that is numbered, measured, and submitted to the cyclical rhythms of the cosmos.[4]

For the Pythagoreans, then, music manifests the order of number, and cosmic harmony entails the circumscription of space and the mensuration of time, in that the proportioned parts of the cosmos are rendered harmonious through their participation in a delimited, macroscopic whole, and time is made regular through its subjugation to the periodic repetition of the same. Although Plato by no means embraces all aspects of Pythagorean doctrine in his writings, he does make frequent use of Pythagorean concepts of harmony and proportion, and he repeatedly affirms that order requires a subjection of the many to the one and the other to the same. In the *Timaeus*, the connection between music, mathematics, and cosmology is elaborately developed, and the ontological status of number, which remains uncertain in the Pythagoreans, is explicitly identified as ideal. In other dialogues, particularly the *Republic*, the concept of harmony is used to characterize psychological and social order, and philosophy itself is often seen as a musical activity. As Edward Lippman observes, the entire Platonic enterprise may finally be conceived of as a form of music: "The musician creates harmony in the pitch and duration of tone and in gesture; man creates harmony in the conduct of his life;

the statesman creates harmony in society; the Demiurge creates harmony in the cosmos; the philosopher creates the harmony of dialectic and the music of discourse" (Lippman 41).

It is essentially this Platonic conception of music that Boethius develops in the *Consolatio* and *De Musica* and that numerous writers later reiterate throughout the Middle Ages and Renaissance.[5] In Boethius's differentiation of *musica instrumentalis* (actual vocal and instrumental music), *musica humana* (the physical, emotional, and spiritual harmony of human beings) and *musica mundana* (the harmony of the spheres), one finds the entire range of Platonic analogies as well as the clear hierarchical ranking of physical and spiritual activities that renders actual music a mere sensual echo of the more significant music of mathematics and philosophy. And holding the entire system together are the notions of number and proportion as all-pervasive forms and cosmic order as the delimitation and regulation of a whole.

RHYTHM AND THE REFRAIN

In virtually every regard, Deleuze and Guattari's treatment of music is the antithesis of the traditional, Platonic approach to the subject. In their view, the cosmos with which music is intertwined is not a circumscribed totality but an open whole whose dimensions can never be given as such.[6] The essence of music is to be found not in the macroscopic order of celestial cycles, but in the molecular domain of transverse becomings. The pulsations that play through music and the world are not measured recurrences of the same but ametrical rhythms of the incommensurable and the unequal. And the time disclosed in music is less that of *chronos* than *aion*, the floating time of haecceities and becoming.

Deleuze and Guattari describe music as "the active, creative operation which consists of deterritorializing the refrain [*la ritournelle*]" (MP 369; 300), a definition that obviously depends for its coherence on a full understanding of the concepts of the refrain and (de)territorialization. Musical refrains, they note, have venerable associations with territoriality, each of the ancient Greek modes or the "hundred rhythms" of the Hindu *deçî-tâlas*, for instance, being associated with a specific region or province as well as a particular mood and character. In this regard, musical refrains resemble birdsongs, which ethologists have long recognized as basic components in the delimitation of bird territories. Abstracting from these instances of geographically associated sonic motifs, Deleuze and Guattari extend the notion of the refrain to refer to any kind of rhythmic pattern that stakes out a territory. Three examples will suffice to indicate the basic ways in which this process takes place: (1) A child afraid in the dark sings a song to reassure herself, and in so doing establishes a stable point in the midst of chaos, a locus of order in a non-dimensional space; (2) a cat sprays the corners of his house and the trees and bushes in his yard and thereby demarcates a dimensional area that he claims as his possession; (3) a bird sings an impromptu aria at the break of day, and thus opens its territory to other milieus and the cosmos at large. A point of stability, a circle of property, and an opening to the outside—these are the three aspects of the refrain. Although the three may be differentiated from one another, they do not represent successive moments in an evolutionary or developmental sequence, but "three aspects of a single and same thing" (MP 383; 312), which manifests itself now in one form, now in another. As stabilizing point, the refrain creates an infra-assemblage with directional components; as surrounding circle, an intra-assemblage with dimensional components; and as opening to the outside, an inter-assemblage with components of passage or flight. "Forces of chaos, terrestrial forces, cosmic forces: all of these confront each other and come together in the refrain" (MP 384; 312).

The elements from which territories are formed are milieus and rhythms, which themselves are created out of chaos. As Deleuze insists at several junctures in his work, chaos is not the dark night in which all cows are black, an undifferentiated and unthinkable blur that is opposed to order, but a genetic medium from which order spontaneously emerges. Chaos has directional vectors from which a point of order may issue. Although we may usefully conceive of this locus of order as a geometrical point, it is not inert but mobile. Nor is it self-contained, but determined by its relations with other loci of order, and hence fluctuating and provisional. In all these senses, then, it delineates a directional space, which Deleuze and Guattari label a "milieu." A milieu is a coded block of space-time, a code being defined by "periodic repetition" (MP 384; 313). Every milieu is in contact with other milieus, however, and "each code is in a state of perpetual transcoding or transduction" (MP 384; 313). We may describe an amoeba's milieu, for instance, in terms of a series of submilieus—its surrounding liquid medium (external milieu), its organs (internal milieu), its exchanges between inside and outside across the cell membrane (intermediary milieu), and its relation to food, sunlight, and other sources of energy (annexed milieu). In each case we may determine the periodic repetition that encodes a given submilieu, the regular patterns that organize a particular block of space-time, and note the fluctuations in patterns that result from the mutual interaction of the various submilieus. The amoeba's milieu is a locus of order in the midst of chaos, but it emerges from chaos along a directional vector, and it remains open to chaos from without and within. Thus chaos, far from being the qualitative antithesis of the milieu, is simply "the milieu of all milieus" (MP 385; 313).

Periodic repetition encodes a milieu, but one must distinguish the measure (or meter) of such repetition from the rhythm that occurs between two milieus, or between a milieu and chaos (as the milieu of all milieus). Measure implies a repetition of the Same, a preexisting, self-identical pattern that is reproduced over and over again, whereas rhythm "is the Unequal or Incommensurable, always in a process of transcoding," operating "not in a homogeneous space-time, but with heterogeneous blocks" (MP 385; 313). Rhythm, in short, is difference, or relation—the in-between whereby milieus communicate with one another, within themselves (as collections of sub-milieus), and with chaos. Rhythm is not a secondary byproduct of a milieu's measure, but a primary constituent of that milieu. Consider the human body. Its internal milieu is made up of various elements—the heart, lungs, brain, nerves, and so on—each with its own rate of periodic repetition. The rhythms of the body, however, take place between various milieus and sub-milieus, the heart's regular measure, for instance, fluctuating in response to neural and hormonal stimuli, changes in breathing rate, alterations in the external environment, and so on. In a sense the heart's periodic repetition produces rhythm, but not by reproducing an identical measure and not in isolation from other milieus. Its regular meter is a vital pulse, not a reproduction of the same, whose regularity and variability are inseparable from the intermilieu rhythms of difference. Hence Deleuze and Guattari assert that "a milieu does indeed exist by virtue of periodic repetition, but such repetition only has the effect of producing a difference through which the milieu passes into another milieu. It is difference that is rhythmic, and not repetition, which, however, produces it; but that productive repetition has nothing to do with a reproductive measure" (MP 385–86; 314).

A milieu, however, is not a territory, for a territory "is in fact an act that affects milieus and rhythms, that 'territorializes' them" (MP 386; 314). Such an action is essentially artistic and appropriative, one whereby milieu components emerge as qualities, and rhythms become expressive. Consider, for example, the brilliant coloring of various species of territorial tropical fish. In many fish, hormonal responses to sexual stimuli or external threats trigger alterations in external body coloration, but such changes are transitory and linked to a specific milieu function. In territorial fish, by contrast, coloration expresses a relation to a given space and attains a temporal continuity that does not vary with the activities within that space. Konrad Lorenz, a pioneer in research on territoriality, observes that the spectacular color displays of tropical fish are like posters ostentatiously signaling the presence of the fish and its claims to a particular area of the coral reef. The more brightly colored the fish, the more aggressively territorial is the species. A similar emergence of expressive qualities is evident in the stagemaker (*Scenopoeetes dentirostris*), a bird that picks leaves from a tree, drops them to the ground, and then turns them upside down to reveal their pale underside and thereby demarcate a territory.[7] Each leaf is a milieu component that has been removed from its milieu and converted into a quality, and the stagemaker's action constitutes a rhythm that is no longer simply a function of a milieu but has become expressive. The leaf is like a poster, a form of *art brut* that declares the oneness of the bird with its proper territory.

With the establishment of a territory, then, "a milieu component becomes at once quality and property, *quale* and *proprium*" (MP 387; 315). A directional milieu becomes a circumscribed, dimensional space, but it is the territorializing function of the expressive quality/property that establishes the dimensional space, not the space that determines the function. It is at the same moment that a quality is abstracted from a milieu component, a possession is declared, and a dimensional space is established. Territory "is in fact an act" (MP 386; 314), although such an act obviously is not necessarily intentional or conscious. (It is doubtful that the stagemaker decides to pluck the leaves, and the tetra certainly does not choose to don its brilliant markings.) Rather, territorialization "is the act of rhythm that has become expressive, or of milieu components that have become qualitative" (MP 388; 315). Rhythm itself—the differential, incommensurable relation between milieus—creates the territory, and with it expressive qualities that stake out a possession.

Ethologists have long stressed the possessiveness of territorial creatures, but Deleuze and Guattari insist that such animals are also artists. "Property is first artistic, because art is first *placard, poster*" (MP 389; 316). The territorial marker is a signature, an expressive quality that creates a domain and names its owner. (Such an owner, we should note, is not a preexisting subject; rather, the owner as subject and the territory are both constituted at the same time through the delineation of an expressive quality.) "One puts one's signature on an object as one plants a flag on a plot of land" (MP 389; 316). Art, then, is connected to property and possession, but not in the reductive sense that art is an outgrowth of a primal acquisitiveness rooted in a self-preservation instinct. Quite the reverse. "The expressive is primary in relation to the possessive" (MP 389; 316). Art, as the disposition of expressive qualities, is the active agent in the formation of territory and the establishment of its occupant's proprietary identity.

What is crucial in the establishment of a territory is the autonomy of qualities and rhythms. In Deleuze and Guattari's terms, a certain level of decoding or deterritorialization must take place if a territory is to be formed. The coloration of the tropical fish must be divested of any fixed connection with sexual or aggressive stimuli if it is to serve as a territorial marker. In the case of the brown stagemaker, if leaf plucking were a constant periodic activity, then all places would be indifferently littered with leaf debris, but since leaf plucking has a certain autonomy and indeterminacy, one space may be differentiated from all others and established as a territory. The establishment of a territory, then, entails a certain degree of decoding, or "unfixing" of qualities and rhythms, and a subsequent recoding of those qualities and rhythms in terms of a specific domain.

Autonomy is evident as well in the shifting relations that link various qualities within a given territory. Qualities and relations occur not in isolation from one another but in complexes that "express" the relation of the territory to the internal milieu of impulses and the external milieu of circumstances. Internal relations constitute *territorial motifs* and external relations form *territorial counterpoints* (MP 390; 317), and both are characterized by nonpulsed, autonomous rhythms that organize patterns of inner impulses and drives on the one hand, and outer connections with environmental variables on the other. Ethologists refer to the formation of such motifs and counterpoints as "ritualization," defining this process broadly as the modification of a behavior pattern to serve a communicative function. They recognize the importance of ritualization in territorial animals, but generally regard territorial rituals as simply stimulus-response patterns made up of the vestiges of other such patterns that have been modified and combined to assume new functions. Deleuze and Guattari argue, however, that the complex of actions that make up a ritual—for example, singing, nest building, grooming, strutting, and displaying colored plumage in a bird's mating ritual—presumes the existence of an autonomous configuration of differences (i.e., rhythms) that puts the heterogeneous impulses and circumstances of the ritual in relation to one another and in relation to a demarcated territory.

The male stickleback fish, for example, engages in a zigzag dance upon seeing a female, thereby signaling his desire to mate. According to Lorenz and others, the "zig" of his dance, a movement toward the female, is a vestige of an attack impulse, and the "zag" toward the nest, a product of the sexual drives. The two movements are combined and given a new function in the dance, which itself assumes a role in a complex sequence of actions: she appears, he dances, she courts, he leads, she follows, he shows her the nest entrance, she enters the nest, he trembles, she spawns, he fertilizes the eggs (see Eibl-Eibesfeldt 185–87). External circumstances affect the dance in various ways, the presence of the female triggering the zigzag movement but only during the mating season and at certain times of day. After fertilizing three or four clutches of eggs, the male's sexual drive wanes and dancing ceases. The male begins to ventilate the eggs with fanning movements of his pectoral fins, apparently in response to increases in carbon dioxide in the water around the nest generated by the oxygen consumption of the gestating eggs (ibid. 54).

The stickleback's zigzag dance is, then, is a territorial motif that organizes internal impulses (a combination of aggressive zig and sexual zag) and a territorial counterpoint that responds to external circumstances (female's presence, season and time of day, carbon dioxide level around the nest). The zigzag dance is a refrain, a configuration of elements that have been decoded from their milieu functions and recoded with new territorial functions. Rather than serving simply as a placard or poster, a mere signature of the male stickleback's possession of its territory, the zigzag dance expresses the relations of internal and external components to the territory. The qualities and relations attain a certain autonomy; it is a question "no longer of signatures, but [of] a style" (MP 391; 318). Hence, internal territorial motifs may be said to form "rhythmic characters" ("*personnages rythmiques*") in which "the rhythm itself is now the character in its entirety," just as territorial counterpoints form "melodic landscapes" ("*paysages melodiques*"), in which contrapuntal relations compose a melody that is itself "a sonorous landscape in counterpoint to a virtual landscape" (MP 391; 318). When a bird sings its territorial song, we do not anthropomorphize in saying that it sings with joy or sadness or that it greets the dawn or competes with a rival, for the song articulates the *relations* among internal impulses and external circumstances that assume a regular pattern in the constitution of a territory. The song is "geomorphic" (MP 392; 319) in that its rhythms are those of all the elements that make up the territory, the territorializing process in a sense singing *through* the bird in an autonomous refrain that expresses the patterning of the ensemble of territorial components. Motifs and counterpoints, in short, are rhythms with a life of their own, not secondary byproducts of stimulus-response reflexes. We may say in somewhat different terms, then, that a territory is characterized by irregular patterns of differential relations that have a certain autonomy in respect to the heterogeneous elements they combine.

Territorialization also induces two important effects, a "reorganization of functions" and a "regrouping of forces" (MP 394; 320), the second of which is particularly important in understanding the cosmic dimension of territorialization. Activities, when territorialized, undergo modification and specialization, and the result is "the creation of new functions such as nest building, the transformation of old functions, such as aggression that changes its nature in becoming intra-specific" (MP 394; 320–21). Besides reorganizing functions, "The territory regroups all the forces of the different milieus in a single sheaf constituted by the forces of the earth" (MP 395; 321). Every territory has a center of intensity where its forces come together, a center that is at once within the territory and outside it, like the kingdom of God, always at hand yet difficult to reach. (Deleuze and Guattari argue that religion is something common to animals and humans, and that in both it is related to the territorial gathering of forces.) The equivocal nature of this center is most evident in the migrations of certain animals whose territory is organized around a distant homeland or gathering place—salmon returning to their spawning grounds, locusts and chaff-inches assembling in masses, spiny lobsters marching single-file for miles across the ocean floor. These are extreme examples of the re-grouping of forces that takes place in territorialization, but they are not exceptions to the basic process, for every territory combines forces in an intense center which itself is an opening whereby the territory issues forth onto the cosmos at large. It is not surprising, then, that territorial forms of social organization may give rise to nonterritorial patterns of group interaction, since territories are by their nature open to a process of decoding, or deterritorialization. Hence, in territorial animals, male-female pairs tend to function as couples only within the territory, whereas in other complex forms of social organization couple bonds have a relative or absolute degree of autonomy in relation to geographic coordinates.

Territorialization, then, is a complex process of decoding and re-coding (deterritorialization and reterritorialization), which transforms milieus and rhythms by creating expressive qualities and autonomous rhythms (both territorial motifs and territorial counterpoints) that in-duce a reorganization of functions and a regrouping of forces. Thus we can elaborate on our initial classification of refrains by saying that they may (1) mark or assemble a territory; (2) connect a territory with inter-nal impulses and/or external circumstances; (3) identify specialized functions; (4) or collect forces in order to centralize the territory or go outside it.

Such refrains form the content proper to music. "Whereas the refrain is essentially territorial, territorializing or reterritorializing, music makes of the refrain a deterritorialized content for a deterritorializing form of expression" (MP 369; 300). Music, it is true, subjects its own materials to systematic rules (such as those of traditional harmony and counterpoint), but Deleuze and Guattari insist that all great composers manage to unsettle the given conventions of their day and invent "a sort of diagonal between the harmonic vertical and the melodic horizon" (MP 363; 296). The process through which a refrain is deterritorialized is essentially one of *becoming*, a becoming-woman, a becoming-child, a becoming-animal or a becoming-molecular, a passage *between* milieus and territories that articulates the nonpulsed rhythms of an unmeasured time. What this might mean should become clearer after a brief examination of the compositional practices of Olivier Messiaen.[8]

MESSIAEN AND THE COMPOSITION OF TIME

At first glance, one might expect to find little in common between a devout Catholic composer and two materialist philosophers such as Deleuze and Guattari. Yet despite the orthodoxy of Messiaen's Christianity and the central role his faith played in his life as a composer, there is much in his thought and practice that is in accord with the remarks about music in *A Thousand Plateaus*. Perhaps in part this is because of Messiaen's mystical proclivities, which led him to emphasize joy and ecstasy in his works rather than pain and suffering: "My music is cheerful, it contains glory and light. Of course suffering exists for me, too, but I've written very few poignant pieces. I'm not made for that. I love Light, Joy, and Glory in the divine sense" (Rößler 92). Many of his religious works, particularly those, like *Les Corps glorieux,* that celebrate the resurrected body (its refinement, mobility, strength, radiance, etc.), could well serve as confirmation of Deleuze and Guattari's observation that "music is never tragic, music is joy" [that] "gives us a taste for dying, a taste less for happiness than for dying with happiness, being extinguished" (MP 367; 299). Perhaps as well Messiaen's ability to move without difficulty from divine ecstasy to human passion and the rhythms of nature, to bring about in his music a "juxtaposition of Catholic faith, the Tristan and Isolde myth and a highly developed use of birdsong" (Samuel 3) is not that far removed from Deleuze and Guattari's practice of creating plateaus of desiring-production that span molecular and cosmic domains.

But obviously what most draws Deleuze and Guattari to Messiaen is the composer's dedication to experimentation in all the parameters of musical expression. Deleuze and Guattari call for a music that puts "in continuous variation all components," that forms "a rhizome instead of a tree, and enters the service of a virtual cosmic continuum, in which even the holes, silences, ruptures and cuts have a part" (MP 121; 95). In this regard, Messiaen's music is exemplary. As early as 1944, Messiaen spoke in his composition classes about the limitations of the Second Viennese School, in whose works pitch structures alone are investigated while conventional rhythmic and formal conceptions remain unexamined (see Goléa 247). Throughout his career, Messiaen experimented with rhythm and harmonic modes, and in his work from *Mode de valeurs et d'intensités* (1949) forward, he explored various serial and modal approaches to dynamics, timbre, duration, and other compositional components.

One of the areas of most intense experimentation in Messiaen's music is rhythm. Rhythmic music, he states, "is music that scorns repetition, straightforwardness and equal divisions. In short, it's music inspired by the movements of nature, movements of free and unequal durations" (Samuel 33). For Messiaen, as for Deleuze and Guattari, rhythm and meter are antithetical concepts, and what passes for "rhythmic music" (jazz, military marches) he sees as the negation of true rhythm. Messiaen defines rhythm as "the change of number and duration":

Suppose that there were a single beat in all the universe. One beat; with eternity before it and eternity after it. A before and an after. That is the birth of time. Imagine then, almost immediately, a second beat. Since any beat is prolonged by the silence which follows it, the second beat will be longer than the first. Another number, another duration. That is the birth of Rhythm.[9]

Rhythm is born of moments of intensity, incommensurable accents that create unequal extensions of duration. Whereas meter presumes an even division of a uniform time, rhythm presupposes a time of flux, of multiple speeds and reversible relations. As Messiaen remarks, the musician must be sensitive to the various "time-scales, superimposed on each other, which surround us: the endlessly long time of the stars, the very long time of the mountains, the middling one of the human being, the short one of insects, the very short one of atoms (not to mention the time-scales inherent in ourselves—the physiological, the psychological)" (Rößler 40). Through rhythm, he says, the musician can experiment with time and disclose new temporal relations: "By means of his rhythms, he can chop up Time here and there, and can even put it together again in the reverse order, a little as though he were going for a walk through different points of time, or as though he were amassing the future by turning to the past, in the process of which, his memory of the past becomes transformed into a memory of the future" (Rößler 41).

Messiaen generates ametrical rhythms in his music through a number of techniques, chief among which are the use of "added values," "rhythmic characters," and "nonretrogradable rhythms."[10] An added value, as Messiaen's defines it in his *Technique de mon langage musical* (1944), is "a short value, added to any rhythm whatsoever, whether by a note, or by a rest, or by the dot" (Messiaen 1:16). To illustrate the three ways in which values may be added, Messiaen provides the following four examples:

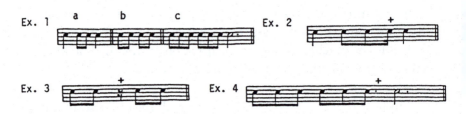

The three measures of example 1 (labeled a, b, and c) are the conventional units to which values are to be added. In example 2, measure (a) is modified by an added note, in example 3 a rest is added to (b), and in example 4 an added dot alters measure (c) (each added value marked by +). The effect is to convert the common meters of example 1 ($\frac{3}{4}$ [a], $\frac{2}{4}$ [b], and $\frac{12}{8}$ [c]) into the complex meters of $\frac{13}{16}$ (example 2), $\frac{5}{16}$ (example 3), and $\frac{25}{16}$ (example 4). When employed frequently in a composition, added values undermine all metrical regularity, and the bar lines, rather than marking fixed units of time, demarcate rhythmic cells of varying duration, their function being reduced to that of convenient reference points for coordinating harmonic relations among the various voices.

Messiaen's concept of "rhythmic characters" (*personnages rythmiques*), which Deleuze and Guattari cite in *A Thousand Plateaus,* may be seen as an extension of the notion of added values. By progressively modifying a figure through the addition or subtraction of rhythmic values, the composer can develop *"personnages rythmiques"* whose dynamic relationships are like those of characters on the stage:

Let's imagine a scene in a play between three characters: the first acts in a brutal manner by hitting the second; the second character suffers this act, since his actions are dominated by those of the first; lastly, the third character is present at the conflict but

remains inactive. If we transpose this parable into the field of
rhythm, we have three rhythmic groups: the first, whose note-
values are always increasing, is the character who attacks; the second, whose note-values decrease, is the character who is attacked;
and the third, whose note-values never change, is the character
who remains immobile. (Samuel 37)

The progressive augmentation or diminution of values in itself is not an
uncommon compositional technique, but in Messiaen's hands it
becomes a complex and original mode of musical development. Messiaen
handles rhythmic units as if they were living entities, and as the table of
fourteen basic augmentations and diminutions in *Technique de mon langage musical* attests (Messiaen 2:3), his conception of the possibilities of
rhythmic cells as generational components is far in advance of that of
most of his contemporaries.

Messiaen's third basic rhythmic innovation is in the use of "nonretrogradable rhythms," which may be defined simply as palindromic
rhythmic patterns with a central common value. Again, Messiaen's technique is not entirely absent in other composers' works, but the palin-
dromes he creates are generally much more complicated and irregular
than those one meets elsewhere. Consider, for instance, example 5, which
is taken from *Technique de mon langage musical:*

Ex. 5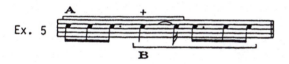

The last three notes are the retrograde of the first three, the two three-
note units framing the central value of the quarter note tied to the six-
teenth. Group B is also the retrograde of group A. The rhythmic structure
of the measure is far from conventional, the values of the measure falling
into sixteenth-note groups of 7, 5, and 7, the entire passage functioning
as a measure in $\frac{19}{16}$ time. Such nonretrogradable rhythms form closed units
that Messiaen generally either uses as rhythmic pedals or develops through
augmentation of the outer units. As Messiaen observes, one senses in
these rhythms "a certain unity of movement (where beginning and end are
confused because identical)" (Messiaen 1:21), a unity of movement that
discloses a time at once circular and reversible.

In added values, then, one encounters an ametrical, staggered time of variable intensities; in rhythmic characters, an active, germinal time of flux; and in nonretrogradable rhythms, a circular and reversible time in which beginning and end are confused. Given Messiaen's general avoidance of metrical regularity and the essentially static and coloristic nature of his harmonic language, it is not surprising that his music often strikes commentators as both timeless and intensely rhythmical. Messiaen's aim, in one regard, is "to suspend the sense of time in his music . . . in order to express the idea of the 'eternal' " (Johnson 183), but it is also to engage the incommensurable rhythms of the cosmos, whose varying time scales range from the infinitesimal vibration of atoms to the endless movement of the stars. His object, in short, is to articulate a "timeless time," ametrical, nonteleological, reversible, and unlimited. As one can readily see, that time is not unlike the time the Stoics called *Aion* (literally, "eternity"), the elusive, fluctuating time of becoming that Deleuze and Guattari describe as "the indefinite time of the pure event or becoming, which articulates relative speeds and slowness independently of the chronological or chronometric values that time assumes in the other modes" (MP 322; 263).[11] Such is the time of the haecceity, the *eventum tantum,* "which has neither beginning nor end, neither origin nor destination; it is always in the middle. It is not made of points, but only of lines. It is a rhizome" (MP 321; 263).

THE MUSIC OF THE BIRDS

Messiaen is unique among composers in his intense interest in the music of birds, which he describes as probably "the greatest musicians existing on our planet" (Samuel 51). He made numerous field investigations of birdsongs around the world, often enlisting the aid of prominent ornithologists in his research, and he notated with great precision the songs of hundreds of birds. Despite a lifelong interest in birds, it was only in *Quatuor pour la fin du temps* (1941) that he first incorporated birdsong in his music. This effort was followed by a series of works in which birdsong supplied the principal material for his compositions, the major works of this period being *Reveil des oiseaux* (1953), *Oiseaux exotiques* (1956), *Catalogue d'oiseaux* (1958), and *Chronochromie* (1960). In his compositions after *Chronochromie,* Messiaen's preoccupation with

birdsong abated somewhat, although it continued to occupy an important, if no longer predominant, role in his scores.

Messiaen stands alone among composers in his extensive utilization
of birdsong, yet Deleuze and Guattari regard his practice of deterritorializing the territorial songs of birds as paradigmatic of the creative process
of all composers. Music is the deterritorialization of the refrain, and all
such deterritorialization entails the engagement of a sonic block whose
content is a "becoming"—becoming-woman, becoming-child, becoming-
animal, becoming-molecular. In the case of a becoming-animal (such as
Messiaen's), the sonic block "does not have as its content a becoming-
animal unless the animal at the same time becomes in sound something
other, something absolute, night, death, joy—certainly not a generality or
a simplification, but a haecceity, *this* death, *that* night" (MP 374; 304).
Such "becoming" above all is not imitative or figurative, no matter what
claims to representational fidelity a composer might make. For even if a
musician should attempt to imitate animal sounds, "Imitation destroys
itself, to the extent that he who imitates enters unknowingly into a becoming, which conjugates with the unknowing becoming of that which
he imitates" (MP 374; 304–5).

Abundant examples of this process of becoming are to be found
throughout Messiaen's works of the bird period, and perhaps none are
more striking than those of the *Catalogue d'oiseaux,* an extraordinary
cycle of thirteen pieces for solo piano that takes almost three hours to
be played. Each piece is dedicated to the portrayal of a specific bird,
whose song Messiaen has attempted to render with great accuracy. Yet
as he describes the process through which he translates a bird's song
into sounds on the piano, one finds that at every stage a deformation
and mutation of the bird's music takes place. "A bird," remarks Messiaen,
"being much smaller than us, with a heart which beats faster and nervous reactions that are much quicker, sings in extremely brisk tempi,
absolutely impossible for our instruments" (Samuel 62). As a result,
Messiaen must transcribe the bird's song in a slower tempo if it is to be
played at all. The extremely high pitch of a bird's voice requires as well
that the song be notated octaves lower than it actually is sounded. A
bird also uses micro-intervals that do not conform to the intervals of
our twelve-tone even-tempered scale. Consequently, in adapting birdsong for use in a piano composition Messiaen preserves the relations
between tones but expands the intervals so that they correspond to the

intervals that may be realized on a piano. Finally, the timbre of a bird's voice is essential to its song, and only through complex harmonic coloration can Messiaen suggest the subtleties of timbre that are part of its music. Hence, says Messiaen, "reproducing the timbre of birdsong has compelled me to constant inventions of chords, sonorities and combinations of sonorities and complexes of sounds which result in a piano which does not sound 'harmonically' like other pianos" (Samuel 75).

The musical "translation" of an individual bird's song may, as Messiaen states, transpose it "into a more human scale" (Samuel 62), but it also deforms the song and renders it other. And when one turns to the actual compositions that utilize birdsong, one encounters further forces of mutation and transformation that modify the sounds of nature. In the *Catalogue d'oiseaux*, for example, Messiaen never approaches an individual bird's song in isolation, but instead juxtaposes it with the songs of other species and situates it within an evocative sonic landscape. Messiaen prefaces each piece with a prose description of the natural setting and the various birds he seeks to render in the work. He then labels the various motifs throughout the score, certain sections identified by the names of specific birds, others by components of the natural scene. "*Le Merle bleu*" ("The Blue Rock Thrush," book I, 3), for example, takes as its subject a seascape in June near Banyuls-sur-Mer, the cliffs and waves providing the setting for the cries of swifts and herring gulls and the songs of the blue rock thrush and the theckla lark. The first twenty measures are marked with the following sequence of labels: cliffs, swifts, cliffs, swifts, water, swifts, water, blue rock thrush, water, swifts, water, theckla lark, water. This rapid succession of motifs continues throughout the piece and is typical of all the works of the *Catalogue d'oiseaux*.

Such pictorialism might suggest that Messiaen's aesthetic is purely mimetic, but the actual results of his practice belie this suspicion. The interplay of various birdsongs induces mutual modifications of the motifs, each song developing as one component of a network of interacting blocks of sound. The landscape motifs insinuate themselves into the birdsongs, birds and natural setting functioning finally as heterogeneous and shifting components of a single sonic continuum.[12] Each piece ultimately creates a specific atmospheric configuration of interpenetrating elements in flux, what Deleuze and Guattari call a "haecceity," which like "a season, a winter, a summer, an hour, a date" has "a perfect individuality and lacks nothing, although it is not to be confused with that of a thing or a subject" (MP 318; 261). Occasionally birdlike phrases emerge from the sonic continuum of each piece, but they are thoroughly subsumed within Messiaen's modal and rhythmic style, so that, as Paul Griffiths observes, "it seems more reasonable to speak of the collection not as a group of attempts at fidelity to nature but rather as a sequence of piano pieces whose realization nature helped facilitate" (Griffiths 183).

In Messiaen's *Catalogue d'oiseaux* we find clear examples of what Deleuze and Guattari mean by the process of becoming-animal, as well as musical elaborations of what they refer to as the time of Aion. Messiaen's intense interest in birdsong is rare among composers, and his extensive exploitation of the complexities of rhythm sets him apart from many of his contemporaries and predecessors. Yet in Deleuze and Guattari's analysis, these apparently idiosyncratic practices point toward a general philosophy of music's relation to the world. Messiaen's rhythmic innovations, rather than being mere formal experimentations, are means of exploring an unmeasured time of multiple speeds and reversible relations that play through subatomic and sidereal domains alike. His transformations of the territorial songs of birds, far from exemplifying a programmatic impressionism, are instances of a dynamic interaction between music and the cosmos, one that discloses both music and world to be open systems of difference engaged in a process of mutual becoming. What Deleuze and Guattari's treatment of Messiaen helps us see is how music can be regarded as a part of nature; what remains is to show how their approach to the refrain leads to a vision of nature itself as music. But before turning to the biological implications of Deleuze and Guattari's thought on music, we will explore a little further the notion of becoming and indicate how the concept of the refrain informs their handling of music history.

Chapter Two

MUSIC IN TIME:
HISTORY AND BECOMING

Music is the deterritorialization of the refrain, and in this sense the refrain is "the block of content proper to music" (MP 368; 299). The refrain itself, of course, is a complex of deterritorialization and reterritorialization, its three aspects being those of a point of order, a circle of control, and a line of flight to the outside. The refrain territorializes chaos in forming a milieu; it deterritorializes milieu components and reterritorializes them in a territory proper; and deterritorializing forces constantly play through the territory, thereby opening it to the cosmos as a whole. Yet the basic function of the refrain is "essentially territorial, territorializing or reterritorializing, whereas music makes of it a deterritorialized content for a deterritorializing form of expression" (MP 369; 300). The refrain, then, is "a way of impeding, of conjuring music or doing away with it" (MP 368; 300). Music takes the refrain as its content and transforms it by entering into a process of "becoming" that deterritorializes the refrain.

BECOMING-WOMAN, BECOMING-CHILD

We have seen how Messiaen's becoming-bird eventuates in the *Catalogue d'oiseaux*. What might seem a mere imitative exercise is actually the inauguration of a creative passage between bird and musician, a process whereby the bird's song becomes other as an unforeseen piano composition takes shape. All musical invention proceeds via such a becoming-other, since music is the deterritorialization of the refrain and deterritorialization is itself fundamentally a process of becoming. Becoming entails an unfixing of commonsense coordinates of time and identity. Drawing on the Stoic opposition of Chronos and Aion, Deleuze and Guattari contrast the measured time of a regulated succession of past, present, and future (Chronos) with an unmeasured and unregulated time that obscures the lines between past, present, and future (Aion), at once an always-already and an always–about to be, "a simultaneous too-late and too-soon" (MP 320; 262). Pierre Boulez distinguishes pulsed from nonpulsed time in music, noting that in modern compositions especially the regular measure of a fixed meter will often give way to a free-floating time, a sort of indefinite rubato unmarked by any organizing pulse; such a free-floating time Deleuze and Guattari call Aion. It is "time out of joint" (or, in the French translation of Hamlet's words, time "*hors de ses gonds*," "off its hinges"), the time of the infinitive—to walk, to sleep, to dream, to die—rather than any specific tense. Besides the coordinates of time, becoming also unfixes the commonsense delineations of spatial entities. In a process of becoming, bodies are determined solely by speeds and intensities, vectors of movement and affective capacities. The individuation of a becoming proceeds via a different course than that of a coded, regular process of identity formation. A becoming has the identity of an atmosphere, a time of day, or a season, a "haecceity" or "thisness" (after Duns Scotus), a specific configuration of relative movements and affective intensities that infuses and in a sense dissolves the heterogeneous commonsense entities that compose it. The identity of a becoming is molecular rather than molar, that of a multiplicity of elements that somehow cohere without entering into a regular, fixed pattern of organization.

Music, then, is a form of becoming, and it is "inseparable" from three specific forms of becoming, "a becoming-woman, a becoming-child, a becoming-animal" (MP 367; 299) (with a becoming-molecular implicit in all three).[1] Evocations of beautiful maidens, childhood games, or bird serenades are not accidental associations with isolated musical compositions but are indications of music's essential relation to the refrain. Why a becoming-*woman*, -*child*, -*animal*? Social coding operates by way of asymmetrical binary oppositions, in Western societies through an implicit privileging of male over female, adult over child, rational over animal, white over colored, etc. A becoming deterritorializes such codes and in its operations necessarily engages the underprivileged term of each of these binary oppositions. Hence, "There is no becoming-man, for man is the molar entity par excellence, whereas becomings are molecular" (MP 358; 292). A becoming-woman, a becoming-child, or a becoming-animal, however, does not involve the imitation of women, children, or animals—an action that would merely reinforce social codes—but an unspecifiable, unpredictable disruption of codes that takes place alongside women, children, and animals, in a metamorphic zone between fixed identities.

If Deleuze and Guattari find in Messiaen's use of birdsong a particularly clear example of a musical becoming-animal, Dominique Fernandez's study of vocal traditions in England, La Rose des Tudors, provides them with especially illuminating instances of becoming-woman and becoming-child in music. Fernandez somewhat whimsically opens his book by noting that in 1833 Rossini abandoned grand opera for haute cuisine, in despair, concludes Fernandez, at "the greatest involution that had ever occurred in the history of vocal art: the passage virtually without transition from an era in which castrati sang the lead roles on all the lyric stages of the world, to an era in which they disappeared completely" (Fernandez 8). Shortly thereafter, Verdi and Wagner rose to prominence, imposing a new order on vocal music, according to which "men must be men, and women must be women" (ibid. 12). Fernandez sees this musical separation of masculine and feminine not as an accidental byproduct of a humanitarian movement against child castration, but as a symptom of capitalism's division of labor, which entails a division of the sexes. He laments this gender partitioning of the voice since the sole purpose of vocal music, he believes, is to allow us to enjoy the undifferentiated pleasures of paradise beyond "the natural mutilation that has divided the two sexes into two camps since the androgynous spheres of Plato were cut into two halves" (ibid. 14–15). The true spirit of vocal music Fernandez finds virtually extinguished in Europe save in England's all-male college and cathedral choirs, whose boy sopranos and countertenors produce ethereal sounds of an unnatural, immaterial transparency. These treble voices are "head voices," produced through the sinuses rather than in the chest, as far as possible from the genitals and the rest of the body, "disincarnated voices, but of a burning sensuality, like a complete act of love, that physical and mystical love whose true dimension is not pleasure—poor respite wrested from time—but the desert, the internal void, death, ecstasy, eternity" (ibid. 36). The only vocalists who rival the English cathedral singers are the boys of Catalonia's Escolania de Montserrat, whose sopranos and altos do not emulate the head-voice technique of the British, however, but sing from the chest and stomach, producing a heavier, more voluminous sound. In their singing, Fernandez speculates, we receive hints of what the great castrati must have sounded like—ethereal, but charged with an intense eroticism. "All the sap which had no other issue from their bodies," he muses, "must have impregnated the air they sent forth from their mouths, transforming that usually aerial and impalpable substance into a pulpous matter, soft, carnal, tangible, sending forth with the volatile oxygen of the lungs the heaviness of their members, the moisture of their flesh, the misunderstood fecundity dislodged from their dead parts. These beings had not lost their sex, but had transferred it to their voices" (ibid. 121–22). The English boys sing as if they had no sex, the Catalan as if they already had the sex they will later possess, the castrati as if their sex had passed into their voices—in each case, as if the voice had been disengendered.

Deleuze and Guattari see in Fernandez's examples a becoming-woman and becoming-child in music, a "machining" of the voice that denaturalizes it, that deterritorializes it by decoding it as masculine or feminine, adult or child. The boy sopranos do not imitate women, any more than the countertenors imitate children. Rather, they submit the voice to a process of metamorphosis that passes alongside women and children, that renders the voice unnatural, other. "It is the musical voice that itself becomes child, but at the same time the child becomes sonorous, purely sonorous. . . . In short, the deterritorialization is double: the voice is deterritorialized in a becoming-child, but the child it becomes is itself deterritorialized, unengendered, becoming" (MP 373; 304). Deleuze and Guattari appreciate the absence of psychoanalytic interpretation in Fernandez, although they are less enthusiastic about his use of myths of androgyny and they reject his narrative of catastrophic loss in the imposition of the Verdi-Wagner separation of the sexes. The eroticism Fernandez discovers in the voices of the boys, countertenors, and castrati is simply the affective intensity evident in any becoming, one that belongs to bodies as vectors of movement devoid of personal or gender organization. What Fernandez regards as Verdi's and Wagner's corruption of vocal music Deleuze and Guattari treat as the deterritorialization of the voice by other means. In Verdi and Wagner gender coordinates may be restored, but at the same time the voice is altered by its relation to the instrumental accompaniment. No longer is the orchestra subservient to a primary vocal line, but the voice becomes merely one more instrument among the many instruments of the orchestral ensemble.[2] The voice is "machined" by the instruments, deterritorialized in a direction that leads eventually to what Deleuze and Guattari see as the "molecularization" of the voice in certain modern compositions.

TRANSVERSE BECOMINGS OF MUSICAL INVENTION

As Deleuze and Guattari's comments on Fernandez make clear, becoming has a historical dimension, although its relation to history is not entirely straightforward. Becoming partakes of the time of Aion, a convulsive, adifferentiated temporal flux, whereas history belongs to the world of Chronos, the time of measure and sequence. In *A Thousand Plateaus*, Deleuze and Guattari oppose traditional history to becoming, associating history with memory and becoming with an antimemory. Memory, they argue, "has a punctual organization since every present refers at the same time to the horizontal line of the *course* of time (kinematic), which goes from a former present to the contemporary present, and a vertical line of the *order* of time (stratigraphic), which goes from the present to the past or to the representation of the former present" (MP 361; 294–95). Becoming is not punctual but linear, a line moving *between* two points, in both directions at the same time. History is a memory that fixes time in discrete points; becoming unfixes those points and generates free-floating lines. History's antipode is Nietzsche's "untimely," which opposes history "not as the eternal, but as the subhistorical or supra-historical" (MP 363; 296). Rather than signifying a mere obliteration of temporal distinctions, the concept of an untimely antimemory points to an alternative mode of temporal differentiation, one according to *blocks* of coexisting "moments" of flux-time, blocks of varying dimensions that may be said in chronological terms to occupy minutes, days, or years, depending on the particular kind of becoming one is dealing with (an atmosphere, a season, an age).

Thus the history of music is always also an antihistory, an account of the various chronological moments in which composers have found means to create sonic blocks of floating time. Pierre Boulez says of Webern that he abolished the contradiction that had formerly existed between the horizontal-melodic and the vertical-harmonic aspects of tonal music, thereby creating "a new dimension, which we might label diagonal, a sort of distribution of points, or blocks, or figures no longer on the flat space, but in the sound-space" (Boulez 383). All genuinely creative composers, according to Deleuze and Guattari, proceed in a similar fashion, inventing diagonal, transverse lines of deterritorialization, whose specific characteristics, however, are determined in each instance by the musical conventions of the composer's era. In this sense, one may approach the history of music in terms of conventional forms and their transverse metamorphosis. Beethoven "produces the most astonishing polyphonic richness with relatively poor themes of three or four notes. There is a material proliferation which is one with the dissolution of form (involution), all the while accompanying a continuous development of form" (MP 331; 270). Likewise, Debussy and Ravel preserve certain late tonal forms in order to break them, *Bolero* being a virtually caricature-like instance of "a machinic assemblage that conserves minimal form in order to lead it to an explosion" (MP 331; 271).

CLASSICAL FORM, ROMANTIC VARIATION

In addition to this continuous history of formal innovation, however, Deleuze and Guattari also recognize the usefulness of a periodization of musical styles and themes, suggesting in *A Thousand Plateaus* a parallel between the traditional period concepts of Classicism, Romanticism, and Modernism and the three permutations of the refrain as milieu point of order, territorial circle, and cosmic line of flight. The problem in Classicism is to bring order out of chaos, to impose form on an amorphous matter and thereby transform it into a shaped substance.[3] Subsuming the Baroque and Classical periods within the same problematic, Deleuze and Guattari note the existence throughout much of the two periods of "a succession of forms compartmentalized, centralized, hierarchized, one in relation to the other" (MP 416–17; 338). Each form is like a milieu, a coded region of order, and the passage between units resembles the transcoding that takes place between milieus. Deleuze and Guattari here are simply echoing the common observation that in Baroque and early Classical works large structures are generally constructed through the juxtaposition of relatively simple formal units, such as the succession of binary and ternary forms of the various dance movements of a suite, the chain of variations sustained in a passacaglia, or the alternation of thematic entrances and nonthematic episodes in a fugue. (Although Deleuze and Guattari do not mention the development of sonata form, one can see this phenomenon as a solution to the period's basic challenge of assimilating small formal units within a broad evolutionary structure, the mature sonata form of Viennese Classicism constituting the great achievement that makes possible the transition to Romanticism.) Yet if each formal unit in a Classical composition is a milieu and the passage between units a transcoding of milieu codes, beneath the surface the forces of chaos continue to move, and between milieu units there is always the risk that chaos will erupt. Hence "the task of the classical artist is that of God himself, to organize chaos, and his only cry is Creation! Creation!" (MP 417; 338). Like Tamino with his golden flute or Papageno with his silver bells, the Classical composer overcomes the chaos of the Queen of the Night, converting birdsong refrains into the music of a newly created, paradisical world.[4]

If Classicism concerns milieu relations and the creation of order from chaos, Romanticism focuses on the earth and the foundation of a territory. In a simple sense Romantic music is territorial in that it frequently summons up associations with evocative landscapes and settings. As Grout remarks, there is a tension in Romanticism between the ideal of pure instrumental music and the desire for poetic expressivity, which is resolved in the development of program music, and though only certain compositions are explicitly associated with texts, "practically every composer of the Romantic era was, to a greater or lesser degree, writing program music, whether or not he publicly acknowledged it" (Grout 495). Hence, when discussing the way in which territorial counterpoints gain autonomy and become melodic landscapes, Deleuze and Guattari cite Liszt as an exemplary creator of sonic landscapes and characterize the Romantic *Lied* as "the musical art of the landscape, the most pictorial of musical forms, the most impressionistic" (MP 393; 319). But several other thematic and formal elements may be subsumed within the dynamics of territoriality. Besides recoding milieu components within a newly demarcated space, we will recall, a territory regroups forces, bringing them together in a mysterious center that is at the heart of the territory and yet outside it, a mythical earth that belongs to the territory and yet remains in tension with it. Rather than taming the evenly distributed forces of chaos (like the Classical composer), the Romantic artist confronts the assembled forces of the earth, whose dangers are figured in the images of hell, the subterranean and the ground-less (*sans-fond*). If the classical artist is a creative god, the Romantic is a hero defying God, like Prometheus or Faust, or one defying the volcanic void, like Empedocles. The Romantic's cry is not creation, but foundation, in the sense that one founds a city by tracing its territorial borders on the consecrated earth. The territorial refrain may find its foundation in the forces of the earth, as at the close of Mahler's *Song of the Earth,* which combines "two motifs, one melodic, evoking bird assemblages, the other rhythmic, the profound respiration of the earth, eternally" (MP 418; 339). Yet the earth as opening to the outside is a deterritorializing force that may undermine the stability of the territory. To the extent that territory and earth are out of sync with one another, the territory becomes a lost homeland and the artist a Romantic wanderer or exile, either seeking a return to the lost territory or pursuing the deterritorializing vector opened up by the earth. "Such is the ambiguity of the natal, which appears in the *Lied,* but also in the symphony and the opera: the *Lied* is at once the territory, the lost territory, the vectoral earth" (MP 419; 340).

Formally Romanticism is characterized by the principle of variation. Whereas the Classical artist imposes form on a chaotic matter and thereby fashions a formed substance (substance and form corresponding to milieu and code), the Romantic makes of form "*a great form in continuous development,* a collection of the forces of the earth," and treats matter as "*moving matter in continuous variation*" (MP 419; 340). Both form and matter, then, are subsumed within a constant process of variation. With the notion of "a great form in continuous development" it would seem that Deleuze and Guattari refer to what commentators on Romanticism have called organic form, distinguishing thereby the fixed structures of traditional genres from the germinative structures that take shape through an elaboration of relations intrinsic to the unfolding of the individual work of art. Such organic forms, manifest throughout Romantic art but especially in music and literature, obviously are forms "in continuous development" and forms that function as active shaping *forces*. That which is shaped by these forms in continuous development is the territorial refrain, which, we will recall, is made up of milieu components that have been decoded and thereby rendered expressive (for example, the leaves of the stagemaker). In the territorial refrain, internal and external milieu relations take on a life of their own, forming rhythmic characters and melodic landscapes whose interrelations constantly shift and change. Hence, in Romanticism matter ceases "to be a matter of content and becomes a matter of expression" (MP 419; 340), and that matter of expression is also a "moving matter in continuous variation."

THE PROBLEM OF THE PEOPLE

Central to Romanticism is the relationship between territory and earth, and it is within this context that Deleuze and Guattari approach the political issue of the role of the people in Romantic art. Questions of national, regional, and ethnic identity, of the dynamics of folk culture and art culture, of the relationship between the individual hero and the broad masses are everywhere apparent in nineteenth-century art, yet despite the efforts of Romantic artists to create works that speak for the collectivity, "that which is most lacking in romanticism is the people" (MP 419; 340). Here Deleuze and Guattari make use of an observation of Paul Klee's, to which they frequently return, that the artist needs the people and yet "C'est le peuple qui manque"—"The people is what is missing."[5] What Klee is suggesting, in Deleuze and Guattari's reading, is that an aggregate of individuals does not necessarily constitute a people, that the collectivity as a functioning entity is not a given but something that must be produced, and that such a functioning entity does not yet exist. The problem of the creation of a people is particularly acute in German Romanticism, where the people remains an ideal abstraction, the hero not a hero of the people, but a mythic hero of the earth. If a people exists, they are mediated by the earth, and the hero occupies the territory as a solitary wanderer, no matter how populous the region. The territory is the domain of the One-Alone, the lone hero, and the earth is the realm of the One-All, from which a people emerge only as a universal ideal. Much more successful are the efforts of Slavic and Italian Romantics, for in their works "the hero is a hero of the people, and no longer of the earth; he is in relation with the *One-Crowd*, not with the *One-All*" (MP 420; 341). Rather than the people being mediated by the earth, "it is the earth that is mediated by the people and that exists only through them" (MP 420; 340).

To a certain degree, in this opposition of Germanic and Slavic-Italian Romanticism Deleuze and Guattari are simply expanding on some of the basic differences often recognized in the operas of Wagner and Verdi (the Slavic-Italian connection being made through an association of Verdi's practices with those of Mussorgsky). Whereas Wagner in large part had to fashion his own dramatic audience, Verdi worked within a vibrant popular tradition, and early on his works became inseparably linked to Italian nationalism, especially through the stirring choruses of such works as *Nabucco* and *I Lombardi,* and were widely adopted virtually as patriotic anthems. Nationalism is equally prominent in Wagner, but generally it is swathed in myth and mysticism, collective identity articulated less in the choruses than in the orchestra, which tends to subsume the lone hero's voice within a homogeneous symphonic texture. In one sense, the differences between Wagner and Verdi are contextual and thematic, functions of historical circumstances and the subjects dramatized in the operas, but in another they are formal and strictly musical. When Klee says that the people is missing, what is at stake is the mode of individuation of a people, which should be that of a *becoming,* a multiplicity that is irreducible to the terms of the One and the Many.

Just such a concern seems to have preoccupied Debussy when he was at work between 1905 and 1908 on two operas based on stories by Edgar Allen Poe. In a letter to Louis Laloy, Debussy spoke of his struggle to develop a new kind of choral writing, more complex than that of Mussorgsky or Wagner. "The people in *Boris* [*Godunov*]," he said, "do not form a true crowd; here one group sings, here another, and here a third, each in its turn, and most often in unison. As for the people of *The Meistersingers,* it's not a crowd but an army, powerfully organized in German style and marching in ranks. What I would like to make is something more sparse, more divided, more relaxed, more impalpable, something inorganic in appearance and yet fundamentally ordered; a true human crowd in which each voice is free, and yet in which all the united voices together produce one impression and one movement" (cited in Barraqué 159). The chorus Debussy envisions is not a homogeneous mass, nor is it an aggregation of autonomous individuals.

Rather, it is a collective phenomenon within which multiple entities come into being and acquire a certain degree of cohesion and group identity, yet do so without dissolving and merging with one another. Such a collectivity is *"Dividual"* (MP 421; 341), neither a composition of the One out of the Many nor a manifestation of the One in the Many. Its cohesion and articulation into multiple elements proceed via the speeds and affects of a becoming: "The people must be individuated, not according to the persons within it, but according to the affects it experiences simultaneously and successively" (MP 421; 341).

The Dividual is a mode of individuation, the process through which a multiplicity comes into existence. It is the mode of individuation of a people, but also of any multiplicity whatsoever. In opera, the Dividual is evident in the handling of the chorus, which Verdi to a degree treats as an affectively individuated people rather than a Wagnerian homogeneous mass. But the Dividual may also affect the relationship between singer and orchestra as a whole. In the Romantic opera, the hero as individual subject undergoes emotions that are reflected in the non-subjective affects of the orchestra. In Wagner, the orchestra functions as a gathering of forces; its mode of individuation is that of the One and the Many, its articulation of elements unfolding via *"the relations proper to the Universal"* (MP 420; 341), the hero's vocal line emerging as an emanation of the One. In Verdi, by contrast, the orchestra's mode of individuation is to a much greater extent Dividual, and the hero's line develops as but one element of an emergent multiplicity. Claudio Sartori says of the great melodramas of the early 1850s, *Rigoletto, Il Trovatore,* and *La Traviata,* that "in truth, the heroes are not alone on the stage: an atmosphere envelops them, sustains and completes them, but it is a purely human, passionate atmosphere" (Sartori 642). Sartori attributes this atmosphere to the subordination of instrumental sonorities to vocal harmonies, but in Deleuze and Guattari's analysis, the affective atmosphere that accompanies Verdi's heroes and determines the relative roles of singer and orchestra is the Dividual, the mode of individuation of a people and a musical multiplicity.

VARÈSE AND THE MODERN SOUND MACHINE

If Deleuze and Guattari read Classicism in terms of milieu relations, and Romanticism in terms of territorial dynamics, they approach Modernism through the third moment of the refrain, the deterritorializing line of flight that opens a territory to the cosmos at large. Classical composers impose form on a chaotic matter, thereby changing that matter into a shaped substance; structural units are so many coded milieus, beneath which and between which the forces of chaos continue to play. Romantics transform the relationship between matter, form and force, treating form as a force of continuous development and matter as an expressive medium in continuous variation. Modern composers, by contrast, discover a third way of handling form, matter, and force, converting matter into a molecular *material* capable of harnessing cosmic forces. Paul Klee says that the object of painting is not to render the visible—to reproduce visual entities—but to *render visible*, to make visible that which is not visible, the forces that play through the visible. "This is the post-romantic turn: the essential is no longer in forms and matters, nor in themes, but in forces, densities, intensities" (MP 423; 343). Cézanne's concern is not to represent apples or mountains, but to render visible the germinative forces that infuse apples, the seismic forces that shape mountains. Similarly, the task of Modern music is to render audible forces that are inaudible. "Music molecularizes sonic matter and thereby becomes capable of harnessing nonsonorous forces such as Duration, Intensity" (MP 423; 343). In this regard, Messiaen's experiments with rhythm are exemplary, for in his compositions he is not simply inventing a new musical vocabulary but also rendering audible the nonsonorous force of time, "the endlessly long time of the stars, the very long time of the mountains, the middling one of the human being, the short one of insects, the very short one of atoms" (Rößler 40).

This Modern conception of music as molecularized sonic matter capable of harnessing forces perhaps has no more articulate a spokesman than Edgard Varèse, whose handful of compositions (eleven complete works, from *Amériques* in 1921 to *Poème electronique* in 1958) have played an important role in the history of the twentieth-century avant-garde. Deleuze and Guattari incorporate much of Varèse's vocabulary in their discussion of Modernism, and a brief consideration of the formation and articulation of Varèse's musical thought may help clarify the aims of their analysis. As a youth Varèse was struck by the speculation in Leonardo's notebook that waves of sound and light are governed by the same laws as those of water, and throughout his life he remained fascinated by the play of waves throughout physical matter. He soon developed a conception of music as an "art-science," whose goal should be the creation of a new alphabet, for "music that lives and vibrates needs new means of expression and science alone can infuse it with an adolescent vigor" (Vivier 31). The nineteenth-century physicist, chemist, musicologist, and philosopher Hoene Wronsky provided him with an apt definition of music as "the corporealization of the intelligence that is in sounds," a notion that led him to think of "music as spatial—as moving bodies of sound in space" (Ouellette 17). Impressed as well by the alchemical concept of the "transmutation of elements," he sought means of transmuting sonic matter, transforming the temporal flow of sounds into spatial blocks, planes, and volumes. Sirens, he found, were capable of generating "beautiful sonic parabolas and hyperbolas that seemed to me analogous to those one finds in the visual world" (Vivier 15). In *Amériques,* he explained, he used two sirens to make a contrast of pure sonorities that functioned as refracting prisms. "It is astonishing to see to what point pure sound, without harmony, gives another dimension to the quality of the musical notes that surround it. . . . In truth, the use of pure sounds in music acts on harmony the way a crystal prism acts on pure light" (ibid. 36).

In *Hyperprism* (1923), Varèse elaborated on this practice, combining pure sounds to create "an auditory impression of prismatic deformation: in my work, in place of the old fixed, linear counterpoint one finds the movement of planes and sonorouos masses, varying in intensity and density. When these sounds collide, phenomena of penetration or repulsion result. Certain transmutations take place on a plane. In projecting them onto other planes one creates an auditory impression of prismatic deformation" (Vivier 45). Some fifteen years later, Varèse studied the phenomenon of crystallization and found there a useful means of describing the generative process that guided his creation of sonic prisms. The external form of a crystal, he noted, depends on its internal molecular structure, "that is, on the most minuscule of arrangement[s] of atoms having the same order and composition as the crystallized substance," yet from a limited number of molecular structures an infinite number of crystal forms may be produced. Thus, in his compositions Varèse begins with an idea, a molecular internal structure, that then "grows, cleaves according to several forms or sonorous groups which ceaselessly metamorphose, changing direction and speed, attracted or repelled by diverse forces. The form is the product of this interaction" (ibid. 50). Yet another figure Varèse adopted to describe his molecular transmutations of sonic matter was ionization, the title of his 1932 composition for percussion. Nicolas Slonimsky, who conducted the New York premiere of *Ionisation,* observed that ionization "signifies the dissociation of electrons from the core of the atom and their transformation into ions. Here an immense force acts within an infinitesimal space" (ibid. 98). In its complex rhythms, textures, and timbres, what *Ionisation* articulates, according to Paul Rosenfeld, is "the life of the inanimate universe" (ibid. 100).

Musically, Varèse's experiments in prismatic deformation, crystallization, and ionization may be described in terms of an elaborate development of rhythmic relations at the expense of traditional linear pitch relations. In an incisive analysis of Varèse's oeuvre, the composer Elliott Carter credits Varèse with having developed "a new way of dealing with musical thought and structure," making "rhythm the primary material of his musical language" (Van Solkema 2). Varèse's basic method, Carter shows, is to combine and interrelate short rhythmic cells, which are varied in three main ways: by the addition or subtraction of notes; by augmentation or diminution of note values according to two-to-three relationships rather than by the more conventional practice of doubling or halving note values; and by distortion of inner cell relations, augmenting or diminishing one portion of a cell while keeping another portion constant. Here one finds clearly expressed in musical terms what Varèse refers to as crystallization, the manipulation of rhythmic cell permutations corresponding to the development of limited inner molecular structures that eventuate in myriad external crystal forms. Varèse does not, however, combine rhythmic development with the development of linear pitch motifs. "Traditionally," notes Robert P. Morgan, "rhythmic structure in Western music has been inseparably bound to the motion of pitches; and it has remained so in virtually all music written during the first half of the present century." Yet in Varèse's music often "the pitches appear to have lost their sense of linear direction, to have relinquished their tendency to form connections defined principally by stepwise motions. The pitches, one might say, don't want to go anywhere" (ibid. 14, 9). Pitches are deprived of temporal continuity, a given pitch not so much moving to another along the trajectory of a melodic line as being displaced by another discrete pitch, each occupying "more a position in musical space than a moment in musical time" (ibid. 10). Thematic development, traditionally dominated by the elaboration of linear pitch relations, is thus shifted to the nonpitched elements of timbre, dynamics, articulation, and, above all, rhythm. The result is a spatialized pitch texture charged with an intense rhythmic energy, for, as Carter remarks, Varèse's great achievement was not to block musical flow but to produce "a new rhythmic structure with a high degree of forward drive not resulting from regular beat patterns" (ibid. 3). In Varèse's handling of pitch, then, we may see a prismatic deformation of sound, a conversion of temporal pitch sequences into spatial units of extended pitch planes, harmonic blocks, and timbral volumes. This sonic space, filled with pitches that "don't want to go anywhere," forms an ionized atmosphere, animated by the complex movement of molecular rhythmic cells.[6]

It is not surprising that over the years Varèse came increasingly to refer to music as "organized sound" and to describe himself as "a worker in intensities, frequencies, and rhythms" (Vivier 126). Nor that he should be a pioneer in electronic music (*Deserts* [1954], *Poème electronique* [1958]), for what he sought was "a completely new means of expression—a sound machine (and not a machine for reproducing sounds)" (ibid. 125), and the electronic manipulation of sound promised to deliver new scales, timbres, rhythms, and harmonies as well as new means of projecting them in space. (*Poème electronique,* created for the Le Corbusier–Xenakis–designed Philips Pavilion at the 1958 Brussels World Fair, was recorded on a three-track tape and disseminated via four hundred speakers lining the pavilion's inside walls.) What must be stressed, however, is that Varèse initially called for such new sonic resources over fifty years before they became available. The technology of sound manipulation, far from generating an aesthetic, simply reinforced it. Throughout his career Varèse sought to dissolve the structures of tonal music and fashion a sonic material capable of capturing vital intensities, frequencies, and rhythms. He created sound prisms that refract nonsonic forces, sound crystals whose inner molecular structures generate multiple external forms, ion machines whose micro-perturbations give rise to sonic transmutations of matter. Advances in acoustical technology merely provided him with better tools for creating a music that "molecularizes sonic matter, but becomes thus capable of harnessing nonsonorous forces such as Duration, Intensity" (MP 423; 343).

If Modern artists shape a molecularized material capable of harnessing forces rather than a Romantic matter in continuous variation, they also have a different relationship to the earth and the people than did their nineteenth-century predecessors. The earth has become more deterritorialized, the people more molecularized. Following the analyses of Paul Virilio in *L'Insécurité du territoire,* Deleuze and Guattari see in modernity a concomitant globalization of powers of control and a molecularization of means of political regulation. If the object of modernity's aerial "total war" is the creation of constant terror, the annihilation of a population, and the destruction of a habitat (such as the DMZ in Vietnam), modernity's "total peace" simply pursues war by other means, instilling a pervasive climate of insecurity, depopulating cities by controlling urban space (citizens visibly disappearing from city landscapes, sheltered in cars, apartments, enclosed malls), rendering habitats increasingly uninhabitable. Modern forces of control engage in constant saturation bombing attacks on consumer-citizens, implementing a micropolitics of media and informational discipline and normalization that creates statistical populations functioning simultaneously as molar masses and molecular aggregates. Romanticism's problem of the "lack" of a people is only exacerbated in modernity; no longer can the artist dream of a universal *Volk* or invoke a constituted regional or national people. The Modern artist's effort remains that of creating a people as Dividual multiplicity, but such a collectivity must increasingly be conceived of as a future people, a becoming as line of incipient elaboration. "Instead of the people and the earth being bombarded everywhere in a cosmos that limits them, the people and the earth must be like vectors of a cosmos that carries them away; then the cosmos itself will be art. To make of depopulation a cosmic people, and of deterritorialization a cosmic earth, that is the desire of the artist-artisan, here or there, locally" (MP 427; 346).

This Modern project of the musical invention of a people may be best approached through the works of two composers to whom Deleuze and Guattari briefly allude, Béla Bartók early in this century, and more recently, Luciano Berio. Bartók sought in Hungarian folk music the inspiration for his own work and for the creation of a new national idiom, and in this sense his work may be seen as an extension of Romantic tendencies of the late nineteenth century. Unlike such Romantics as Liszt and

Brahms, however, who merely exploited Hungarian folk motifs for vague and picturesque coloration, Bartók engaged in intensive ethnomusicological research, collecting and publishing nearly two thousand folk tunes and eventually identifying among multiple crosscultural influences the core elements of a Magyar musical sensibility. This music of the people, however, did not directly feed into Bartók's compositions but instead guided him in his extension of the possibilities of modern Occidental art music.

As Gisèle Brelet shows, Bartók did not so much imitate Hungarian folk songs as extract their key practices and exploit them in the development of his own modern idiom. The asymmetrical rhythms and complex meters of folk tunes furnished Bartók with tools for disassembling the temporal regularities of the nineteenth century, but unlike those of many Modern composers, his rhythmic experiments did not issue from an abstract manipulation of numerical permutations but retained the vibrancy and physicality of the dance and song practices of a popular culture. His harmonic language developed from tendencies within folk melodies, the pentatonic and modal scales and relaxed cadences of folk tunes suggesting means of extending tonality without embracing atonality. Rather than starting from a theoretical commitment to chromaticism, as in serial practice, Bartók arrived at an intense chromaticism through a fusion of modes and combination of tonalities intimated in the flexible structures of folk melodies. He developed a supple and mobile harmony, one that exploits chromaticism and intense dissonance while maintaining a tonal center. "The harmony of Bartók," as Brelet observes, "is the atonal mastered by the tonal" (Brelet 1052).

His development of form also grew out of his encounter with folk motifs, but again without resorting to a simple imitation of popular techniques. As Brelet points out, the primary obstacle to the appropriation of folk song within art music is that folk melodies are generally self-enclosed, complete in themselves and in no need of further development, whereas the themes of great art compositions are incomplete and open-ended, and the form of such compositions is generated from the expansion and elaboration of the potential inherent in those themes. Bartók's great achievement, argues Brelet, was to absorb the essence of Hungarian folk melody, and without echoing any particular tunes, to invent open-ended, generative themes that eventuate in extended, complex musical forms.

What is important to note is that despite his intense engagement with the remnants of a rich folk tradition, Bartók was in no way presuming the existence of a popular culture within which he could function. His ethnomusicological research was an effort to rediscover a lost heritage and use it to reinvent Hungarian musical culture within the larger practices of Western art music. In Deleuze and Guattari's terms, a process of mutual deterritorialization passed between Magyar folk song and Western Modernism in Bartók's music, making possible an extended, chromatic tonality and a rhythmic complexity that are neither ethnically traditional nor academically experimental. As Deleuze and Guattari remark, in extracting from self-enclosed melodies the elements of open-ended themes, Bartók converted territorializing refrains into deterritorializing refrains, thereby constructing "a new chromaticism" and creating " *'themes'* that assure a development of Form or rather a becoming of Forces" (MP 432; 349–50). The discovery of a popular tradition, in short, in no way spared Bartók the modern task of inventing a people, and that invention proceeded in his music via the deterritorialization of folk and art practices alike.

In the Italian composer Luciano Berio, the Modern dilemma of the invention of a people is even more pronounced than in Bartók. Here, we find a similar if somewhat less intense interest in the interrelationship of folk and art music, as well as a pronounced concern with the problem of the Dividual, or the articulation of collectivities. "I return again and again to folk music," says Berio, "because I try to establish contact between that and my own ideas about music. I have a Utopian dream, though I know it cannot be realized: I would like to create a unity between folk music and our music—a real, perceptible, understandable continuity between ancient, popular music-making which is so close to everyday work and our music" (Berio 148). That utopian project is perhaps best represented by *Coro* (*Chorus*), Berio's composition for forty voices and forty-four instrumentalists, first performed in its extended form in 1977. In *Coro*, Berio makes explicit use of folk material, alternating settings of various folk texts and fragments from Pablo Neruda's *Residencia en la Tierra* in thirty-one continuously played sections. Like Bartók, Berio does not quote specific folk melodies, but writes lines that freely develop microthemes extracted from general folk practices. Unlike Bartók, Berio does not concentrate on a single ethnic tradition, but includes in his composition texts from North and South America, Polynesia,

Africa, Europe, and the Middle East. Although the Italian and Hebrew sources are performed in those languages, most of the non-Western texts are sung in a literal English translation, with Croatian texts set in French translation, and Persian texts in German. A similar pancultural heterophony prevails musically, as, for example, in Berio's exploitation of the performance techniques of African wooden-trumpet bands, which he freely adapts in his setting (in section 9) of a Gabon text to the melodic contours of a Macedonian tune—the result of which, as David Osmond-Smith remarks, sounds "as close to a fourteenth-century European hocket as to a Central African trumpet band" (Osmond-Smith 83). In this conjunction of multiple cultural, linguistic, and musical motifs, transmuted through the compositional techniques of Berio's sophisticated late Modern idiom, we hear echoes of a global, ethnic past, but one in which folk motifs have been deterritorialized, cut loose from their specific contexts and juxtaposed in unstable, shifting relations. Amid the amalgamation of cultural voices, however, we hear as well the sounds of a people in the process of formation, one that has yet to be born and that Berio is attempting to create.

In *Coro* Berio also tries to solve the technical problem of imagining a collective identity outside the universalizing relation of the One and the Many. Throughout his work, Berio is interested in exploring the relationship between voices and instruments, and in *Coro* he pairs each singer with an instrument of a similar range, placing the pairs in a complex arrangement across the performance space. Each vocalist's line is conceived as an interactive development of its matched instrument's capabilities, just as each instrument explores the expressive and gestural potentials of its accompanying voice. The voice is denaturalized through its use of intervals, timbres, attacks, and so forth typical of its paired instrument, but also through the interjection of cries, clicks, wheezes, stutterings, and laughter amid the fragments of recognizable linguistic text. At times Berio alternates contrasting duets of isolated voice-instrument pairs, at others he combines pairs to form chamber ensembles of various sizes and textures. In the sections devoted to Neruda's text, however, massed *tutti* forces create sonic blocks of prolonged chords in which instruments and voices blend, emerge momentarily as discernible entities, and then reenter the sonic mix. As voices become perceptible within the *tutti* chords, vague syllables and fleeting stammerings seem to emerge from the sound mass as if a collective utterance were in gestation but not yet fully formed. What *Coro* presents, in sum, is the composition of a molecular population, created through a "machining" of voices and instruments, words and nonlinguistic utterances, that appears in various groupings and combinations of musicians as Berio explores the possibilities for composing a Dividual collectivity, each assemblage with its prospects of defining an affective multiplicity, each with its dangers of collapsing into a homogeneous mass or a concatenation of discrete individuals.

The three periods Deleuze and Guattari identify, the Classical, the Romantic, and the Modern, correspond to the three moments of the refrain—as organizing point, territorial circle, and cosmic vector. Yet the moments of the refrain, we will recall, do not follow one another in an evolutionary sequence, but function "as three aspects of a single and same thing" (MP 383; 312). As one might expect, then, Deleuze and Guattari stress that the three periods "must not be interpreted as an evolution, nor as structures, with signifying breaks" (MP 428; 346). The Modern task of molecularizing matter and harnessing forces is the task of all art. Painters have always sought to render visible invisible forces, composers to render audible inaudible forces. The difference is that in Modernism forces are seized directly, whereas in Classicism and Romanticism they are "reflected in the relations of matter and form" (MP 428; 346). The history of art, then, is a history of perception and discernibility, of the changing ways in which forces and the molecular operations of deterritorialization manifest themselves. Hence, the problem of the creation of a people emerges in the nineteenth century, but the mode of individuation proper to the formation of a people, the Dividual, is already present in Classicism, though undiscerned as such. In Romanticism the Dividual is perceived in terms of ethnic, regional, or national identity, and in Modernism in terms of statistical masses and micropolitical populations, but what becomes increasingly explicit in Modernism is that the invention of a people is part of a general process of becoming, one that embraces the phenomena of becoming-woman, becoming-child, and becoming-animal in a single becoming-molecular. "In this sense, there is hardly any history other than one of perception, whereas that from which history is made is rather the matter of a becoming, not of a story [*histoire*]" (MP 428; 347).

The music history Deleuze and Guattari trace, then, is always a double history: a *history* of perception and discernibility, of individual composers' formal innovations, and of the varying problems and solutions evident in different periods; and an *antihistory* of becoming, an antimemory of temporal blocks of differential speeds and affective intensities. Deleuze and Guattari state that there is no evolution in the periodization they outline, but it is decidedly Modernist in orientation, with its emphasis on innovation and experimentation as the prime movers in all art. This orientation, however, may simply be a function of the history of discernibility, the hermeneutic perspective of Modernism being necessarily the one from which we discern our position in history. But whatever the contours of their periodization or the particular judgments they offer of individual composers, most significant are the interconnections Deleuze and Guattari's double history makes possible between what are conventionally regarded as musical and extramusical matters. The various themes enunciated in opera librettos, song lyrics, program notes, and composition titles, the diverse connections drawn by composers between their works and mythical, religious, philosophical, and social ideas—these are not extraneous impositions on a musical form, but indexes of becomings, elements proper to music yet unassimilable within a mimetic model of musical imitation or representation of a discursive content. Music's emotional dimension also is proper to its history, not as a coded translation or direct expression of emotions but as a complex intermingling of personal and interpersonal feelings with the nonpersonal affective intensities of becomings. And finally, there is a politics proper to music, that of the invention of a people, but one that avoids reductive schemes of sociological causation or reflection and resists ready appropriation by any given agenda, since the history of the Dividual is an antihistory of becoming, whose opening to the future is forever uncharted.

Chapter Three

NATURA MUSICANS:
TERRITORY AND THE REFRAIN

According to Messiaen, birds are probably "the greatest musicians existing on our planet" (Samuel 51). As we have seen, this conjunction of birds and music points in one direction toward a conceptualization of human music as a cosmic art, one that is directly in touch with the differential rhythms of the natural world. But it also points in another direction, toward a biological contextualization of music and the other arts. Are birds musicians? Do animals have art? If so, what is the relationship between human art and the art of other creatures? These are some of the questions Deleuze and Guattari explore in plateau 11 of *A Thousand Plateaus,* the guiding thread of their discussion being the concept of "territoriality." Our concern here is to show how this discussion affects our understanding of ethology, developmental biology, and evolutionary theory, and how we might begin to relate aesthetics to these sciences.

ETHOLOGY AND TERRITORIALITY

The concepts of territorialization, deterritorialization, and reterritorialization have long played an important role in the thought of Deleuze and Guattari. As early as 1966, Guattari made use of these concepts in discussions of group psychology, speaking of mass identification with a charismatic leader as "an imaginary territorialization, a fantasmatic group corporalization that incarnates subjectivity," and of capitalism as a force that " 'decodes,' 'deterritorializes' according to its *tendency*" (PT 164). Guattari's effort here is to extend to the domain of the social Lacan's essentially psychological use of "territorialization" to refer to the process whereby parental caregiving invests the infant's libido in specific body regions, the infant's initially free-floating "polymorphous perversity" giving way through parental care (feeding, cleaning) to a "territorialized," or fixed, localized organization of the body into erogenous and nonerogenous zones. Guattari's broadly social application of the Lacanian concept is developed further in *Anti-Oedipus,* where "deterritorialization" and "reterritorialization" figure prominently in tandem with the concepts of "decoding" and "recoding," the first pair largely relating to bodies and physical investments of energy, the second pertaining to symbolic representations and mental investments of energy. As Eugene W. Holland has pointed out, in *A Thousand Plateaus* decoding and recoding tend to recede in importance, whereas deterritorialization and reterritorialization become increasingly significant concepts, their relatively circumscribed function in *Anti-Oedipus* of describing material investments in human desiring-production being extended in *A Thousand Plateaus* to characterize phenomena ranging from geological formations to DNA strands and interspecies relations.[1] It is only at this juncture of their work that Deleuze and Guattari turn to what biologists call "territoriality."

Observers since Aristotle and Pliny have noted that certain animals defend their domains against intruders, but the formal concept of territoriality has been slow in taking shape. Henry Eliot Howard is often credited with first developing the biological concept of territory in his *Territory in Bird Life* (1920), although Ernst Mayr points out that many of his findings were anticipated in Bernard Altum's *Der Vogel und sein Leben* (1868), a work that has remained untranslated and generally unknown in the English-speaking world. Stokes notes as well that the concept of territoriality may be found in C. B. Moffat's largely ignored essay, "The Spring Rivalry of Birds" (1903). In the 1930s and 1940s, Huxley, Tinbergen, Lorenz and others extended analyses of territoriality in birds to other animals, and gradually the concept became established as a basic notion in ethology. From the earliest studies by Altum, Moffat, and Howard, the idea of territoriality has been related to aggression. In a 1956 survey of the literature on territoriality in birds, Hinde reviews a number of definitions of the concept and concludes that Noble's 1939 characterization of territory as "any defended area" may serve as a standard minimal formulation of the notion.[2] Several functions have been attributed to territorial behavior: limitation of population density, facilitation of pair formation and maintenance of the pair, reduction of interference with reproductive activities, defense of the nest, defense of food supplies, reduction of losses to predators, reduction of time spent in aggression, prevention of epidemics, prevention of inbreeding and crossbreeding (see Hinde). But the predominant view is that territoriality is a mode of social organization whereby the strongest males (generally) secure mates and desirable habitats, establishing through various aggressive communicative actions with conspecifics an equilibrium of population density across a given area.

Perhaps the best-known and most fully developed study of aggression and territoriality is Konrad Lorenz's *On Aggression* (1966), a work that articulates with particular clarity the assumptions predominant in the field. Lorenz sees hunger, sex, fear, and aggression as the four great biological drives. Intraspecies fighting has Darwinian survival value in that "it is always favorable to the future of a species if the stronger of two rivals takes possession either of the territory or of the desired female" (Lorenz 30). Territorial aggression ensures that the resources of a region will not be exhausted through overcrowding, that the strongest will obtain the most desirable mates, and that progeny will be sheltered within the defended domain: "The environment is divided between the members of the species in such a way that, within the potentialities offered, everyone can exist. The best father, the best mother are chosen for the benefit of the progeny. The children are protected" (ibid. 47). Various territorial signals—the "bright poster-like color patterns" (ibid. 18) of certain tropical fish, the songs of numerous birds, the olfactory markings of deer, rabbits, or dogs, diverse ritual behavior patterns such as the zigzag dance of the stickleback—all serve as substitutes for fighting, and hence as derivative means of establishing and maintaining distance between rivals.

According to this familiar mechanistic, stimulus-response model, territoriality is simply a random outgrowth of the primary drives that has proved to possess survival value. Birdsong, far from being an animal art form, is merely an instinctual communicative signal at the service of the drives of sex and aggression. Lorenz's influential thesis, in Deleuze and Guattari's judgment, "seems to us ill-founded" (MP 388; 316). Deleuze and Guattari do not deny the connection between aggression and territoriality, but they do question the primacy granted aggression as explanatory cause. Aggression is organized differently in a territorial than in a nonterritorial species, just as other functions (mating, rearing, food gathering, etc.) are differently configured, or in some cases, newly created (various forms of dwelling construction). But no function explains territoriality; rather, it is territoriality that explains the reorganization of functions. "These functions are organized or created only because they are *territorialized,* and not the reverse. The T factor, the territorializing factor, must be sought elsewhere: precisely in the becoming-expressive of rhythm or melody, in other words, in the emergence of proper qualities (color, odor, sound, silhouette . . .)" (MP 388; 316). There is "an auto-movement of expressive qualities" (MP 389–90; 317), Deleuze and Guattari claim. Expressive qualities are "auto-objective, in other words, they find an objectivity in the territory they draw" (MP 390; 317). They express the relation of the territory to internal and external milieus, but this expressiveness is not the result of an impulse triggering an action. "To express is not to depend upon; there is an autonomy of expression" (MP 390; 317).

Deleuze and Guattari's response to Lorenz may seem no response at all, in that they claim "the T factor," the becoming-expressive of rhythm or melody, is its own explanation. In fact, what Deleuze and Guattari are proposing is an alternative conception of nature, one that is expressive rather than mechanistic and that builds especially on the work of the pioneering ethologist Jakob von Uexküll and the philosopher Raymond Ruyer.

VON UEXKÜLL AND MUSICAL MILIEUS

Deleuze and Guattari cite von Uexküll as the author of "an admirable theory of transcodings," one that treats milieu components "as melodies in counterpoint, the one serving as a motif for the other, and vice versa: Nature as music" (MP 386; 314). The work in which the nature-music connection is most evident is von Uexküll's 1940 study *Bedeutungslehre (Theory of Meaning),* which appeared in French translation in 1956 as *Théorie de la signification.*[3] Living beings are not mechanical objects regulated merely by cause-and-effect forces, according to von Uexküll, but subjects inhabiting worlds of meaning. When von Uexküll meets a furiously barking dog on his daily walk and throws a paving stone toward it to scare it away, the stone does not change its physical properties, but its *meaning* for the dog does change. What had been an object functioning in the human world as a support for the steps of pedestrians (and probably as an indifferent feature of the ground for the dog) has been converted into a menacing projectile in the dog's world, into a bearer of meaning. "It is only by way of a relation that the object is changed into a bearer of meaning, meaning which is conferred on it by the subject" (ibid. 86). Von Uexküll distinguishes between plants, which are immediately embedded in their habitat, and animals, which occupy a milieu (*Umwelt*), but "on one point the planes of organization of animals and plants coincide: both effect a precise choice among the events of the external world that concern them" (ibid. 93). An animal milieu "constitutes a unity closed in on itself; each part of it is determined by the significance it receives for the subject of this milieu" (ibid. 90). Perhaps von Uexküll's best-known example of this concept is the tick, whose milieu is constituted by a very limited number of factors. The tick climbs to the top of a branch or stalk and drops on a passing mammal, whose blood it then sucks. The tick has no eyes, the general sensitivity of its skin to sunlight alone orienting it in its upward climb. Its olfactory sense perceives a single odor: butyric acid, a secretion given off by the sebaceous follicles of all mammals. When it senses a warm object below, it drops on its prey and searches out a patch of hair. It then pierces the host's soft skin and sucks its blood. The tick's milieu is made up of those elements that have meaning for it: sunlight, the smell of butyric acid, the tactile sense of mammalian heat, hair and soft skin, and the taste of blood. Its milieu is a closed world of elements, outside of which nothing else exists. Although it seems that animals all inhabit the same universe, each lives in a different, subjectively determined milieu. Hence, the stem of a wildflower is a different object for the tick that climbs it, the girl who plucks it, the locust larva that pierces the stem and extracts its sap, and the cow that eats it. "The same components, which in the stem of the flower belong to a precise plane of organization, separate into four milieus and with the same precision join four totally different planes of organization" (ibid. 89).

From a behaviorist's perspective, von Uexküll is simply saying that animals respond to different stimuli. Von Uexküll insists, however, that the passage from perception to action is to be understood not as an induction of an electrical current through a wire, but as "the induction which passes from one sound to another in the unfolding of a melody" (von Uexküll 93), that is, as a unifying theme that expresses a meaning. Furthermore, such melodies uniting perceptions and actions are inseparable from the developmental melody that guides the gestation and maturation of each living being, "a melody of growth or an imperative of growth that regulates the individual tonalities of the germinative cells" (ibid. 98). Hence, von Uexküll can refer to gastrulation as "the simple melody with which every superior animal's life begins" (ibid. 98). To emphasize the interconnection of biological beings and their habitats/milieus, von Uexküll speaks of the relationship between an interpreter and a bearer of meaning as a contrapuntal relation, that is, as a harmonious concurrence of two or more melodies. For an oak tree, rain is a bearer of meaning that it utilizes as nourishment. The oak's leaves, which are fashioned with gutterlike veins and which spread like the tiles of a roof, form a melodic point in harmony with the counterpoint of the rain. In a similar fashion, the formation of the octopus's muscular pocket, which it contracts in order to swim, is a developmental melody in counterpoint with the incompressibility of water, which makes such hydraulic locomotion possible.

More complex are the contrapuntal relations between species, such as that between bats and certain nocturnal butterflies. The chief predator of such butterflies is the bat, which uses sound for a variety of purposes. The butterfly possesses a very limited sonic apparatus, capable of recognizing only a narrow band of frequencies; that band, however, corresponds precisely to the cry of the bat. The same sound emitted by the bat has different meanings for the two species. "Given that the range of perceptive signals of the bat is extended, the sharp sound it perceives is only one tone among others. By contrast, the range of perceptive signals of the nocturnal butterfly is very limited, for its milieu contains only one sound: that of its enemy" (von Uexküll 114). How is it that the structure of the butterfly contains an apparatus suited to perceiving its enemy? "The rule of development of butterflies contains from the beginning instructions for forming an auditory organ attuned to the cry of the bat" (ibid. 114). Clearly, the butterfly's behavioral melody of perception and action presumes a developmental melody, both butterfly melodies being constituted in counterpoint with the melody of the bat.

And it is meaning that is the guiding concept in this analysis, "not the miserable rule of causality which can see no further than one step in front or one step behind, and remains blind to broad structural relations" (ibid. 106).

The same determinative role of meaning in relation to development may be seen in the spider. The spider spins a web that is ideal for capturing flies: the web's tensile strength is sufficient to withstand the fly's struggles, the gaps in the mesh proportioned to the dimensions of the fly; the radial filaments are more solid than the circular arcs, and hence well suited for the spider's perception of vibrations in the web and its movement to the site of a disturbance; the finer circular strands, unlike the radial spokes, have a sticky glue for imprisoning the fly; and all the threads of the web are so fine that they escape detection by the fly's eyes. What is most surprising is that the spider "weaves its web before even having encountered a real fly. Its web, consequently, cannot be the copy of a physical fly, but represents its archetype, which is not given physically" (von Uexküll 105).

Von Uexküll regards a territory as simply a specialized milieu, and one that reveals very clearly the subjective nature of milieus. A fly may have a dwelling, but the space it traverses does not constitute a territory. The spider, by contrast, has both dwelling and territory in its web. The mole also has dwelling and territory in its central nest and radiating network of tunnels, which occupy and control a given region like an underground spider web. What one sees more clearly in the mole's territory than the spider's, however, is that a territory is "a pure active space" (von Uexküll 63), the tunnels marking the repeated and familiar movements whereby the animal constructs its milieu in accordance with its particular array of senses. In the case of territorial birds and fish, dwelling and territory are distinct. Such territories may be marked in various ways, but they tend to be more abstract and less visible than the territories of the spider and mole; like the mole's burrow—and more obviously so—they are pure active spaces created through patterns of movement that define an extended milieu.

Deleuze and Guattari do not adopt all aspects of von Uexküll's analysis of nature as music, but much of it they are in sympathy with. Von Uexküll's stress on "meaning" they rephrase in terms of "affects" and "bodies," the tick aptly illustrating the thesis that a body may be defined by its power of affecting and being affected by other bodies (see

MP 67-68; 51, and MP 314; 257; S 167-68; 124-25). But this shift in terminology merely reinforces von Uexküll's basic point that milieus are inextricable from the creatures that create and inhabit them. Deleuze and Guattari, like von Uexküll, speak of milieu components as "melodies," thereby emphasizing the organization of pragmatic and developmental patterns as temporal unfoldings that possess a thematic coherence. But they stress as well the role of differential rhythms and periodic metrical repetitions in the construction of milieus; hence, by isolating the characteristic common to sonic and nonsonic motifs—the temporal disposition of their elements—they provide a literal rather than a figurative means of speaking of milieu components. Von Uexküll's analyses of such contrapuntal relations as those between bats and butterflies, and spiders and flies, merely reinforce Deleuze and Guattari's contention that milieus must be considered as relational concepts. And though Deleuze and Guattari's differentiation of milieu and territory differs somewhat from von Uexküll's—the spider, for example, is not territorial according to Deleuze and Guattari (MP 386; 314)—they all regard territory as a specialized rhythmic organization of milieu components.

RUYER AND THE MELODIES OF DEVELOPMENTAL BIOLOGY

Von Uexküll recognizes the importance of developmental melodies in the symphony of nature, but for a detailed elaboration of this notion one must turn to Raymond Ruyer, a philosopher whom Deleuze and Guattari cite with some frequency.[4] In a series of books, including *La Conscience et le corps* (1937), *Eléments de psycho-biologie* (1946), *Néo-finalisme* (1952), and *La Genèse des formes vivantes* (1958), Ruyer articulates a philosophy of biology centered on the formative activity of all living beings. Ruyer's controlling insight is that the morphogenesis of a living entity can never be explained via a mechanistic causality-through-contiguity, but must presume the existence of a formative theme or melody controlling its development. Following Whitehead, Ruyer distinguishes between living forms—self-shaping, self-sustaining, and self-enjoying entities—and aggregates, quantitative collections of entities whose forms are determined by external forces, and hence are explicable in terms of mechanistic causal relations. Examples of aggregates are clouds, ocean currents, geological formations, and human crowds.

Living forms extend from the smallest self-sustaining subatomic particles through viruses and bacteria to the most complex multicellular organisms.

A living form is a process, an ongoing formative activity that Ruyer equates with consciousness: "Consciousness *is* every active process of formation, in its absolute activity, and every process of formation *is* consciousness" (Ruyer 1958, 240). Ruyer is not advocating a mind-body dualism, or a vitalistic dualism of "entelechy" and organic machine. Consciousness is not a separate ingredient or a spiritual substance. It is an "intelligent or instinctive act, always in the process of organizing, according to the theme that it assumes, subdomains themselves in the midst of a process of organization" (ibid. 244). Ruyer also differentiates his position from panpsychism, which adopts human consciousness as its model and then ascribes such a consciousness to other entities. Ruyer's point is that human consciousness is a very specialized, idiosyncratic instance of a general formative activity exhibited by all living entities. Hence, one should regard embryologists as former embryos, who, in the course of their morphogenesis, have developed a most complicated and indirect cognitive tool—adult human consciousness—with which they try to learn what every embryo already knows: how to grow into a mature individual.

According to Ruyer, morphogenesis proceeds in a temporal, "horizontal" sequence, but always according to a "vertical," trans-spatial and transtemporal theme, "an individualized melodic theme which can either be repeated as a whole or can be distributed in variations, in which the initial, repeated theme serves as its own 'development' (in the musical sense of the term)" (Ruyer 1958, 96). This organizing and regulating theme exists in a virtual, ideal domain immanent within the entity undergoing actualization. The theme, however, is not a complete blueprint or code for the construction of a living being, for Ruyer is not proposing to replace a mechanistic preformationism (which he finds in conventional explanations of morphogenesis as the implementation of genetically coded instructions) with a metaphysical version of this doctrine. Morphogenesis proceeds in accordance with the theme, but not as the copy of a fully formed model. "The organism forms itself with risks and perils, it is not formed. . . . The living being is at the same time agent and 'material' of its own action. . . . The living being forms itself directly according to the theme, without the theme having first to become idea-image and represented model" (ibid. 261–62).

The vertical melodic theme, a virtual motif immanent within the actualizing process of morphogenesis, is consciousness, which is "nothing other than form, or rather the active process of formation, in its absolute existence" (Ruyer 1958, 240). To emphasize the derivative, specialized nature of human consciousness, Ruyer distinguishes between three different kinds of forms. Form I is the fundamental form, the self-sustaining, auto-conducting, self-enjoying activity common to all living beings. Form II is a particular case of Form I, that of a reflective, representational consciousness created through the development of organs of perception and motor schematization. Form III, a subset of Form II and found only among humans, "appears when utilitarian perception, which serves only as a signal or index of instinctive life in animals and in humans insofar as they lead an animal life, changes its role, and when the signal becomes a symbol, manipulable by itself, and detachable from every context of vital or immediate utility" (ibid. 220). In this sequence of forms Ruyer sees evident the nature of morphogenesis as a conquest of space and time, "a conquest and also a creation" (ibid. 221). Form I, as exemplified in atoms and molecules, is a structuring activity "for constituting a domain of space" (ibid. 221). Form II creatures, provided with faculties of perception and schematization, gain possession of an extended space as *Umwelt*. And with the advent of Form III, "the 'subject' or 'perceiving consciousness' seems detached from extension and duration, as a sort of point of view" (ibid. 221). Territoriality marks a specific stage in the conquest of space and time, one that reveals the intimate connection between Form I and Form II. Territoriality requires the development of a Form II consciousness, but the inhabited territory is defined and fashioned by the body that inhabits it—that is, by the body as actualization of the Form I process of morphogenesis. Territory and animal constitute a single biological field, "a morpho-genetic theme directing at once the organic and the extra-organic, internal circuits and external circuits, the biotope and the psychotope, that which is inside and that which is outside the skin. . . . Organic movement includes the milieu. The *Umwelt* is a subordinated theme in the organic form before being differentiated into a distinct extra-organic form as territory" (Ruyer 1958, 230).

Ruyer does not discuss the role of birdsong, display markings, or other indexes used to demarcate territories, but his remarks on the relationship between animal and human artistic activity suggest what his analysis would be. The display feathers of the peacock form a complex, organized pattern, each feather developing as if it could see from the outside its position in the overall design. The mystery of such self-decoration, however, only arises when we analyze it from the perspective of a human artist before a canvas. Instead, we should reverse the situation and treat human art as a subcategory of organic creativity. A man tattooing himself is essentially no different from a peacock forming its ornamental display, except that in the human being the ornamental theme appears first as an idea in the cerebral tissues, and then is executed through a complex neuromotor circuit of eye-hand-brain activity, whereas in the peacock there is no such specialization of functions, the morphogenetic formative activity of the organism operating as the equivalent of an undifferentiated eye-hand-brain circuit. Human art, then, is merely a specialized and indirect manifestation of the organism's ongoing formative activity, one that is increasingly detached from other life functions. "The expressivity of perceived forms is detached from the vital situation, which permits artistic play and the gratuitous creation of aesthetic forms . . . that live their own life and develop as if by themselves, although they are naturally always attached to possible perceptions, that is to Form II, itself always attached to the Form I of the organism" (Ruyer 1958, 220–21). Birdsongs and display markings, we may infer, are simply components of the territorial time-space system that reflect a certain level of specialization in the organism's morphogenetic formative activity and a specific degree of detachment from other life functions.

What is important to note here, however, is the continuity among living forms that Ruyer exhaustively establishes, as well as the increasing degrees of specialization and detachment he points out at various stages in the development of complex organisms. Every living form is the unfolding of a virtual melodic theme, but in the emergence of Form II from Form I, and of Form III from Form II, one sees a growing autonomy in the organization of time and space, an increasing separation of subjectivity from morphogenetic formative activity, and an augmenting independence of aesthetic forms from their vital context. In essence, what Ruyer is describing at such length are biological instances of de/reterritorialization, of the detachment or unfixing of elements and their reorganization within new assemblages. Ruyer's work, then, supports Deleuze and Guattari's contention that a *territory*, in the biological sense of the term, is created through the general processes of *deterritori-alization,* whereby milieu components are detached and given greater autonomy, and *reterritorialization,* through which those components acquire new functions within the newly created territory. Deleuze and Guattari emphasize the distinction between milieus and territories, but the continuity of living forms across that divide is suggested in their concept of the refrain, which can serve as a point of organization for a milieu, which can delimit the dimensional space of a territory, and which can open a line of flight from a territory toward the cosmos, but whose three manifestations are "not three successive moments in an evolution," but "three aspects of a single and same thing" (MP 383; 312).

STRUCTURAL COUPLING AND NATURAL DRIFT

One might concede that Ruyer and Deleuze-Guattari have demonstrated the ubiquity of de/reterritorialization yet still question whether this is a self-explanatory phenomenon (and hence challenge the assertion that a territory emerges through the "self-movement of expressive qualities"). What remains is to see how von Uexküll's ethology of contrapuntal *Umwelten* and Ruyer's developmental biology of melodic living forms might be accommodated with evolutionary biology. It is, after all, the neo-Darwinian model that supplies the primary explanatory power of Lorenz's account of territoriality, and any alternative to that account must address the issues raised by evolutionary theory. A useful approach to the subject that embraces many of the insights of von Uexküll and Ruyer and that largely accords with Deleuze and Guattari's thought is the so-called Santiago theory of Humberto Maturana and Francisco Varela (which Guattari refers to briefly in *The Three Ecologies* [TE 60; 100] and *Chaosmosis* [CH 20; 7 and 61; 56]).[5]

Maturana and Varela are among a number of researchers who have been studying self-organizing systems, or systems whose patterns of order emerge spontaneously from chaotic states. Maturana and Varela characterize living systems as self-organizing, self-maintaining, and self-referring systems, coining the term "autopoiesis" to describe this process of autogeneration and autoregulation. What differentiates living systems from other self-organizing systems is the manner in which they interact with the world. Not only do they act on and react to the outside world, but they specify which external perturbations will be incorporated into their circular, self-regulating organization. They engage in a "structural coupling" with selected features of their surroundings, thereby "bringing forth a world." This autopoietic process of structural coupling Maturana and Varela equate with cognition. Hence Maturana's statement that "living systems are cognitive systems, and living as a process is a process of cognition" (Maturana and Varela I 13).

In *The Embodied Mind* (1991), Varela and his colleagues Evan Thompson and Eleanor Rosch offer a critique of neo-Darwinism and outline an alternative approach to evolutionary theory based on the notions of autopoiesis, structural coupling, and natural drift. They point to several problems inherent in the neo-Darwinian model, but especially the severe restrictions on genetic variation imposed by pleiotropy, or the interdependent linkage of genes to one another, and by the complex genic interconnections that orchestrate the developmental sequence of morphogenesis; the puzzling phenomenon of genetic drift and the gratuitous existence of "junk DNA"; and the evolutionary stasis of some organisms through pronounced environmental changes over long periods of time. Neo-Darwinism presumes a fixed, given environment to which an organism must adapt, genetic variation serving as the motor of that adaptation. Varela, Thompson, and Rosch insist, however, that living beings and their environments are mutually specified, or codetermined, and that genetic codes cannot be separated from their material context.

This point requires some elucidation, given the prevailing orthodoxy of genetic determinism in much contemporary biological thought. Varela, Thompson, and Rosch here follow the analyses of Susan Oyama, who in *The Ontogeny of Information* carefully demonstrates that current genetic research argues against the notion that DNA alone provides the "blueprint," "plan," or "code" for biological development, despite researchers' continuing talk as if this were the case. Raff and Kaufman, she points out, marshal strong evidence that in the fertilized egg three components are necessary for development: nuclear DNA, regionalized cytoplasmic macromolecules (mRNA, which derives from the mother's genome, not the embryo's own), and the cytoskeletal matrix (the structure of the cell). The cytoplasm is not a passive medium for the reception of DNA instructions, nor is the cell structure a neutral context for DNA activity. All three are active participants in a developmental system, and as ontogenesis proceeds, multiple factors, both internal and external to the growing organism, affect its development. Signals between developing embryonic cells, as well as environmental influences such as heat and light from outside the embryo, at times initiate sequences of differentiation, at others maintain differentiation in surrounding cells. "Development thus proceeds in 'cascades' of sequential inductions and 'networks' of multiple influences on a given induction" (Oyama 130). And, of course, the embryo does not exist *in vacuuo,* but within a maternal organism, which itself functions in an extended environment. What all this means, concludes Oyama, "is not that genes and environment are necessary for all characteristics, inherited or acquired (the usual enlightened position), but that there is no intelligible distinction between inherited (biological, genetically based) and acquired (environmentally mediated) characteristics" (ibid. 122).

Organisms and environments, then, are "mutually unfolded and enfolded structures" (Varela, Thompson, and Rosch 199) engaged in a process of bringing forth a world. And that world is not ruled by a logic of the "survival of the fittest." Natural selection (if one must use the term) does not prescribe what life forms will exist, but simply proscribes those life forms that are not viable. Within the broad constraints of survival and reproduction, mutually enfolded organisms and environments engage in a process of "natural drift," exploring a vast range of possible lines of development. Those possibilities do not have to be the best (survival of the *fittest*) but simply good enough. The evolutionary process is "*satisficing* (taking a suboptimal solution that is satisfactory) rather than optimizing," and it proceeds via "*bricolage,* the putting together of parts and items in complicated arrays, not because they fulfill some ideal design but simply because they are possible" (ibid. 196).

Maturana and Varela conclude *The Tree of Knowledge* (1987) by positing love as the controlling principle of evolution, thereby stressing the cooperative values of mutual enhancement and interdependence as opposed to the competitive values of struggle and domination that reign in neo-Darwinism.[6] But what Varela, Thompson, and Rosch suggest, in their notion of natural drift as satisficing *bricolage*—an assembling of parts "simply because they are possible"—is that *creation* is the primary force active in evolution. Living systems emerge from chaotic states as loci of self-organization, and as they develop, they bring forth multiple worlds, over time interchanging components in heterogeneous structural couplings, fashioning new enactive couplings for no other reason than that they can be formed. The broad constraints of survival and reproduction allow myriad structural couplings, but dictate none; ever new couplings emerge simply because living systems are inherently creative, inventive, formative processes.

What Maturana, Varela and their colleagues provide is an evolutionary biological justification for the claim that the transmutations of the refrain, whose transverse, differential rhythms pass between milieus and territories and beyond, are, indeed, self-explanatory. Von Uexküll's contrapuntal harmonies of intertwined milieu melodies are structural couplings, spontaneously generated codeterminations of organisms and environments. The varying degrees of deterritorialization and reterritorialization manifested in the passage from Ruyer's Form I to Form II and Form III, and from milieus to territories and other modes of spatial organization, are evidence of no teleological design, but simply the products of a ubiquitous experimental *bricolage*, an inventive construction of machinic assemblages across a wide range of structural possibilities.

FUNCTION AND AESTHETICS

If we return to the question of whether animals have art, we might say in a general sense that all living beings have art, in that all are inherently creative. Following Ruyer's analysis of the relationship between the peacock's feather display and the painter's canvas, we might argue that there is a continuity between animal and human creativity, although animal invention involves Forms I and II but not the more deterritorialized Form III. Yet we may still ask whether animal creativity is an aesthetic activity, whether, for example, birdsong is really music. For Ruyer, the answer would be no, for only with Form III is the expressivity of perceived forms "detached from the vital situation, which permits artistic play and the gratuitous creation of aesthetic forms" (Ruyer 1958, 220). Lorenz would obviously respond negatively as well, since for him birdsongs and other territorial markings are simply functional signals in the service of aggressive and sexual drives. Hartshorne and Thorpe, who have discussed the relationship of birdsong to music with particular care and insight, have concluded that birds are indeed musicians, since they play with sounds and appear at times to enjoy song for its own sake.

All these responses assume an opposition of the functional and the aesthetic, of activities that are purposive means and those that are self-sufficient ends. Deleuze and Guattari concur with Hartshorne and Thorpe that birds make music: "Art is not the privilege of human beings. Messiaen is right in saying that many birds are not only virtuosos but artists, and above all through their territorial songs" (MP 389; 316–17). But their approach to the question entails a realignment of the functional and the aesthetic that allows for their mutual interpenetration in the work of art.

From the point of view of neo-Darwinism, birdsong exists only because it serves the purposes of species survival and reproduction. From the perspective of an autopoietic universe of natural drift, birdsong might serve any number of functions, some (possibly) ensuring survival and reproduction, others promoting different activities of the living system, including but not limited to the activities we call artistic creation and aesthetic enjoyment or contemplation. The birdsong as territorializing refrain is a milieu component that has gained autonomy and become expressive, in the process creating a territory and concomitant reorganization of functions (MP 394–97; 320–23). As territorialized motif, the birdsong takes on various roles within the territory, combining with diverse functions to promote different activities. The refrain itself, however, as differential, incommensurable rhythm passing between milieus and territories, has a life of its own, a nonorganic life that functions only as a creative line of flight, an autonomous, deterritorializing transverse vector of invention.

If birdsong is a form of art, as Deleuze and Guattari assert, then the work of art is embedded in the world and enfolded in various functions. Art therefore cannot be construed in terms of a pure formalism, as a "purposiveness without purpose" divorced from the world (if we adopt here a common narrow reading of Kant). Those functions, however, extend over such a wide range that the concept of function as pragmatic purpose is undermined, in that there is no longer any clear criterion for distinguishing pragmatic and nonpragmatic ends. The functionalism of natural drift ultimately tends toward the functionalism of molecular desiring-production described in *Anti-Oedipus*, one in which "functioning and formation, use and assembly, product and production are merged" (AO 342; 288). The functional question in such desiring-production is not "What is it for?" but simply "Does it work? Does it make something happen?" "Only that which is not produced in the same way as it functions has a meaning, and also a purpose, an intention. Desiring-machines on the contrary represent nothing, signify nothing, mean nothing, and are exactly what one makes of them, what one makes with them, what they make in themselves" (AO 342; 288).

Two examples from *Anti-Oedipus* should clarify Deleuze and Guattari's approach to the "functioning" of components in desiring-production. In the opening pages of the book, Deleuze and Guattari characterize the interconnection of desiring-machines by referring to a section from Beckett's *Molloy* (Beckett 69–74), in which the narrator exhaustively describes the movement of sixteen "sucking stones" distributed in two greatcoat pockets and two trouser pockets, the stones passing from one pocket to another via the mouth that sucks the stones. The stones, pockets, transferring hands and sucking mouth form a circuit of clearly delineated components whose interrelations are demarcated by a discrete and regular series of operations. Together, the components make up a simple, well-oiled machine, yet one that seems devoid of any purpose other than its own functioning. This is in contrast to the Rube Goldberg machines that Deleuze and Guattari cite as examples of desiring-production in the appendix to the expanded edition of *Anti-Oedipus*. Here, the pragmatic purpose of each machine is clear, in one case to remind a man to mail a letter (*You Sap, Mail That Letter*), in the other to help someone diet (*Simple Reducing Machine*), but the means of fulfilling its purpose are ludicrously convoluted and improbable. (*Simple Reducing Machine:* peas from the diner's plate shoot in the air and strike a bell; a disoriented boxer answers the bell and falls on a mattress; air compressed from the mattress arouses a rabbit, whose leap activates a phonograph that plays the *Theme of the Volga Boatmen;* a Volga boatman heaves on a rope tied to the diner's wheeled chair, which pulls the diner away from the table.)

These extremes of desiring-production—maximal efficiency with no clear purpose, and clear purpose with minimal efficiency—are the extremes observable in a cosmos governed by natural drift. When describing the complex of components that makes up the territorial assemblage of the stagemaker, Deleuze and Guattari speak of "a veritable *machinic opera* that unites heterogeneous orders, species and qualities" (MP 408; 330), the male bird's song being indissociably linked to his position on his singing stick, his situation in relation to his particular display ground and the leaves he manipulates, his exposure of yellow feathers below his beak, his contrapuntal responses to other singers and to the presence of prospective mates, etc. The stagemaker's song is but one element of an intricate circuit of actions and objects, whose functioning is so fascinating precisely because it is so involved and so unlikely. It seems a mere *bricolage* of randomly gathered pieces held together by improvised means. And in no way can this be considered an anomalous assemblage, as one may see from any cursory review of the array of improbable circuits that inform many relationships between predator and prey, parasite and host, male and female, parents and progeny, etc. Even the developmental patterns of individual organisms, so often thought to be the result of a mechanical efficiency, seem as *ad hoc* and improbable as the machinic opera of the stagemaker. In an article titled "Why Is Development So Illogical?," Roger Lewin describes Sydney Brenner's effort to detail the genetic code of a nematode worm, which always has the same number of cells in each of its organs and in its body as a whole. After determining the complete developmental history of each of the nematode's 959 cells, Brenner found that " 'what the lineage of the cells has taught us . . . is that there is hardly a shorter way of giving a rule for what goes on than just describing what there is.' " Observes Lewin, "There is no simple logical series of cell divisions from which the groups of organ assembly might have been predicted. The lineage is, in a word, baroque" (Lewin 1328). As Oyama remarks in her review of Lewin's article, "Even the most apparently clockworkish developmental systems on closer inspection seem more like Rube Goldberg devices" (Oyama 178). If, then, the universe of natural drift gives rise to ubiquitous Rube Goldberg machines and gratuitous Beckettian stone-sucking circuits, there is no clear means of distinguishing the functional from the nonfunctional. Of course, if species survival determines functionality, then every aspect of a successfully reproducing species' life world is functional, no matter how baroque, bizarre, or preposterous it might seem. But this is simply another way of saying that a creature's activities are embedded in a life world, whether we conventionally label those activities pragmatic or aesthetic, necessary or gratuitous. All that one can say, finally, is that they are part of the same machine, and that somehow the machine works.

THE AUTONOMOUS REFRAIN

In *The Ontogeny of Information,* Susan Oyama demonstrates at length the remarkable persistence with which the Cartesian mind/matter dualism continues to haunt biological thought. Time and again organisms are treated as physicochemical machines, and then ghosts (usually genes) are surreptitiously slipped into the machines in order to explain how passive, inert matter can be animated by a shaping form. Time and again, these ghost-driven machines are situated within a world of mechanical forces to which they adapt with greater or lesser flexibility (depending on the analyst's stand in the nature/nurture debate). Genetic determinism reduces organisms to robots constructed by preexisting programs, and behavioristic determinism regards organisms as stimulus-response devices reacting to environmental forces. To counter the mechanism of such thought, von Uexküll speaks of biological subjects and meaning, while Ruyer equates living form with consciousness and Maturana and Varela define living systems as cognitive systems. Their use of such mental concepts as subject, meaning, consciousness, and cognition, however, must not be construed as revivals of panpsychism or vitalism, but instead as efforts to overcome the mind/body and form/matter dualisms that continue to control much of the discussion in developmental biology, ethology, and evolutionary theory. Von Uexküll's reference to subjects and meaning simply stresses the active coinvolvement of organisms and milieus in their mutual determination. Ruyer's talk of consciousness serves primarily to naturalize human consciousness as a particular version of a general self-shaping activity manifest in all living forms. And Maturana and Varela speak of cognition in order to stress that organisms specify their environments and thereby bring forth co-enacted worlds.

In *A Thousand Plateaus* Deleuze and Guattari avoid such mentalistic terms, occasionally resorting to an antimentalist vocabulary of desiring-machines, machinic assemblages, machinic phylums, and so forth in order to counter the same Cartesian dualisms, though from the opposite direction. The danger they run, of course, is that of being read as simple mechanists, and it is for this reason they stress so often that desiring-machines are not the same as industrial machines. What von Uexküll and Ruyer offer them, however, is an alternative vocabulary for describing nature, not one of minds or machines but one of music—melodies, counterpoints, harmonies, refrains—and by avoiding any reference to subjects, consciousness, or cognition, they stress that the cosmic refrain produces itself and is its own explanation.[7]

Does it finally make sense to speak of a self-generating refrain, a refrain divorced from a specific, producing agent or subject? One need simply ask, Where is the refrain? Is it in the contraction of the octopus's muscular pocket or in the water the octopus expels as it swims? Is the refrain in the tick or in the mammal whose blood it sucks, in the spider and its web or in the fly for whom the web seems so specifically designed? The refrain is the differential rhythm constituted in milieus, the relation between milieu components, and though one can speak of the melody of the octopus and the countermelody of the water, their contrapuntal *relation* is the refrain, one that belongs to both but in a sense to neither. Likewise, the stagemaker sings its territorial song, yet its musical motif is part of a refrain that includes its perching stick, the leaves it turns, the mate it attracts, the songs of its competitors, and the space it controls. The refrain is the set of relations that constitutes the territory, produced by its components but not contained exclusively in any one of them. The stagemaker's song expresses the territorial relations, but the refrain is immanent within the territorial assemblage as a whole. Can one locate the refrain in the developmental melodies Ruyer studies? Ruyer insists that ontogeny is a formative activity that proceeds according to a melodic theme, one that does not preexist its own activity and that is not exhausted until its action ceases. It is immanent within the process of morphogenesis but at no specific point present save as movement toward the completion of its form. Often we hear that the developmental refrain is in the DNA sequence, but in a fertilized egg, the nuclear DNA, regionalized cytoplasmic macromolecules, and the cell's structure are all necessary, active components of ontogenesis, and in the process of cellular differentiation, temporal factors, intercellular relations and extracellular influences mutually determine the formation of the organism. Once again, the refrain is not in any one component, but in the relations between elements within an unfolding activity.

The refrain is autonomous, unlocalizable, and, as we have seen, self-explanatory. Neo-Darwinians such as Lorenz regard behavioral patterns as functions of biological drives (such as hunger, sex, fear, and aggression), the pressure of natural selection assuring that those drives are the primary determinants of behavior. But in a world of natural drift, self-preservation and reproduction alone do not specify paths of evolutionary development. Multiple paths are possible, with varying degrees of efficiency and complexity. Within the broad constraints of survival and reproduction, viable structural couplings may assume the most baroque and improbable of configurations, incorporating whim-sical Beckettian sucking devices or forming intricate and unlikely Rube Goldberg machines. The motor of such a universe is not survival of the fittest but creation, an experimental assemblage of heterogeneous forms for no other reason than that they are possible. Those forms display varying levels of autonomy in their organization of time and space and in their differentiation of functions, a general process of decoding and recoding, of deterritorialization and reterritorialization, marking the emergence of various milieu relations, territorial configurations, and nonterritorial social structures. But this variability is as much aesthetic as pragmatic, the manifestation of an inventive *bricolage* and spontaneous functioning without purpose or goal beyond its own operation.[8]

What we have, then, is a grand *natura musicans,* a creative intertwining, enfolding, and unfolding of differential rhythms that play through milieu points of order, territorial domains, and transterritorial openings to the outside. Human music is a deterritorialization of the refrain—a formed substance wrested from chaos in the Classical age, a form in continuous development shaping a moving matter in continuous variation in Romanticism, a molecular material capable of capturing nonsonic forces in the Modern era—but its deterritorialization is only one manifestation of a general process that pervades the physical and biological universe. Birds are musicians, but so are crickets, ticks, atoms, and stars. And the musical motifs composed by a Varèse or a Messiaen are intertwined with those developmental themes that unfold in the embryo and its coenacted world as it eventuates in the ongoing biological activity we call Varèse or Messiaen. The becoming of human music—becoming-woman, becoming-child, becoming-animal, becoming-molecular—passes between entities, and in this regard it simply takes the path of the cosmic refrain, the differential rhythm that passes between milieu components, through territorial assemblages and beyond. The refrain is a territorializing force, in that it encodes milieus and organizes territorial assemblages, yet it is also a deterritorializing force. Hence Deleuze and Guattari's opposition of the territorial refrain to another kind of refrain, the refrain as "prism," as "crystal of space-time," "as final goal of music, the cosmic refrain of a sound machine" (MP 430–31; 348–49). Human music is a deterritorialization of the refrain, but the refrain deterritorializes itself, and in harnessing forces through molecular sound machines modern composers make discernable processes that permeate the world. We speak of composers and their compositions, but at a certain level of analysis it is difficult to tell who or what is composing. Where is the refrain? It is not contained in the composition, in the forces it harnesses, or in the developmental theme of the composer as unfolding biological entity and coenactive world, though it passes through them. Music, finally, is the refrain composing itself.

Part II

PAINTING

Chapter Four

FACES

The central tenets of Deleuze's philosophy of painting are to be found in two major texts: *A Thousand Plateaus* (1980), especially "Plateau Seven: Year Zero—Faciliaty," and *Francis Bacon: The Logic of Sensation* (1981). In this chapter we will examine the first of these texts, focusing on the rather elusive concept of "faciality," which treats the human face as a key component not simply in painting, but also in the functioning of language and sign systems, the formation of subjectivity, and the deployment of power relations. In chapters 5 and 6 we will turn to *Francis Bacon* and what Deleuze calls the "logic of sensation," considering first the "harnessing of forces" that Deleuze regards as the main object of painting, and then the role Deleuze attributes to color in painting's engagement of those forces.

HAND AND MOUTH, TOOL AND FACE

Each art confronts a different problem it addresses in heterogeneous ways, according to Deleuze and Guattari. Painting's problem is "the face-landscape," whereas music's is the refrain (MP 369; 300). Before examining painting's problem, however, we should note first that this opposition of face-landscape and refrain need not be taken too strictly. The broad concept of the refrain as differential rhythm clearly allows for visual as well as sonic components in the formation of milieus and territorial assemblages. The stagemaker not only sings but also manipulates inverted leaves to demarcate its territory, and its visual display Deleuze and Guattari describe as a form of "*art brut*" (MP 389; 316). Most strikingly, the three basic moments of the refrain may be described in visual terms, Paul Klee's remarks on the "gray point" providing Deleuze and Guattari with a lucid explanation of this concept. In his discussion of the genesis of art, Klee posits an initial chaos which he calls a "nonconcept," a "nowhere-existent something" or a "somewhere-existent nothing" that defies the laws of contradiction. Its pictorial symbol is "the point that is not properly a point, the mathematical point" (Klee 3). Chaos is the gray point, neither white nor black, cold nor warm, high nor low, without determinate dimensions. There is a fundamental instability in this chaos, however, and the origin of the world comes from the automovement of the point. "A point in chaos: Once established the gray point leaps into the realm of order. . . . The order thus created radiates from it in all directions" (Klee 1961, 4). The gray point is the refrain's initial figure as point of milieu order; its automovement creates lines that eventuate in demarcated territorial space. And as the point continues to move, it "launches forth and leaves itself, under the action of wandering centrifugal forces that unfold to the sphere of the cosmos" (MP 383; 312).

Rhythm is the element common to painting and music, and there is a fundamental continuity between the two arts that allows for their mutual accommodation within the concept of the refrain and territoriality. Nonetheless, the fact remains that musicians work with sounds and painters with lines and colors, and the refrain in its strictest sense is a sonic notion. Hence, rather than approach painting as the deterritorialization of the refrain as differential rhythm, Deleuze and Guattari choose to discuss painting via a specifically visual concept, that of *visagéité*, a neologism formed from *visage*, the French word for face, that Deleuze and Guattari's translators have generally rendered as *faciality*. Painting and music have their own specificity, based in an opposition between the face and the voice: "The face with its visual correlates (eyes) relates to painting, the voice, with its auditory correlates (the ear is itself a refrain, it has the shape of one), relates to music" (MP 371; 302). Painting deterritorializes the face just as music deterritorializes the voice.

This opposition of face-painting and voice-music is less straight-forward than it might at first appear, not simply because voices issue from the mouths of faces, but also because, according to Deleuze and Guattari, faces and voices are themselves essential components in the functioning of language. Indeed, it is only via a discussion of language and what Deleuze and Guattari call "regimes of signs" that we will be able to appreciate the significance of their association of the face with painting. In their treatment of language as one configuration of the strata of the cosmos (plateau 3 of *A Thousand Plateaus*), Deleuze and Guattari cite André Leroi-Gourhan's speculations on the development of human language in relation to the evolution of the body. Leroi-Gourhan argues that the use of tools and the use of language are inter-related, and that their emergence is dependent on the anatomical modifications of *Homo sapiens* that set the species apart from other primates. The fabrication of tools requires the liberation of the hands and arms from the activity of locomotion, something that is made possible when humans stand erect on two feet. Not only are bipeds able to handle tools, but they can also capture prey with their free hands. Once the mouth is no longer needed for seizing prey, as it is in four-legged primates, it may assume other functions. The snout-shaped face with its muzzle jaw, essential for grasping prey, grows flat, and the lips, tongue, throat, and larynx are able to assume a form that makes them suitable for the articulation of speech. (Many researchers point out that the obstacles to language use among nonhuman primates derive as much from anatomical limitations in the reproduction of sound as from limitations in cerebral capacities.) The relative flattening of the face also makes possible a reconfiguration of the skull and enlargement of the cranial cavity to accommodate a brain capable of producing and processing language. Thus in Leroi-Gourhan's analysis there is a complementary relationship between tool use and language use and between the anatomical development of the hand and the face, the configuration of the face being inextricably tied to the evolution of the voice.

Deleuze and Guattari use this opposition of hand-tool and face-language to develop a theory of language that emphasizes the interrelationship of discursive and nondiscursive elements in the formation of sign systems. Broadly put, hand and face correspond to the poles of technology and language, the manipulation of things and the manipulation of words, and Deleuze and Guattari insist that the two poles are closely related, though in no simple correspondence of representing word to represented thing. Rather than seeing language as a self-referential system of acoustic images (signifiers) and mental concepts (signifieds), as do many of the structuralist descendants of Saussure, Deleuze and Guattari situate language within a larger sphere of action. They argue that the common subordination of pragmatics to linguistics should be reversed, that language should be regarded as a specific kind of action related to other forms of action. (Here, of course, Deleuze and Guattari are expanding on some of the implications of speech-act theory, as developed by Austin, Searle, Grice, and others.) To speak is to do things with words, to effect transformations of bodies through language, as when the pastor says "I thee wed" and the couple thereby become man and wife. Language presupposes a complex structure of actions, a regular pattern of socially sanctioned practices that inform the transformations of bodies effected by words. Such a pattern constitutes a "collective assemblage of enunciation" or "regime of signs." Likewise, the "bodies" or "things" transformed by words are themselves shaped by a pattern of sanctioned practices, and hence they belong to a "machinic assemblage of bodies" or a "social technological machine." Collective assemblages of enunciation and machinic assemblages of bodies reciprocally presuppose one another, but they remain functionally independent. Signs do not represent things so much as they intervene in them, "work on things themselves, just as things extend into and deploy themselves across signs" (MP 110; 87). In a given social field, then, one encounters two "formalizations," or ways of shaping the world, one of content, and one of expression, each autonomous but each interacting with the other. "For content is not opposed to form, it has its own formalization: the hand-tool pole, or the lesson of things. But it is opposed to expression, which has its own formalization: the face-language pole, the lesson of signs. Precisely because content has its own form no less than does expression, one can never assign to the form of expression the simple function of representing, of describing or attesting to a corresponding content: there is neither correspondence nor conformity" (MP 109; 85–86).

REGIMES OF SIGNS AND THE FACES OF POWER

Leroi-Gourhan correlates the anatomical modifications of hand and face with the emergence of technology and the development of language, but

Deleuze and Guattari view this association of the face with language as more than a mere accident of evolutionary history. The face, they argue, is a basic component of at least two collective assemblages of enunciation, or regime of signs, and its function varies with the configuration of each of the two regimes. Throughout their discussion of language, Deleuze and Guattari emphasize the power relations inherent in sign systems, insisting that language's purpose is less to communicate than to impose order. Language enforces a codification of the world according to orthodox categories and classifications, its various speech-acts shaping, guiding and policing thought and behavior. Hence, the regular pattern of socially sanctioned practices effected by language may be said to constitute a *regime* of signs, a power structure that forms individual subjects and places them in social and political relation to one another. In plateau 5 of *A Thousand Plateaus,* Deleuze and Guattari outline four general categories of regimes of signs: a presignifying primitive regime, a signifying despotic regime, a postsignifying passional regime, and a countersignifying nomadic regime (with no suggestion that this classificatory schema is exhaustive or comprehensive). The face plays a different role in each regime (although Deleuze and Guattari do not specify what that role might be in the nomadic regime, which they treat only in a cursory manner).

One of the objects of Deleuze and Guattari's analysis of regimes of signs is to demonstrate that Saussurean linguistics does not reveal the universal aspects of language, but only discloses the characteristics of a specific organization and disposition of signs. The biunivocal correlation of signifier and signified, the dominance of the arbitrary signifier over the signified, the identification of the signifier with law and authority (especially in the Lacanian thematics of the master signifier and the *Nom du Père*), the positioning of signifiers in an infinite chain of self-referential interpretation—all are characteristics of the despotic regime of signs, which Deleuze and Guattari associate with the state form of social organization. In their account, primitive societies that lack a state also lack a centralized organization of signs. Animals, plants, places, celestial objects, bodies, lineages, gods, and so on have significance, but their interconnections remain local, specific, and heterogeneous. "It is a segmentary semiotic, but one that is plurilinear, multidimensional, which fights in advance any signifying circularity" (MP 147; 117). With the advent of the state, such primitive codes are detached from their various domains and reassigned to the omnipotent despot, whose body functions as the body of the state. The despot becomes the unifying source of all signification, his signs being interpreted endlessly by the inner circle of courtiers and priests and the radiating circles of provincial administrators, regional officers, and local functionaries. All signs refer back to the despot, and they are registered on his frontal face, which beams forth as the coded body of authority. Opposition to the despot's reign of universal signification is figured in the faceless scapegoat, whose expulsion from the state negatively codes the regime's line of flight. Thus the signifying despotic regime may be seen as a spiral: in the center is the Master Signifier, the despot-god whose voice issues from on high and whose face bears the codes of state authority; surrounding the despot are widening circles of interpretation; and at the limit of the regime the spiral straightens into a line of flight that is blocked by the city wall, beyond which the expiatory scapegoat is driven into exilic wandering.

In a sense, the postsignifying passional regime of signs begins where the despotic regime leaves off—with the line of flight, which this regime inhabits, tames, and encodes. Here, one might think of Moses and the Israelites wandering in the desert. Moses is not a temple priest interpreting the despot's past and present edicts, but a prophet possessed and overwhelmed by God, seeking at each stage of the people's journey a path to the future. In his encounter with the Lord on Mount Sinai, he turns his face away from the God whose face is hidden, and he returns to the Israelites with tablets that encode the people. But the journey does not end at this point. The people betray God's covenant, their wandering continues, and other prophets succeed Moses, as do further betrayals that occasion still new wanderings, whether literal or figurative. What Deleuze and Guattari find in this example is an authoritarian rather than a despotic regime of signs, one whose figure is not a spiral but a line divided into discrete segments, each segment representing an instance of a process of "subjectification," whereby a subject is constructed in relation to a dominant reality. Signs are organized not around a central power, but in relation to an obsessional "point of subjectification," an object of fixation from which issue two forms of the subject, the subject of enunciation (*sujet d'énonciation*) and the subject of the statement (*sujet d'énoncé*). (Deleuze and Guattari are here making use of a common structuralist distinction that allows one to discriminate in a sentence such as

"I am dying" between the actual person speaking, the *sujet d'énonciation*, and the "I" spoken of in the sentence, the *sujet d'énoncé*.) From the point of subjectification "issues the subject of enunciation, as function of a mental reality determined by this point. And from the subject of enunciation issues in its turn a subject of the statement, that is, a subject tied to statements in conformity with a dominant reality" (MP 162; 129). In our example, God is the point of subjectification, Moses the subject of enunciation, and the Israelites the subject of the statement. From God issues the mental reality that determines Moses' position as a subject, and from his interaction with God issues the dominant reality of the covenant people. Moses, of course, is a member of that people, and hence there is a doubling of the two subjects, "an imposition of the one on the other, the subject of the enunciation on the subject of the statement" (MP 162; 129), a process that is crucial to the fixing and regulating of codes in this regime. Here, signs are organized in discontinuous encounters, each establishing a local order, yet each initiating a meandering movement toward further encounters. The doubled subject engages the point of subjectification in a relationship of perpetual absorption and betrayal, a covenant in errancy. The face in profile replaces the frontal face of the despot, Moses' averted face signaling at once his bond with God and his people's inevitable betrayal of that bond.

We must not focus too closely on the example of Moses, however, for the postsignifying passional regime may be manifest in many different forms. Anorectics find in food a point of subjectification, their position as subject of enunciation and subject of the statement emerging from that relationship of alimentary obsession and betrayal. Lovers may take each other as points of subjectification, Tristan and Iseult serving as models of this version of the passional regime—seized by an all-consuming passion, yet perpetually denied fulfillment of their love, wandering from encounter to encounter toward the black hole of their eventual union in death. The Cartesian subject also may be seen as an instance of the passional regime, the idea of the infinite functioning as point of subjectification, the *cogito* as subject of the enunciation, and the *sum* as subject of the statement redoubling the *cogito* as determinate existence in conformity with the dominant reality of common sense (see MP 160; 128). Likewise, the signifying despotic regime may take on many different guises in multiple settings—in families, schools, factories, armies, hospitals, wherever the radiating circles of perpetual signification are focused on a centralized master signifier. Even the presignifying primitive regime may appear in multiple contexts, although its dynamics become less clearly discernible when it functions outside traditional tribal social structures. It is convenient initially to conceive of regimes of signs in terms of a schematic narrative of pre-state primitives, despotic empires, and wandering desert peoples, but regimes of signs are finally highly general patterns of sanctioned actions that make possible different modes of organization of signs. Nor does a given regime of signs necessarily appear in a pure form. Indeed, Deleuze and Guattari assert that "every semiotic [i.e., regime of signs] is mixed, and only functions in that fashion" (MP 169; 136), an important object of a semiotic analysis being to discern the ways in which various regimes of signs combine and interact in a given context. Hence, in the psychoanalyst's office one might detect a passional regime in the analysand's bond with the analyst as point of subjectification, a despotic regime in the analyst's endless interpretations, and a primitive regime in the analysand's dream and symptom associations. Likewise, in the history of the Israelites one might differentiate the passional regime of prophetic wanderings, the despotic regime of the centralized kingdom and temple, and the countersignifying nomadic regime of the numbered troops organized for battle (on this last, see MP 149; 118).

WHITE WALL, BLACK HOLE

In differentiating social technological machines from regimes of signs, Deleuze and Guattari make use of Leroi-Gourhan's opposition of hand-tool and face-language, which would imply that the face is a part of *every* regime of signs. Yet they also assert that "the face is not a universal" (MP 216; 176), and they associate faciality primarily with the despotic and passional regimes of signs. Indeed, they state that "if one considers primitive societies, little takes place through the face: their semiotic is non-signifying, non-subjective, essentially collective, polyvocal and corporeal, playing with quite diverse forms and substances of expression" (MP 215; 175). There is no real inconsistency here, however, for Deleuze and Guattari are making two separate points. The first is that language is part of a larger sphere of action, in which linguistic and nonlinguistic signs of various kinds are inextricably combined, facial expressions being a particularly prominent component of speech action.

Hence, they assert that "it is absurd to believe that language as such can carry a message. A language is always embedded in the faces that announce its statements and anchor them in relation to the signifiers in process and the subjects concerned" (MP 220; 179). The second point is that in different societies the face plays a different role, in some a relatively minor role, in others a quite significant one. In societies dominated by the mixed semiotic of the signifying despotic regime and the postsignifying passional regime, the face is especially important, its features highly coded and its function coextensive with language as a whole. To emphasize this point, Deleuze and Guattari say that primitives do not so much have faces as heads, and in their discussion of faciality they use the word "face" to refer primarily to the coded face generated in the despotic and passional regimes.

Before proceeding to an exposition of the concept of faciality, we might assess briefly the plausibility of Deleuze and Guattari's fundamental claims. Since the 1930s, considerable research has been dedicated to uncovering the significance of facial expressions, and over the last three or four decades the dominant view in experimental psychology has been one that does not accord with Deleuze and Guattari's. The orthodox position, sometimes referred to in the literature as the Facial Expression Program, is that facial expressions constitute a genetically determined, universal signaling system whose components consist of a set of discrete expressions that manifest a limited number of basic emotions (between five and nine, the most common list including happiness, surprise, fear, anger, contempt, disgust, and sadness). Complex facial expressions reflect mixtures of the basic emotions, an anxious face, for example, manifesting a combination of fear, sadness, and anger. Voluntary facial expressions can simulate spontaneous ones, and different cultures establish different rules for the expression or suppression of genuine emotions as well as the production of deceptive facial signals, but the communication of basic emotions remains constant across cultures.

In the last few years, however, the Facial Expression Program has been challenged by a number of researchers, whose efforts are usefully summarized in a recent volume edited by Russell and Fernández-Dols, *The Psychology of Facial Expression* (1997). A good bit of evidence suggests that facial expressions are much less involuntary responses to inner stimuli than social signs and that the distinction between genuine, spontaneous expressions and simulated, deceptive expressions is far from clear-cut. Happy people smile more in the company of others than when alone; babies at an early age make more intense facial expressions in the presence of caretakers than before strangers or nonhuman objects; and viewers of films react more demonstratively when observed by others than when unobserved. The interpretation of facial expressions is also much more a contextually dependent activity than the Facial Expression Program allows. Photographs of facial expressions are interpreted differently when juxtaposed with other expression images, when associated with differing verbal narratives, or when modified to remove situational markers. Many researchers have questioned the primacy granted emotion in the Facial Expression Program, arguing that the face may serve several functions other than that of signaling inner affective states. Fridlund's influential ethological model, for instance, treats facial expressions as messages about social interactions, a happiness smile saying "Let's play," a sad face, "Take care of me," a contentment face, "Keep doing what you're doing," etc. Bavelas and Chovil study the facial action of conversants in dialogue and argue that "the facial displays of conversants are *active, symbolic* components of *integrated* messages (including words, intonations, and gestures)" (Russell and Fernández-Dols 334). Finally, reviews of cross-cultural research have called into question the strong claims of universality in the interpretation of facial expression, challenges being raised both to the persuasiveness of the data on their own terms and to the presumed cultural neutrality of the methodology used in generating the data.

There is empirical evidence, in short, to support Deleuze and Guattari's claims that facial expressions have complex social interactive functions, that they play an important role in language use, and that their significance varies from culture to culture. But Deleuze and Guattari's assertions go well beyond these. They stress the power relations inherent in speech acts and hence treat facial expressions as part of a larger system of social discipline. "A child, a woman, a mother, a man, a father, a boss, a teacher, a police officer—they do not speak a language in general, but a language whose signifying traits are indexed on specific traits of faciality. Faces are not at first individual; they define zones of frequency or probability, they delimit a field which neutralizes in advance expressions and connections that are rebellious to conforming significations" (MP 206; 167–68). Approving nods, disapproving frowns, angry glances, disbelieving stares, looks of disappointment, shock, pity, disgust, shame, and so on—all are part of a general pedagogy whereby authorities of various sorts reinforce proper behavior and orthodox codes. In the despotic regime, language as a whole is registered in the face of power. If we distinguish in Hjelmslevian terms between a level of expression (a regime of signs) and a level of content (a social technological machine), and if we recall that each level may have its own form and substance (a substance being defined as a matter shaped by a given form), we may say that the despotic *form of expression* is the signifier and its *substance of expression* is the face. "It is the face that gives substance to the signifier, that gives itself to be interpreted, that changes, that changes traits when interpretation gives the signifier back to its substance. Look, his face changed. The signifier is always facialized" (MP 144–45; 115). This means not simply that facial expressions accompany language, but that "the face crystallizes the totality of redundancies, it emits and receives, releases and recaptures signifying signs. It is itself a whole body: it is like the body of the center of significa-tion" (MP 144; 115).

In the passional regime, signs are also related to the face, though not through a system of self-referring signifiers but through a process of subjectification. Deleuze and Guattari distinguish between two forms of redundancy in detailing the connection between faces and signs, one of *frequency* that affects "signs or elements of signs (phonemes, letters, groups of letters in a language)" (MP 166; 132) and ensures redundancy in the relationship of signifier to signified and of each signifier to all other signifiers; and one of *resonance* that affects "above all shifters, per-sonal pronouns and proper names" (MP 166; 133). In the despotic re-gime, signs form a kind of endless wall of interconnected signifiers; in the passional regime, by contrast, signs coalesce in discontinuous pack-ets, each related to a specific point of subjectification which functions as a type of black hole, a center of fascination that absorbs signs in a sys-tem of subjective identities. Here, the redundancies of the code enforce resonances between the subject of the enunciation and the subject of the statement (between Moses and his people, between the *cogito* and the *sum*, between Tristan and Iseult, etc.). The point of subjectification cre-ates a mental reality and thereby opens a world unto itself, detaching signs from their multiple external connections and fixing them in a sin-gle centripetal vortex. Hence, the passional regime deterritorializes signs to a much greater extent than does the despotic regime, with its solid wall of interrelated signifiers, but only to reterritorialize them again within closed processes of self-identification. "Every consciousness pursues its own death, every love-passion pursues its own end, attracted by a black hole, and all black holes resonate together" (MP 167; 133).

Although Deleuze and Guattari are careful to distinguish between the despotic and passional regimes, they find a fundamental affinity between the two, such that there is no despotic signification "that does not include a seed of [passional] subjectivity; no subjectification that does not carry with it remnants of the signifier" (MP 223; 182). Though they oppose the frontal despotic visage to the averted passional profile, the face that interests them most is one that combines the two regimes, a *"white wall–black hole* system" (MP 205; 167) that brings together a despotic wall of interconnected signifiers and passional black holes of subjective absorption. The full integration of the two regimes is met with in the Christian and post-Christian West, and it is the face of this mixed semiotic that they refer to when remarking that "the face is not a universal." This face is "is not even of the white man, it is the White Man himself, with his broad white cheeks and the black hole of his eyes. The face is Christ. The face is the typical European. . . . Jesus Christ Superstar: he invented the facialization of the entire body and transmitted it everywhere" (MP 216–17; 176).

THE ABSTRACT MACHINE OF FACIALITY

Specific faces manifest the mixed semiotic of the despotic and passional regime in various concrete ways, but that which produces them is an *abstract machine of faciality*, and it is to this abstract machine that Deleuze and Guattari refer when speaking of the "white wall–black hole system." What is an abstract machine? Transformational grammarians posit the existence of "deep structures" in language, fundamental patterns and transformational rules that speakers unconsciously utilize to produce actual utterances. Deleuze and Guattari insist, however, that such structures are not deep enough, not sufficiently abstract. In any linguistic utterance, one may distinguish between a level of expression (a regime of signs) and a level of content (social technological machine), each with its own form and substance. But immanent within expression and content is something that corresponds to Hjelmslev's unformed matter, a virtual domain of pure becoming that puts the levels of expression and content in relation to one another and thus serves as language's genuine "deep structure." As we have seen, the domain of becoming disrupts commonsense temporal and spatial distinctions; its time is that of Aion, and its spatial coordinates are those of differential speeds and affective intensities. Here, there is no distinction between expression and content, form and substance. "Substances, forms, are of expression 'or' of form. But functions are not yet formed 'semiotically,' and matters are not yet formed 'physically'" (MP 176; 141). A "pure Function-Matter," this domain consists of "a matter-content which has only degrees of intensity, resistance, conductivity, heating, stretching, speed or slowness; and a function-expression that has only 'tensors,' as in a mathematical or even a musical notational system" (MP 176–77; 141). Deleuze and Guattari define the abstract machine as "the aspect or moment at which there is no longer anything but functions and matters" (MP 176; 141). The abstract machine is a "diagram" of this pure function-matter that plays a "pilot role." An "abstract or diagrammatic machine does not function in order to represent, even something real, but in order to construct a real-yet-to-come, a new type of reality" (MP 177; 142). The abstract machine, in short, is simply a name for the domain of becoming in its role as abstract diagram that guides the formation of levels of expression and content and puts them in relation to one another. The abstract machine of *faciality*, then, is one component of the larger abstract machine immanent within regimes of signs (level of expression) and social technological machines (level of content). It is the diagrammatic function-matter of pure becoming that guides the formation of the face as an element of a regime of signs.

In the mixed semiotic of the despotic and passional regimes, the abstract machine of faciality functions as a white wall–black hole system, which guides the formation of individual, concrete faces as substances of expression. Deleuze and Guattari distinguish two operations of the abstract machine of faciality in the production and regulation of individual faces. The first consists of a coding by binary oppositions: "It is a man *or* a woman, a rich or a poor person, an adult or a child, a leader or a subject, 'an x *or* a y'" (MP 217; 177). Here, the black hole acts like a central computer traversing the blank wall as general surface of reference, establishing facial types as functions of proliferating codes. "The face of the teacher and the student, father and son, worker and boss, cop and citizen, accused and judge . . . : concrete, individuated faces are produced and transformed according to these units, these combinations of units" (MP 217; 177). The second involves a selective response or choice involving a given individual face. "The binary relation this time is of the 'yes-no' type. The empty eye of the black hole absorbs or rejects, like a half-senile despot still able to make a sign of acquiescence or refusal" (MP 217; 177). Are you a woman, yes or no? Are you crazy, yes or no? At each moment, a process of evaluation and sorting, a disciplining of faces that categorizes and regulates. Although a face may be rejected as deviant at a given moment, it is only rejected so that it may be judged again according to other yes-no choices until it is assigned its properly coded identity. The purpose of both operations is to carry out the work of the despotic and passional regimes—that of creating an all-encompassing network of centrally controlled, self-contained, and inter-related signifiers, and that of assigning subjects their fixed positions within that network.

What the despotic and passional regimes share is a common effort "to crush all polyvocality, to make language an exclusive form of expression, to operate by signifying biunivocalization and subjective binarization" (MP 221; 180). The mixed semiotic of the two regimes is a specific power formation that has "the singular need of being protected against any intrusion from outside" (MP 219; 179). It requires a single, all-inclusive substance of expression to which its form of expression may correspond. The abstract machine of faciality produces that single substance of expression, not only in individual human faces but also in an extended "face-ified" world. The human body as a whole, for instance, is facialized by this abstract machine, though not in the sense that it is made to resemble a face. Rather, the volume-cavity system of the proprioceptive body is replaced by the surface-hole system of faciality.[1] The body's volume-cavity system is polyvocal and multidimensional, its parts interconnected in heterogeneous and divergent paths and tendencies. In the despotic-passional regime, the head, which forms a part of this polyvocal, multidimensional corporeality, is first decoded, detached from the body's volume-cavity system, and then overcoded as a face. In a similar fashion, the abstract machine of faciality decodes the rest of the proprioceptive body and overcodes it as part of a surface-hole system, in other words a single, unified dimension that comprises a substance of expression suitable for correlation with the form of expression of the mixed despotic-passional regime. Fetishism and erotomania are clear instances of this process, the foot fetishist, for example, decoding

the corporeal foot and overcoding it as a facialized surface capable of
entering into a network of significations and subjectifications. But
again, there is no resemblance between the foot and the face—"No
anthropomorphism. Facialization does not work by resemblance, but
by an order of reasons. It is a much more unconscious and machinic
operation which makes the entire body pass across the holey surface,
and in which the face does not have the role of a model or image, but
that of an overcoding of all of the decoded parts" (MP 209; 170).

Facialization extends beyond the body as well, encompassing a world
that has been detached from its polyvocal, multidimensional connections and overcoded in a single, unified landscape. "Now, the face has a
correlate of great importance in the landscape, which is not simply a
milieu but a deterritorialized world" (MP 211; 172). In the despotic-
passional regime, the face and the landscape enter into complex relations with one another, the two forming a continuous surface: "There is
no face that does not envelope an unknown, unexplored landscape, no
landscape that is not peopled by a loved or dreamed-of face, that does
not develop a face to come or one already past. What face has not called
forth landscapes that it amalgamates, the sea and the mountain, what
landscape has not evoked the face that would complete it, that would
furnish it with an unexpected complement of lines and traits?" (MP 212;
172-73). The world is facialized, the face "landscape-alized," the two
constituting a face-landscape "holey surface" generated by the abstract
machine of faciality.

What Deleuze and Guattari mean precisely by this connection of
the face with the landscape is not easily articulated, precisely because, in
a strict sense, it is not verbal. At first glance, Deleuze and Guattari seem
simply to be suggesting that there are vague, subjective associational
links that may be established between faces and landscapes, the one
"evoking" the other, "calling the other forth," "developing" it, "com-
pleting" it, "complementing" it. They cite a passage from Chrétien de
Troyes's *Perceval* in which Perceval stares at spots of blood in the snow
and associates the landscape's vermilion and white with the colors of his
beloved's face. They allude as well to Swann's associations of Odette's
face with landscapes, paintings, and musical phrases in Proust's *A la
recherche du temps perdu*. These examples are potentially misleading, however, for the point is not that faces and landscapes are linked through
personal, sentimental ties. Nor is it that faces and landscapes are always

interpreted through a unified semantic system. It would be easy to argue, for instance, that language *causes* us to identify a given facial type and expression as, say, the "look of an angry foreman"—that certain aspects of his body, clothes, and gestures conform to the codes of his occupation, gender, class, religion, and so forth; that those codes are only comprehensible through the discourses that make sense of the world at large; and that the factory and its urban environs are saturated by semantic associations that intersect and combine with those of the foreman and his angry expression. But this is precisely the explanation offered by Saussurean semiology, which, in Deleuze and Guattari's analysis, is generated by the despotic-passional regime. What they argue is that the face is an important component of the despotic-passional regime, but that it is not reducible to language. The abstract machine of faciality produces faces

> that trace all sorts of arborescences and dichotomies. . . . And doubtless the binarities and biunivocalities of the face are not the same as those of language, of its elements and subjects. They do not resemble each other at all. But the former underlie the latter. When translating the formed contents of whatever kind into a single substance of expression, the machine of faciality already submits them to the exclusive form of signifying and subjective expression. It carries out a prior gridding that makes possible the discernment of signifying elements, the execution of subjective choices. The machine of faciality is not an annex of the signifier or the subject, it is rather connected to it and conditioning: the biunivocalities, the binarities of the face double the others, the redundancies of the face form redundancies with the signifying, subjective redundancies. Precisely because the face depends on an abstract machine, it does not presuppose an already present subject or signifier; but it is connected to them, and it gives them their necessary substance. (MP 220; 180)

The difficulty we encounter in describing faciality is that, in the commonsense world we inhabit, words and things come to us premixed, intertwined, and intermeshed. Once we notice the conventional, coded aspects of things, it is all too easy to assume that language alone has created the codes and thereby guided the conventional shaping of things.

Only with great care can we sift through this mixture and separate its constituents and generative processes. We might propose the following hypothetical reconstruction of the concept of faciality. Initially, we find in the face a component of a discursive practice. That face component is essential to discourse yet irreducible to language—it is a gestural, expressive, visual surface that accompanies verbal enunciations and interacts with them in ways that reinforce power relations. Recognition of this face component of a discursive practice then leads us to widen this apprehension by noting the existence of similarly gestural, expressive, visual appearances of the body that resonate with the facial surface and create an echo effect with the face component's nondiscursive encodings. Finally, we discover, especially through the arts, resonances outside the body that give the landscape a "physiognomy," a "look" that corresponds to faces in some nonrepresentative way. Rather than interpreting such correspondences outside the body as subjective associations, we read these as hints or indirect signs of a generative process that escapes common sense. That generative process is a process of facialization whereby a gestural, expressive, visual gridding unfolds and extends through facial expressions to cover the world. Such a facialized world, finally, comes to constitute an overcoded surface capable of serving as the substance of expression for the biunivocal signifiers and binary subjectivities of the despotic-passional form of expression.

THE FACE AND THE GAZE

What does all this mean in concrete, visual terms? What examples might we provide of a "facialized" body or landscape? Deleuze and Guattari offer only fleeting hints in A Thousand Plateaus, and these hints are by and large easily misconstrued. Perhaps the easiest way to approach this question is through Jean Paris's L'Espace et le regard, which Deleuze and Guattari cite in their opposition of frontal and profile faces. Indeed, in some respects one might see their discussion of faciality as a rewriting of Paris's analysis of painting. Paris's project is to found a theory of painting on le regard, the "gaze," or "look," a concept much discussed following Sartre's extended analysis of the objectifying regard in Being and Nothingness but one Paris finds curiously undervalued in treatments of painting. Using a wide variety of examples from the Western tradition, Paris demonstrates the centrality of the gaze, showing how the formal and thematic focus of various paintings is met with in the looks of the individuals portrayed in them. He opens by contrasting three gazes: the frontal stare of the *Christ Pantocrator*, a twelfth-century mosaic from the cathedral of Cefalù, Sicily; the reciprocal three-quarter glances that unite Jesus and Saint Peter in Duccio's *The Calling of Saint Peter and Saint Andrew* (Washington, National Gallery, reproduced in *A Thousand Plateaus*); and the crossing, yet noncoinciding looks found in the canvas *Allegory* (*Alfonso d'Este and Laura Diante?*), painted by a follower of Titian (Washington, D.C., National Gallery), in which a clothed nobleman studies the face of a nude woman observing herself in a mirror. In the *Christ Pantocrator* we meet the archetype of the portrait, a commanding face on a blank background, an "absolute look" in an "absolute space" (Paris 15). Duccio's painting combines the frontal face of the portrait in the figure of Saint Andrew, who is looking toward the viewer, with the mutually absorbing profiles of Jesus and Peter, the arc of the apostles' boat and the curve of the mountain behind Jesus reinforcing the line of sight that connects Jesus and Peter and organizes the postures of their bodies. The follower of Titian's *Allegory* presents a zigzag of intersecting glances that require a third gaze for their completion—that of the viewer, who unifies the looks of the courtier watching the woman watching her reflection. And though the glances of man and woman do not coincide, their trajectories establish a grid of perpendicular, horizontal, and diagonal coordinates that structure the composition, from the individuals' faces, to the eyelike breasts of the nude, to the contrasting landscapes that frame the heads of the two figures. Three instances of the gaze—the single gaze of frontal power, the dual gaze of profile absorption, the triple gaze of interrelated pictorial figures and unifying observer—each determining a complex visual space.

Relying on extensive evidence from world mythology and visual artifacts, Paris argues that the gaze is a primary mode of power, a means of conquering, dominating, and knowing the world. Hence, the absolute gaze is that of God, the all-seeing and all-knowing, whose glance is found in the divine face of Christ, but also in the cosmic eye of the sun (and occasionally the proliferating eyes of other heavenly bodies). The dominating gaze is extended pictorially in various ways, in the halo that magnifies and multiplies the look, in shafts of light and trails of fire, in touching and pointing hands, in stigmata implanted through visible rays of light or invisible glances, in piercing arrows, threatening spears and aiming rifles. Paris also links the gaze to breath, the common figure of ocular breasts (Bosch, Bouts, Huys, Brueghel, Redon, Picasso, and Dalí, among others) indicating that the eye absorbs the landscape in the same manner that the lungs take in air. Seeing, like breathing, "integrates us in nature, founds existence on a rhythmic exchange with the environment" (Paris 44), an alternation of active and passive instants whereby the eye takes in and acts on the world. Yet, though the gaze is related to the eye, it is finally not an organ function. Paris, like Sartre, argues that the gaze disappears as soon as we become aware of the eyes as such. The gaze is a generalized power function, one that passes through the eyes but extends its effects into the face, the body, and the surrounding world.

Paris offers numerous examples of the ways in which the gaze structures space in painting, a particularly interesting instance for our purposes being that of Giotto's *Saint Francis Giving His Cloak to a Poor Knight* (Basilica of San Francesco, Assisi). The focus of the painting is the head of Saint Francis, surrounded by a halo centered on his right eye. His gaze is met by that of the knight on his left, the saint's face in three-quarter view, the knight's in full profile. The force of Francis's gaze is indicated in the arc of the knight's back as he bends toward the saint, a line that is echoed in the curved back of the docile horse on Francis's right. Two hills oppose one another to the left and right, their diagonal descents converging at the saint's head. A city sits at the top of the hill on the left, a church on the right hill's crest, the slightly inclined line of sight between city and church paralleling the line of sight that connects Francis and the knight. Clearly, the landscape features echo and explicate the relations between the human figures: "The mute dialogue which unites the saint and the mortal below is that which, in heaven, unites the church and the city" (Paris 190). But Paris insists as well that in Giotto "it is the landscape, finally, that sees [*se fait voyant*]" (ibid. 189). Not only is there a symbolic link between the landscape and the gaze, but the landscape itself gazes forth. The windows and doors of the city and church, the rock faces of the hills and the trees function as points of vision within the painting, multiple *regards* that fill the space. This proliferation of the gaze Paris finds throughout Giotto's art: "The angels who tirelessly streak through space, the animals who populate his provinces, already witness to the power that the clouds and the earth have to see us as we see them. But the most humanly constructed settings

Giotto di Bondone. *Saint Francis Giving His Cloak to a Poor Knight,* or *Saint Francis Gives His Mantle to a Beggar.* © Alinari/Art Resource, NY.

share this faculty. Doors, windows, garret openings, rose windows, lamps: so many organs by which stone accedes to the 'clairvoyant seeing' [*voyance*] of the azure sky" (ibid. 190).

Even in paintings without human subjects, Paris discovers the controlling power of the gaze, albeit in an indirect rather than a direct manner. A painter's vision, he asserts, is always intentional, in the Husserlian sense, an actively shaping force that gives things a particular look and significance. Paris supports this thesis with an analysis of three still lifes, Baugin's *Nature morte à l'echiquier* (*Les Cinq Sens*) (Louvre), de Heem's *Still Life* (Prado), and Cézanne's *Nature morte à la commode* (Bavarian State Gallery, Munich). The objects of Baugin's canvas are presented with a Cartesian clarity and order, neatly disposed in a uniform light and a regulated perspective measured by the geometric squares of the chessboard; yet the heterogeneous compositional elements, with their unresolved appeal to the five senses and their allusions to interrupted, casual activities, make visible "a debate between the formal ideal of the intellect and the chaotic reality of life" (Paris 134). De Heem's still life, by contrast, offers an opulent, sensuous overflow of possessions, a euphoric celebration of wealth, ripeness, and splendor; yet the disequilibrium of the half-peeled orange, the teetering oyster shell, and the overturned fruit bowl instill a fundamental instability in the composition, suggesting a subterranean awareness of the precarious and ephemeral status of worldly goods. In Cézanne's canvas, as in de Heem's, the ephemeral is evident, but in this case, one sees "the perfection of the ephemeral" (ibid. 137), a calm space occupied by carefully modulated volumes, angles, and tones that bespeak a direct engagement with primary sensations; these objects, however, stand against an implicit background of nothingness, a haunting darkness just outside the canvas that impresses on the scene "the tragedy of our existence, the impossible union of time and the eternal" (ibid. 138).

FROM THE GAZE TO THE FACE

Much of what Paris says about the gaze may be applied directly to the face produced by the abstract machine of faciality. From Paris's phenomenological perspective, of course, the gaze is foundational and universal, whereas in Deleuze and Guattari's view the gaze as Paris describes it is the product of a specific regime of signs.[2] Paris's association of the gaze with domination, power, and knowledge aptly characterizes the face of the despotic regime, and his differentiation of the commanding frontal stare and mutually absorbing profile gazes maps the dual tendencies of the mixed semiotic of the despotic-passional regime. As Paris proceeds through his lengthy demonstration of the centrality of the divine gaze in Western religious art, one sees how Deleuze and Guattari can assert that the essential face of the despotic-passional regime is that of Christ, whose Caucasian male features function in painting after painting as a commanding norm of cultural regulation, controlling the gazes and facial expressions of the Madonna, the apostles, various saints, sinners, and so forth. Paris's distinction between the gaze and the eye, although drawn primarily to stress an opposition between the visual poles of active apprehension and passive reception, serves to emphasize the radiating power effect of the gaze, which, although perhaps centered on the eye, is diffused throughout the face and extended to the body.

The ocular breasts that Paris cites as metaphors of vision's rhythmic exchange between inside and outside perhaps could be used as illustrations of the facialization of the body, although Paris's point seems to be that the breasts look like eyes, and Deleuze and Guattari assert that the body's facialization does not proceed by resemblance. Paris's discussion of other pictorial figures of the gaze, however, does shed light on the facialized body, and particularly useful are his remarks on the function of stigmata. Paris finds a telling revelation of the stigmata's relation to the gaze in Giotto's *Saint Francis Receiving the Stigmata* (Louvre). A winged Christ soars above Saint Francis, Christ's arms outstretched and his feet together, rays of light shooting from his wounds and connecting to the corresponding wounds in Saint Francis's hands, feet, and side. The faces of Christ and Saint Francis are surrounded by halos, and their gazes are fixed upon one another. For Paris, the painting demonstrates the power of the gaze, the rays of light emanating from Christ's wounds being visible manifestations of the invisible gaze issuing from his enhaloed face. Deleuze and Guattari cite the same painting and remark that "the stigmata effect a facialization of the body of the saint in the image of Christ" (MP 219; 178). (This is in fact the only concrete example of the body's facialization they offer.) Paris's point seems well taken. Clearly, it is the commanding gaze of Christ that arrests Francis in his posture of surprise and vulnerable surrender, and the rays of light do indeed seem extensions of that gaze. But one can see as well in the fixed gazes of

Giotto di Bondone. *St. Francis Receiving the Stigmata.* © Réunion des Musées Nationaux/Art Resource, NY.

Christ and Francis an imprinting of codes and subject positions through the face, which provides a visual substance for various religious values (humility, pity, concern, detachment, etc.) without itself being wholly subsumable within a system of discursive signifiers. The posture of Francis and the visible lines connecting his body to Christ's establish a clear correspondence between the two figures that resonates with the interplay of their faces. The signifying and subjectifying force of Christ's face extends to his body, and the coordinated effect of his face and body instill parallel configurations in Francis. The saint's body is facialized, but in no way does it resemble a face. Rather, Francis's facial *imitatio Christi* extends to a corporeal imitation, the two providing irreducibly visual analogues of a particular cultural order.

Paris's treatment of the space of the gaze also provides a useful means of understanding the interplay of face and landscape that Deleuze and Guattari see as an essential feature of facialization. Paris offers copious examples of paintings in which the formal relations among compositional elements are determined by the gazes of the figures. Though his delineations of structural lines of orientation, planes of organization, patterns of hue, texture, volume, and so on make use of the standard tools of formalist analysis, his demonstration of the primacy of the gaze suggests a concrete way in which the eye "breathes in" the world and actively determines the configuration of space. If we read the effects of the gaze as those of Deleuze and Guattari's faciality, we can see in the ramifying formal patterns emanating from faces and extending to the landscape an interpenetrating process of facialization-landscapization that operates through correspondences without resemblance. Yet Paris also argues that at times the landscape itself "sees," as do the city and church windows, trees and rock faces of Giotto's *Saint Francis Giving His Cloak to a Poor Knight.* (Perhaps it is in the context of this analysis that we should read Deleuze and Guattari's observation that "architecture places its ensembles, houses, villages or cities, monuments or factories, which function as faces, in a landscape that it transforms. Painting takes up the same movement, but reverses it as well, giving a landscape the function of a face, in treating one as the other" [MP 211–12; 172].) It might seem that Paris is merely playing with resemblances, noting that the windows of Giotto's buildings look like eye sockets and amplifying such resemblances in other landscape features. But Paris's point goes beyond this. The landscape in Giotto takes on a dispersed, interactive look, as if the divine gaze were equally partitioned among all objects of creation, emanating from them and constituting a particular visual field. A similar dispersed gaze informs each of the three still lifes Paris analyzes, the elements of each tableau participating in the constitution of a given world with its own special light, weight, texture, and feel.

Deleuze and Guattari also speak of objects that see: "Even a practical object [*objet d'usage*] may be facialized: one might say of a house, a tool, or an object, a piece of clothing, etc., they are *looking at me*, not because they resemble a face, but because they are taken up in the white wall–black hole process, because they are connected to the abstract machine of facialization" (MP 214; 175). Such a facialization of objects they find in painting when a still life "becomes from within a face-landscape ... A tool, a cup on a tablecloth, a teapot, is facialized, as in Bonnard, Vuillard" (MP 215; 175). We should note, however, that unlike Paris, Deleuze and Guattari inject a hint of paranoia in their description of facialized objects—not only do the objects see, but *they're looking at me*. In this respect, Deleuze and Guattari are simply echoing the basically paranoid nature of the concept of the gaze as Sartre formulated it. When differentiating the gaze from the eye in *Being and Nothingness,* Sartre says that the eye is merely the support for the gaze, which seems to go *"in front of"* the eyes (Sartre 258). When soldiers on a night mission see the silhouette of a farmhouse or hear rustling in a bush, they sense that they are being watched; though "the bush, the farmhouse are not the look [*regard*]" but only "the support for the look," the bush and farmhouse do not "refer therefore to the actual eye of the watch hidden behind the curtain, behind a window in the farmhouse. In themselves they are already eyes" (Sartre 258). Awareness of the gaze implies being seen, and the gaze in Sartre is basically hostile and threatening. The possibility of being seen converts the objects of the world into so many eyes, each the site of a potential gaze that fixes, limits, and accuses. Paris explicitly rejects Sartre's negative characterization of the gaze, arguing that the gaze may embrace a wide range of attitudes, including care, tenderness, acceptance, and so forth. By contrast, Deleuze and Guattari preserve Sartre's emphasis, regarding the menacing Sartrean gaze as simply a manifestation of the despotic regime, a panoptic power structure that seeks to impose ubiquitous surveillance and control. For them, no universal gaze creates paranoid object-eyes, but a specific regime of signs does so. It is only when an object is facialized—gridded, positioned, and normalized within the despotic regime—that it begins to look back.

"Landscapes that see," such as Giotto's and still lifes imbued with a particular look, then, are considerably less benign phenomena for Deleuze and Guattari than for Paris. What Paris identifies as the permeation of the world by the gaze Deleuze and Guattari regard as the organization of a visual field through a process of universalizing signification and subjectification. One further point about the facialization of objects may help clarify this distinction. When speaking of objects that look back, Deleuze and Guattari cite Sergei Eisenstein's remarks on the close-up in the films of D. W. Griffith. Eisenstein notes that in Dickens's opening line of *The Cricket on the Hearth,* "The kettle began it," the kettle functions "as a typical Griffith-esque close-up. A close-up saturated, we now become aware, with typically Dickens-esque 'atmosphere,' with which Griffith, with equal mastery, can envelop the severe face of life in *Way Down East,* and the icy cold moral face of his characters, who push the guilty Anna (Lillian Gish) onto the shifting surface of a swirling ice-break" (Eisenstein 199). What Eisenstein suggests is that Dickens's kettle is a telling detail that evokes a particular world and that the function of the close-up in Griffith is to provide a similar visual detail—a face, a knife, a watch—that creates a specific atmosphere appropriate to the drama the film is unfolding. The atmospheric object, it would seem, is a legible object that may be read in terms of conventional codes, the kettle, say, summing up a world of humble, domestic intimacy, or alternatively, one of exasperated poverty. The same may be said of the facialized object, with the proviso that its evocative power not be construed simply as a function of discursive codes. The facialized object is a visual entity shaped in conformity with a dominant configuration of power, and it serves as a substance of expression for linguistic signifiers. But its facialization is part of a specifically visual process of formation that is separate from that of discursive signs. The kettle may be the bearer of many linguistic associations, but as facialized kettle, it fulfills its atmospheric function through its specific "look," its particular "kettleness," which resonates with other visual elements that make up a domain regulated by a single regime of signs.

The face of despotic-passional power identifies, classifies, *recognizes.* Its role is "to permit and guarantee the omnipotence of the signifier, as well as the autonomy of the subject. You will be pinned to the white wall, stuffed in a black hole" (MP 222; 181). The facialized object is recognized, pinned to the wall, or stuffed in a hole, imprinted with a look that it returns as a reverberation of the force that shapes it. The object looks back as the eye of a dispersed power effect, its participation in a network of recognized visual elements imbuing it with an atmospheric suggestiveness that may evoke a complex semiotic domain. In Giotto's *Saint Francis Giving His Cloak to a Poor Knight,* the connection between face and landscape is made explicit, the mutually inclined faces of Francis and the knight structuring the surrounding space, imparting to the landscape objects an atmospheric configuration in conformity with the dominant look of Saint Francis, instilling in them an identified, recognized look that looks back. In the still lifes Paris analyzes, the face of the despotic-passional regime looks back in the elements of the canvases, the specific way of seeing that Paris points to in each still life being the manifestation of a constitutive cultural recognition, an atmospheric coherence that reinforces a specific order of signs.

DETERRITORIALIZING THE FACE

But this is only half of the story. Painting, say Deleuze and Guattari, "is inscribed in a 'problem,' which is that of the *face-landscape* [*visage-paysage*]," just as music is inscribed in "an entirely different problem, that of the refrain" (MP 369; 301). The face-landscape *problem* may elicit quite varied responses. Artists may indeed reinforce despotic-passional encodings by producing facialized compositions. But they may also undermine those encodings by deterritorializing the face and its extended facializations. In either case, they engage the abstract machine of faciality, which in a sense operates in two directions. The abstract machine is immanent within the real, but it is virtual rather than actual. It serves a pilot role in the actualization of faces and a facialized world. Yet it is a deterritorialized, unformed matter with unspecified functions, and as such it points the way for a decoding of facialization coordinates, a metamorphic undoing of the regularities of signification and subjectification. Such deterritorialization may take the form of a mutative modification of facial features in a portrait, an expressive elongation or contortion of a body, an eccentric orientation of a landscape, a disjunctive handling of light in a still life, and so on.

Hence, though one does indeed find in Western Christian art canonical impositions of the face of divine authority, there is also "a jubilation in painting of the Middle Ages and Renaissance, like an unrestricted freedom. Not only did Christ preside over the facialization of the entire body (his own body), over the landscapization of all milieus (his own milieus), but he also composed all elementary faces and made use of all deviations: athlete-Christ at the fair, Christ-Mannerist queer, Christ-Negro, or at least black Virgin on the edge of the wall" (MP 219; 178). In Giotto's *Saint Francis Receiving the Stigmata* we see the facialization of the body, but also "the greatest madness" authorized by Catholicism: "Against the white background of the landscape and blue-black hole of the sky, the crucified Christ, turned kite-machine, sends the stigmata of Saint Francis via rays; the stigmata effect the facialization of the saint in the image of Christ; but the rays that bring the stigmata to the saint are also the strings by which he moves the divine kite" (MP 219; 178). In *Francis Bacon*, Deleuze makes a similar point in remarks about El Greco's *The Burial of Count Orgaz* (San Tomé, Toledo): "A horizontal divides the canvas in two parts, lower and upper, terrestrial and celestial. And in the bottom part, there is indeed a figuration or narration that represents the burial of the Count, although already all the coefficients of the deformation of bodies, and notably their elongation, are already at work. But on high, where the Count is received by Christ, there is a mad liberation, a total freedom: the figures rise up and grow longer, refined without measure, beyond all constraint" (FB 13).

If we were to do justice to Jean Paris's analyses, then, we would have to distinguish those aspects of the gaze that confirm a dominant order from those that introduce aberrant, metamorphic tendencies. And if we were to extend those analyses to the history of painting generally, we would need at every stage to weigh the relative degrees of facialization and deterritorialization that affect a given artist, movement, or period. Thus in much twentieth-century art we would simply find a more explicit deterritorialization of the face-landscape than in the painting of earlier centuries, the well-known experimentations on the face in such artists as Picasso, Francis Bacon, and Willem de Kooning being the most obvious examples of this tendency, but any number of modern defamiliarizing treatments of human forms, still lifes, and landscapes serving likewise as illustrations of this point. It might seem that abstract art would lie outside the problem of facialization, but Deleuze and Guattari insist otherwise: "Even when painting becomes abstract, it only rediscovers the black hole and white wall, the great composition of the white canvas and the black slash. Tearing, but also stretching the canvas along an axis of flight, a vanishing point [*point de fuite*], a diagonal, knife cuts, slash, or hole: the machine is already there, a machine that always functions in producing faces and landscapes, even the most abstract" (MP 212; 173). Mondrian would thus be correct to refer to his geometric compositions as "landscapes," according to Deleuze and Guattari, for they are instances of a "pure landscape deterritorialized to the absolute" (MP 370; 301).

PRIMITIVE HEADS, CHRIST-FACE, PROBE HEADS

Although the facialization of the body and landscape does not operate through mimetic representations of concrete faces, it remains the case that in the despotic-passional regime the face is a privileged site of visual coding. The despotic signifier and the passional subject take the face as their substance of expression, and the extension of facial coding to the body and landscape may create effects such that a torso, a clock, a building, or a cloud may look like a face, but resemblances of this sort are only secondary effects of a primary process of facialization, which is exercised by the abstract machine of faciality. Its system of white wall–black hole is not controlled by mimetic relations of likeness and similarity, but the visual encodings it directs may well result in elements that allow one to discern facial resemblances in nonfacial entities. The point is that in the despostic-passional regime the processes of universal signification and subjectification are coordinated with the creation of a similarly uniform visual encoding of the world, which has as its most important component the human face, but which is extended beyond the face through the nonmimetic operation of virtual relations of forces.

In developing the concept of faciality, Deleuze and Guattari oppose the frontal face of the despotic regime and the profile of the passional regime, concluding that in the West especially the two regimes tend to combine in a mixed semiotic that brings together the facializing operations of despotic signification and passional subjectification. In contrast to the despotic and passional regimes is the primitive regime, which does not privilege the face but treats it as simply one among many elements interconnected through multiple, heterogeneous, decentralized codes and practices. Hence, Deleuze and Guattari argue that in the despotic-passional regime, clothing and masks fulfill the function of facializing the body, whereas primitive costumes, decorations, and masks serve diverse purposes, the mask countering any facializing tendency within primitive cultures and assuring that physiognomic features operate as disparate elements of a head that belongs to a polyvocal body. It is important to note, however, that in contrasting the despotic-passional regime and the primitive regime Deleuze and Guattari are not advocating any form of neoprimitivism: "It is never a question of a return to. . . . It's not a matter of 'returning' to the presignifying and presubjectifying semiotics of primitives" (MP 231; 188). The primary thrust of Deleuze and Guattari's argument is simply that the face does not have a universal, unchanging role in communication, but varies in its social and cultural function. Whether the sharp delineation between primitive and non-primitive regimes may be maintained is difficult to tell. Deleuze and Guattari offer only one instance of the polyvocal, decentralized disposition of facial expressions in primitive cultures—through a brief allusion to Jacques Lizot's account of the unexpected and discontinuous shifts of facial expression among Nambikwara Indians in various social contexts—and it appears unlikely that any empirical testing of their hypothesis will ever be possible, given the rapid, and by now virtually complete, disappearance of traditional cultures unaffected by the industrial modern world. Nonetheless, the claim that the face varies in its cultural significance seems plausible, and one that current research in experimental psychology would tend to support.

Yet even if the existence of cultural universals in facial expression were conclusively demonstrated, Deleuze and Guattari would still assert that the codification of the face is not necessary and inevitable. They are advocating not an alternative organization of the face, but a mutation of the face, an exploration of metamorphic possibilities for its deregulation and dissolution. What they seek is the development of "probe heads" (*têtes chercheuses,* literally "searching heads," a term used to describe automated guidance devices), "which in their passage undo strata, which pierce the walls of significance and gush forth from the holes of subjectivity, flatten trees in favor of veritable rhizomes, and pilot fluxes along lines of positive deterritorialization or creative flight" (MP 233; 190). In the primitive regime, facial features and expressions participate in heterogeneous circuits, but they are nevertheless regulated and codified, albeit in a decentralized, polyvocal fashion. Even if it were possible for moderns to return to a primitive regime, there is no guarantee that it would be superior to the despotic-passional regime. Only through the mutative decomposition of the face, through the experimental launching of probe heads, can alternative dispositions of facial elements be opened up.

Deleuze and Guattari suggest finally that an analysis of the face may be reduced to three basic models: "primitive heads, Christ-face, and probe heads" (MP 234; 191). Primitive heads engage "semiotics of corporeality (these semiotics are already present and flourish among animals, the head is part of the body, the body has for its correlate the milieu, the biotope)" (MP 369; 301). The Christ-face system offers "an organization of the face, white wall–black holes, face-eyes, or face seen in profile and oblique eyes (this faciality semiotic has for its correlate the organization of the landscape: the facialization of the entire body and the landscapization of all milieus, Christ being the European central point)" (MP 369; 301). And probe heads activate "a deterritorialization of faces and landscapes, . . . with lines that no longer follow any form, which no longer form any contour, with colors that no longer lay out any landscape" (MP 371–72; 301). As we can see, with this basic taxonomy we return to the thematics of the refrain, primitive heads corresponding roughly to milieu points of order; the Christ-face to decoded milieu components that have been recoded in a single territorial domain; and probe heads to cosmic lines of flight that open territories to the outside. It would seem, then, that ultimately the attribution of specific modes of facial organization to individual regimes of signs is less important than the delineation of three coexisting moments in the disposition of the face: corporeal codings, facialized overcodings, metamorphic decodings.

Painting, according to Deleuze and Guattari, "has never ceased to have as its goal the deterritorialization of faces and landscapes, either through the reactivation of corporeality, or through the liberation of lines and colors, or both at the same time" (MP 370; 301). Through the reactivation of corporeality painters engage aspects of the primitive regime, but their primary means of creative experimentation lies with probe heads and their metamorphic deterritorialization of the face-landscape. Such a deterritorialization initiates a becoming-other, and in this sense we may link the becoming-other of the face's deterritorialization with those becomings we encountered earlier in our discussion of music and the refrain—becoming-woman, becoming-child, becoming-animal, becoming-imperceptible. In this regard, painting shares the goal of all art, "for it is through writing that one becomes animal, it is through color that one becomes imperceptible, it is through music that one becomes hard and without memory, at once animal and imperceptible" (MP 229–30; 187). Yet art itself is not the goal: "It is only an instrument for tracing lines of life, that is all real becomings, which are not simply produced *in* art, all these active flights, which do not consist only of fleeing *into* art, taking refuge in art, these positive deterritorializations, which do not come to be reterritorialized in art, but rather carry art along with them, toward the regions of the asignifying, the asubjective and the faceless" (MP 230; 187).

In *A Thousand Plateaus*, Deleuze and Guattari offer few concrete examples of painting's deterritorialization of the face-landscape, of the face's becoming-other, of the probe head's movement toward regions of the asignifying, the asubjective, and the faceless. For an extended discussion of specific paintings we must turn to Deleuze's *Francis Bacon: The Logic of Sensation*. Here, we will find many instances of probe-head deformations, becoming-animal, becoming-imperceptible. But we will also find a reconfigured argument, one centered not on the face and landscape, but on forces and sensations.

Chapter Five

FORCES

The paintings of Francis Bacon would seem to provide ideal instances of the dynamics of faciality, and indeed in *Francis Bacon: The Logic of Sensation* (1981) Deleuze does discuss the deformation of the face so evident in most of Bacon's work. Deleuze says that Bacon is a "painter of heads and not of faces," the head belonging to the body, the face functioning as a "structured spatial organization that covers the head" (FB 19). Bacon's object is to undo the face and bring forth the head beneath it, thereby making the head an element of an affective, intensive body. Bacon's decoding of the face proceeds through the disclosure of animal traits within the face, but Deleuze insists that such traits do not operate via formal correspondences or mimetic representation. A smeared eyebrow may resemble a bird wing, a twisted nose a pig's snout, or a slashed grin a dog's muzzle, but such animal traits must be seen as zones of indiscernibility or undecidability between the human and the animal. They are instances of a becoming-animal, a passage between identifiable entities toward some unknown figure, elements of an experimental probe-head engaged in a process of uncharted mutation. Rather than turning humans into animals, Bacon reveals their common zone of undecidability, which Deleuze associates with the body as flesh or meat. Bacon's obsessive treatment of butcher shop imagery—rolled roasts, racks of ribs, trussed loins, crucified dressed carcasses—Deleuze sees as part of a general becoming-animal of the human. Meat is the "fact" (one of Bacon's favorite words) common to animals and humans, as well as a state in which flesh and bone "confront one another locally, rather than composing themselves structurally" (FB 20). Face and head oppose one another as bone to flesh, the structuring skull imposing form on the malleable flesh. In meat, bone no longer exercises its organizing and shaping force on the flesh. Likewise, in Bacon's portraits the flowing currents of flesh defy the hold of the face's cranial scaffolding.

THE FIGURAL

Yet Deleuze's primary subject in *Francis Bacon* is not the face, nor does he here address the topics of the facialization of the body or the interplay of face and landscape. Instead, his focus is on three topics: the problem of representation, the harnessing of forces, and the logic of sensation. Deleuze's point of entry into the first topic is the observation that Bacon consistently isolates the human figure in his paintings, placing it in rings, squares, parallelepipeds, or other limiting forms. As Bacon explains, his object is to avoid "illustration," to reveal in the figure a "matter of fact." Deleuze argues that Bacon's problem—and the problem of all painters—is that the blank canvas on which he paints is not really blank at all. It is already full of images—clichéd images that bring with them a host of cultural associations, a panoply of trite symbols, ready-made meanings, and well-worn narratives. "Figuration exists, it is a fact, it is even preliminary to painting. We are assaulted by photos that are illustrations, by magazines that are narrations, by cinema images, by television images. There are psychic as well as physical clichés, ready-formed perceptions, memories, fantasies. There is a very important experience here for the painter: an entire category of things one can call 'clichés' already occupies the canvas, before the beginning" (FB 57). One might think that the solution would be to embrace abstraction and abandon representation altogether, but Bacon adopts another course, one that attempts to render the figure without figuration, to escape the clichés of illustration and narration and disclose what Jean-François Lyotard calls the "figural." Although Deleuze does not embrace all aspects of Lyotard's concept, much of what Deleuze says about "the figure" derives from Lyotard's analysis, and it is useful to consider briefly the way in which Lyotard develops this notion.

In *Discours, figure* (1971), Lyotard's primary object is to counter structuralism's rampant textualization of the world and to insist that the visual constitutes a domain unassimilable within codes and regulated oppositions. Using Merleau-Ponty's phenomenological analysis of vision and space, Lyotard argues that language always refers to an outside world, even if the relations among signifiers within language may be characterized in terms of a self-contained system. Hence, one must distinguish between a dimension of signification, involving linguistic signs and their differential relations with one another, and a dimension of designation, a gestural dimension in which language points to a world outside itself and thereby opens itself to the visual. Lyotard then contrasts the differential relations among linguistic signs (signification) with those among visual entities (designation), asserting that the opposition of a present sign to the absent signs from which it differs is fundamentally unlike the difference between co-present objects in a single visual space. The visual, then, is presupposed in the textual through the gestural dimension of designation, whereby words point to a world of mutually situated and co-present objects.

But this phenomenological critique of Saussurean structuralism is only a preliminary stage in Lyotard's argument, for the visual itself requires examination if what Lyotard calls its "truth" is to be disclosed. To the extent that the visual is recognized, comprehended, and assimilated within a rational order, Lyotard contends, its truth is lost, for it is thereby coded, made "readable," and textualized. Its truth is only revealed in "the event," which "presents itself as a fall, as a sliding and an error: what is called a *lapsus* in Latin. The event opens a space and a time of vertigo" (Lyotard 135). The time of the event is one that ignores the order of past, present, and future, and hence escapes the fundamental structure of Husserl's "living present" (*présent vivant*) (ibid. 152–55), with its "retention" of an ongoing past and its "protention" toward an upcoming future. Likewise, the space of the event disturbs the organized dimensionality of Merleau-Ponty's "lived body" (*corps vécu*) and discloses a dimension of disorganized visibility that Lyotard labels a "figural" space. Merleau-Ponty's analysis of the lived body's prereflective experience of space reveals a visible realm below the level of consciousness, but it presumes the existence of a primary space in which objects are recognized and directional coordinates are coherently organized. Lyotard argues that even the Gestaltist distinction between figure and ground already represents a secondary rationalization of space. The visual field is constantly subject to an organizational movement of the eye that regularizes and systematizes objects in space, corrects them and imposes "good form" on them. "Attention has as its end to recognize. To recognize only proceeds through comparison. The eye moves here and there, and composes its familiar web" (ibid. 155). The movement of the eye constructs a recognizable space, and "it is only through the suspension of movement . . . that the essential heterogeneity of the visual field can be approached. . . . To learn to see is to unlearn to recognize" (ibid. 157).

Lyotard's guide to the figural in modern art is Paul Klee, whose theoretical approach to form Lyotard contrasts with that of the painter André Lhote. For both Klee and Lhote, representational art has become impossible after Cézanne. Lhote argues that the only alternative to the representation of nature is to abstract ideal geometric forms from it. Klee rejects this problematic of "constituting and making recognizable an intelligible world" and takes on instead the problematic of "an 'interworld,' another possible nature, one that extends creation, rendering visible that which is not visible, without however becoming a slave to the subjective imagination" (Lyotard 224-25). In Lyotard's analysis, the problem of representation is not simply one of clichés but also one of symptoms, for as Klee shows, a fundamental and spontaneous element of design is to give visible form to fantasies and obsessions. Yet even in Klee's descriptions of his early childhood drawings one finds two forces at work: a force of desire, which seeks to represent fantasies and obsessions, and a force of deformation, which ironically critiques representational forms through their exaggeration and distortion.

Klee speaks of his desire to create an "interworld" (*Zwischenwelt*), midway between an objective exterior domain and a subjective, internal imaginary realm, a natural world but one that in ordinary experience is not seen—an invisible nature *in potentia*, a possible world made visible through art (Lyotard 224). Klee's interworld is the world of art as *natura naturans*, as force and energy in the process of constructing its own cosmos. According to Lyotard, Klee's work "attests to the fact that creation exceeds created nature, and that the artist is a place where creation continues to produce its fruits. Nature and art are two kingdoms of creation. But the second owes nothing to the first. . . . Klee says that the artist is nothing more than a tree trunk through which the sap rises; but the fruit the tree bears is something no one has ever seen before" (ibid. 237-38).

Klee's interworld, however, is not simply an alternative kingdom; it is a world revealed through critical deformation. The "truth" of the visible is covered over and hidden by the "good form" of Gestaltist figure and ground, by the fixed temporal sequence of past, present, and future in Husserl's "living present," and by the regularizing movement of the eye of Merleau-Ponty's "lived body." The interworld discloses that truth through "bad forms," through coexisting incommensurable moments and perspectives, through shifting curvatures, topological twists, unreconcilable reversals, distensions, contractions, ablations, excrescences, and so on. The compositional elements of an interworld artwork engage forces that act on the eye and body of the spectator, and hence the artwork is situated "in the field of sensibility, indeed of sensuality" (Lyotard 238).

For Lyotard, then, there exist two ontologically distinct spaces: a textual space of recognizable, coded entities, and a figural space of metamorphosing unconscious forces (Lyotard 211). Figural space is unmarked by the coordinates of a regular dimensionality, of a fixed up and down, left and right, foreground and background; its objects defy "good form," ready categorization, or denomination; and its time is that of the event, a time free of sequential demarcations of past, present, and future. The opposition of the textual and the figural does not coincide with the traditional opposition of representational and nonrepresentational art, for abstract paintings may well observe the canons of "good form," Cartesian dimensionality and recognizability (in regular geometric lines and shapes) just as fully as the most conventionally constructed figurative works. Conversely, the figural may be disclosed as easily in the deformations and distortions of a human portrait as in the meanderings of an abstract line. The figural itself is unrepresentable. Only the trace of its action appears, and the function of the artwork is to reveal its effects and thereby open up an interworld between an objective, codified world and a subjective fantasy world. This interworld has the autonomy of a self-creating *natura naturans* and the dynamism of an energetic field of activity. The figural forces of deformation that play through the artwork directly invest the eye and hence engage the domain of the sensible, while at the same time manifesting the operations of the unconscious.

Lyotard expends a great deal of energy linking the figural to the Freudian unconscious, and in this enterprise he and Deleuze part company. Yet much of what Lyotard says about the figural is compatible with Deleuze's approach to painting. In appropriating the concept of the figural Deleuze, too, wishes to resituate discussions of figurative and abstract art and delineate a space of sensible autonomous forces. As we shall see, Deleuze has his own way of relating the figural to sensation, affect, and the play of material forces, one that engages what might be loosely called psychological forces and physical-phenomenal forces but without resorting to the theoretical presuppositions of Freudian psychoanalysis or conventional phenomenology.

SYSTOLE AND DIASTOLE

Lyotard identifies the figural as an energetic space of forces, but he does not indicate precisely why this is the case nor how forces are related to the sensible and the aesthetic. These questions are addressed by Deleuze, and they are best approached via another source upon whom Deleuze relies heavily, Henri Maldiney, who in a remarkable series of essays collected in *Regard Parole Espace* (1973) outlines a theory of rhythm and its relation to form that establishes the connection between sense experience, the work of art, and the dynamic play of force in the world.

Maldiney's thought is essentially phenomenological, though the primary orientation of his arguments comes not so much from Husserl as from the psychologist Erwin Straus, who offers a broad exposition of his views in *Vom Sinn der Sinne* (1935, translated as *The Primary World of Senses: A Vindication of Sensory Experience*). Straus posits a fundamental distinction between *perception* and *sensation,* arguing that perception is a secondary, rational organization of a primary, nonrational dimension of sense experience. The primary world of the senses is one we share with animals, an unreflective, alingual being-with the world in an eternally becoming Here and Now which possesses only an emergent delineation of subject and object:

> The being present of sensory experience—and thus sensory experience in general—is the experiencing of a being-with (*Mit-Sein*)
> which unfolds into a subject and an object. The sensing subject
> does not have sensations but, rather, in his sensing he has first
> himself. In sensory experience, there unfolds both the becoming
> of the subject and the happenings of the world. I become only

insofar as something happens, and something happens (for me) only insofar as I become. The Now of sensing belongs neither to objectivity nor to subjectivity alone, but necessarily to both together. In sensing, both self and world unfold simultaneously for the sensing subject; the sensing being experiences himself and the world, himself in the world, himself with the world. (Straus 351)

Thus, in this primary sensory experience there can be no Husserlian intentionality, for there is no fully delineated subject to bear that intention. Nor can there be a uniformly organized space and time, since these require a conceptual objectification of the world in which the subject is separated from its surroundings and space-time is demarcated according to an abstract, nonperspectival system of coordinates. Sensation and movement are inseparable in Straus's view, and hence the time of sensation is that of the becoming of a perpetual Now. The space of sensation is perspectival, a surrounding environment (*Umwelt*) delineated by its shifting horizon. We do not move *in* space so much as space moves with us, as our Here, with its unfolding perspective and horizon, transforms across time. Sensing "is always an unfolding toward the poles of world and self" (Straus 202), yet an unfolding that is never completed, a process of ongoing union and separation whereby self and world communicate through mutual movement and interaction. Hence, sensation is neither "within" nor "without," for "the body is the mediator between the self and the world. It belongs fully neither to the 'inner' nor to the 'outer' " (Straus 245).

Straus elaborates on the distinction between perception and sensation by contrasting the space of *geography* and the space of *landscape*. The perceptual world, he remarks, "is a world of things with fixed and inalterable properties in universal objective space and universal objective time" (Straus 317). Geographical space is perceptual, the space of the map, with its system of coordinates and unspecified perspective. The landscape, by contrast, is sensory, a perspectival world enclosed by a horizon that constantly moves with us as we move. It is only with great difficulty that we separate the landscape from geography, since conceptual perception is so much a part of our everyday dealings with the world. But in landscape painting Straus finds an entrance to the world of sensation. "Landscape painting does not depict what we see, i.e. what we notice when looking at a place, but—the paradox is unavoidable—it makes visible the invisible, although it be as something far removed. Great landscapes all have a visionary character. Such vision is of the invisible becoming visible" (ibid. 322). In such a landscape, we gain access to the *Mitwelt* of an unfolding self-world that knows no clear differentiation of subject and object. Hence, "the more we absorb it, the more we lose ourselves in it" (Straus 322).

As Maldiney observes, Straus's characterization of the landscape as a making visible of the invisible is strikingly similar to Klee's dictum that "art does not render the visible but renders visible" ("*Kunst gibt nicht das Sichtbare wieder, sondern macht sichtbar*") (Klee 1961, 76). Maldiney argues that all art is like the landscape, a means of making visible the invisible world of sensation, the "Real" which "one never expects—and yet which is always already there" (Maldiney 152). Straus's analysis makes clear for Maldiney the connection between the two senses of the "aesthetic" that we meet in Kant—the aesthetic as sense experience in the *Critique of Pure Reason* and the aesthetic as the domain of art in the *Critique of Judgment*. It also counters the common tendency to treat art as a mode of representation or a means of expressing concepts, for in the realm of Strausian sensation there are no completely delineated objects to represent and no articulable concepts to express. Hence, even in a figurative painting or drawing, "the image's essential function is not to imitate but to appear" (154–55), its appearance being its emergence as a rendering visible of sensation. Maldiney concludes, then, that the aesthetic (in both senses) "concerns not a *what* but a *how*" (137), not the what of represented objects but the how of *style*, which "signifies without representing" (131).

Maldiney characterizes style in terms of *form* and *rhythm*, and it is through these concepts that he elaborates on the way in which Strausian sensation "appears," or manifests itself, in the work of art. Art is not a discourse; hence it is not made of signs but of forms. As Henri Focillon observes, "The sign signifies, the form signifies *itself*" ("*Le signe signifie, la forme se signifie*") (cited in Maldiney 131). By form, however, Maldiney does not mean a static shape or a set of fixed relations—concepts of form that would obviously be inadequate for Maldiney, since the pathic communication of sense experience is inseparable from movement, and in the domain of sensation, there are no fully articulated objects. Rather, form is to be understood dynamically as a process of spontaneous emergence and self-shaping. The "appearance" of the artwork, its manifestation, is one with its form, which "is the sudden arising [*surgissement*] of itself to itself" (ibid. 132). As Klee remarks, "*Werk ist Weg*," the work is the way—the work is the *process* of its genesis and formation. Hence, "The action of form is that by which *a form forms itself*. It is its autogenesis" (Maldiney 155). And rhythm is the unfolding pattern of this self-shaping activity. "This sense of form in formation, in perpetual transformation in the return of the same, is properly the sense of rhythm" (ibid. 157).

Maldiney identifies three moments in the manifestation of form: a vertiginous disclosure of the chaotic world of sensation; a systolic condensation of elements toward definite shapes; and a diastolic eruption of forces that dissolves those shapes and establishes a pathic communication among the components of the whole. The first moment is suggested by Straus's observation that humans inhabit both sensory and perceptual worlds, and that when we have the rare experience of encountering the animal world of sensation without the perceptual coordinates of an objective space and time, we feel lost: "In twilight, darkness, or fog I am still in the landscape. My present location is still determined by the next adjacent location; I can still move. But I no longer know *where* I am, I can no longer determine my position in a panoramic whole. Geography can no longer be developed from the landscape; we are off the path; as human beings, we feel 'lost' (forlorn-*verloren*)" (Straus 319). The aesthetic, then, has its origin in a moment of dislocation, an unexpected experience of vertigo as the world of commonsense temporal and spatial markers ceases to cohere. In Maldiney's opinion, no one has better described this instant than Cézanne, when he remarked to Gasquet: "At this moment I am one with my canvas [not the painted canvas, Maldiney comments, but the world to be painted]. We are an iridescent chaos. I come before my motif, I lose myself there . . . We germinate" (Maldiney 150). The unfamiliar domain of sensation is an "iridescent chaos," an "abyss" Cézanne says elsewhere, but it is also an opening toward creation. As Klee teaches, chaos is a "nonconcept" (*Unbegriff*) a "nowhere-existent something" or "somewhere-existent nothing" (Klee I, 3), whose graphic symbol is the gray point, neither black nor white, cold nor warm, high nor low, "a non-dimensional point, a point between dimensions." As such, the point is sterile and unproductive. But miraculously, the point "leaps into the realm of order" (Klee 1961, 4). This originary leap is the germinative moment of chaos when the cosmogenic line begins to move.

Without the originary leap, no artwork would come into existence. With it, the second moment of systolic condensation arises. At this juncture, says Cézanne, the "stubborn geometry" and the "measure of the earth" begin to assert themselves. "Slowly the geological strata appear before me.... Everything falls straight down.... I begin to separate myself from the landscape, to see it" (Maldiney 150). As Straus argues, the world of sensation is an "unfolding toward the poles of world and self" (Straus 202), and hence the sensing being is "related to it simply in uniting and separating" (ibid. 197). This systolic separation from the world is never complete in sensation, but the subject and objects begin to unfold toward the poles of self and world at this juncture as definable forms come into being. At this stage, from the multiple possible worlds of a confused chaos a particular line of development emerges, a rhythmic articulation of space and time that is "the most unpredictably necessary. Such, among a thousand possible, is the right line [ligne juste], whose reality annuls the possibility of all the others" (Maldiney 166).

Yet the "stubborn geometry" of emergent shapes and definable objects is soon countered by a third movement, a diastolic expansion in which demarcated entities crumble and dissolve. What Straus calls the "uniting" of sensation takes over, an envelopment that puts the *Mitwelt* in an ecstatic communication. Cézanne speaks of "the radiation of the soul, the look, the mystery of light . . . the colors! An aerial, colored logic suddenly replaces the stubborn geometry. The geological strata, the preparatory labor, the moment of design collapse, crumble as in a catastrophe" (Maldiney 185). At this moment, Cézanne says that he "breathes the virginity of the world" (ibid. 150). Man is "absent," he states, "but everywhere in the landscape" (ibid. 185). When Cézanne exclaims in ecstasy to his coachman, "Look! The blues! The blues down there under the pines!" (ibid. 138) he is gesturing toward the pathic communication that unites an enveloping world. Likewise, observes Maldiney, when van Gogh writes of his efforts to "attain the high yellow note of this summer," he uses the musical metaphor "because in this yellow the world sounds; and it sounds to the extent that van Gogh, in this yellow, inhabits a world which has not yet crystallized into objects, and with which he communicates in the rhythm of an ascending vertigo" (ibid. 137).

This interplay of systole and diastole in perpetual emergence from a generative chaos gives rise to the time of form, its *rhythm,* the time of "form in formation, in perpetual transformation in the return of the same"

(Maldiney 157). Rhythm is not to be confused with cadence or meter, says Maldiney, for the rhythm of form is not regulated by an external time measure. The time of rhythm Maldiney relates to Boulez's amorphous, nonpulsed, "smooth" time, one unmarked by a standardized pulse. Citing the work of the linguist Gustave Guillaume, Maldiney defines the rhythm of a form as "the articulation of its implicated time" (ibid. 160).[1] The rhythm of systole and diastole that plays through the self-shaping activity of form in an artwork creates its own temporal framework, and when we experience the artwork we also enter into the implicated time of its form, a perpetual Now outside commonsense coordinates.

Clearly, Maldiney's views converge with Lyotard's on a number of points. Both stress the nondiscursive nature of the visual and find in phenomenological analyses an entry into the space-time of an uncoded domain of visibility (although each distances himself from certain tendencies within phenomenology, Maldiney by adopting the framework of a preintentional Strausian *Mitwelt*, Lyotard by rejecting the presuppositions of a dimensionally regulated *corps vécu*). Both see painting as a rendering visible of the invisible, a moment of "truth" which induces a chaotic vertigo with its own time (for Lyotard, the time of the "event," for Maldiney the "implicated time" of form's rhythmic unfolding within a perpetual Now). Both emphasize the autonomy of the artwork's emergence and self-shaping: Lyotard speaks of the "interworld" artwork as *natura naturans*, and Maldiney of the autogenesis and self-formation of form. Although Lyotard relates the invisible rendered visible by painting to the Freudian unconscious and Maldiney identifies it with the pathic world of Strausian sensation, both associate it with a dynamic manifestation of force. As we shall see, Deleuze's strategy in part is to thematize force and to treat Lyotard's figural deformation as a means of engaging the systolic and diastolic rhythms of Strausian sensation. And if justification for Deleuze's synthetic appropriation of Lyotard and Maldiney is necessary, it is to be found in the remarks of Francis Bacon himself on painting and its relation to force.

THE BRUTALITY OF FACT

In a series of interviews with David Sylvester, Francis Bacon speaks repeatedly of his desire while painting to avoid "illustration," or visual narrative, and to impart an intense sensation directly on the nerves.

"Can you analyze the difference, in fact, between paint which conveys directly and paint which conveys through illustration? This is a very difficult problem to put in words. It is something to do with instinct. It's a very, very close and difficult thing to know why some paint comes across directly onto the nervous system and other paint tells you the story in a long diatribe through the brain" (Sylvester 18). When paint touches the nerves, it renders what Bacon calls a "fact," a term that emphasizes the objective as opposed to the subjective nature of sensation, for what Bacon wants is to engage "the force of the image" (ibid. 126) rather than express an inner state. Hence, when contrasting illustrational and non-illustrational form he says that "illustrational form tells you through the intelligence immediately what the form is about, whereas a non-illustrational form works first upon sensation and then slowly leaks back into the fact" (ibid. 56). In this sense, painting is a type of "recording," a kind of "report," and what Bacon misses in abstract art is that "there's no report, there's nothing other than the aesthetic of the painter and his few sensations" (ibid. 60).

But fact cannot be rendered intentionally and consciously. "One of the things I've always tried to analyze is why it is that, if the formation of the image that you want is done irrationally, it seems to come onto the nervous system much more strongly than if you knew how you could do it. Why is it possible to make the reality of an appearance more violently in this way than by doing it rationally?" (Sylvester 104). Bacon believes that "the mystery of fact is conveyed by an image being made out of nonrational marks" (ibid. 58). His effort is to take advantage of accidents that occur while painting and thereby "set a trap . . . to catch the fact at its most living point" (ibid. 54). Bacon's method is most clearly described in his account of the genesis of *Painting* (1946, Museum of Modern Art, New York), a canvas of a dark-suited individual surrounded by various cuts of meat whose upper face is shadowed by an overspreading umbrella and whose mouth is stretched wide in a toothy grin. Bacon relates that he was attempting to "to make a bird alighting on a field," but that "suddenly the lines that I'd drawn suggested something totally different, and out of this suggestion arose this picture. I had no intention to do this picture; I never thought of it in that way. It was like one continuous accident mounting on top of another" (ibid. 11). When asked if the bird suggested the umbrella, he answers that "it suddenly suggested an opening-up into another area of feeling altogether.

And then I made these things, I gradually made them. So that I don't think the bird suggested the umbrella; it suddenly suggested the whole image" (ibid. 11). The development of the image, in other words, does not proceed by resemblance from one representation to another; rather, an accident discloses the path of a self-forming activity. The involuntary marks, intermittent swipes with a brush, rag, or sponge, sporadic blotches of paint, or splatters of turpentine that Bacon uses while painting a subject are all ways of breaking "the willed articulation of the image, so that the image will grow, as it were, spontaneously and within its own structure, and not my structure" (ibid. 160). The image does not develop according to a preconceived plan, for "I don't really think my pictures out, you know; I think of the disposition of the forms and then I watch the forms form themselves" (ibid. 136).

We may recognize here a version of Klee's artwork as interworld *natura naturans* and of Maldiney's form as self-forming activity whereby the *ligne juste* opens up the path of unpredictable necessity through which various possibilities are eliminated and one course of development is realized. The involuntary marks are accidents, aleatory moments of chaos like Klee's gray point that introduces the *Ursprung* of a cosmogenic line of creation. Bacon says that these marks serve as "a sort of graph" (in the French edition of Bacon's interviews "graph" is translated as *diagramme*, a word Deleuze comments on frequently in his works). Within the graph one can see "the possibilities of all types of facts being planted. This is a difficult thing; I'm expressing it badly. But you see, for instance, if you think of a portrait, you maybe at one time have put the mouth somewhere, but you suddenly see through this graph that the mouth could go right across the face. And in a way you would love to be able in a portrait to make a Sahara of the appearance—to make it so like, yet seeming to have the distances of the Sahara" (Sylvester 56). The irrational, involuntary, accidental marks, comments Deleuze, "are neither significant nor signifying: they are asignifying" (FB 66). They bring about "the intrusion of another world in the visual world of figuration" (FB 66), the world of Lyotard's figural deformation but also of Klee's interworld creation, for the graph or diagram "is indeed a chaos, a catastrophe, but also the seed of order or rhythm" (FB 67).[2]

Bacon's graphs of germinative chaos—the Sahara that opens out of an extended mouth, the landing bird that develops into an umbrella-covered individual—are means of deforming figurative into figural images.

"What I want to do is to distort the thing far beyond the appearance, but in the distortion to bring it back to a recording of the appearance" (Sylvester 40). That appearance Deleuze identifies with Cézanne's and Straus's "sensation," which has one face turned toward the subject and one toward the object. "Or rather it has no faces at all, it is the two indissolubly, it is being-in-the-world, as the phenomenologists say: at the same time I *become* in sensation and something *arrives* through sensation" (FB 27). Yet Deleuze, like Lyotard and Maldiney, must distance himself from standard phenomenological analyses of sensation. As Lyotard argues, Merleau-Ponty's *corps vécu* accounts for the body's being-in-the-world, but it is still too rational, too organized to account for the disequilibrium of the figural. And as Maldiney points out, Husserlian intentionality is irrelevant to the Strausian *Mitwelt* of primary sensation. Sensation "is in the body" (FB 27), says Deleuze, but it is traversed by something that surpasses the lived body, by "a Power [*Puissance*] that is deeper and almost unlivable" (FB 33). The body of sensation is a "body without organs."

Deleuze takes the term from Antonin Artaud, who writes, "The body is the body/ It is alone/ And has no need of organs/ The body is never an organism/ Organisms are the enemies of the body" (FB 33). It is perhaps the best known and most puzzling of Deleuze's coinages, first introduced in *Anti-Oedipus* (1972) and later the subject of an extended discussion in plateau 6 of *A Thousand Plateaus* (1980). The body without organs is in one sense the catatonic body of the schizophrenic, the hallucinatory body as experienced by Daniel Paul Schreber, who reports that he "lived for a long time without a stomach, without intestines, almost without lungs, with a torn oesophagus, without a bladder, and with shattered ribs" (AO 14; 8). Hence, in associating the body of sensation with a psychotic body Deleuze emphasizes the irrational disorientation of sensation. But in *Francis Bacon* Deleuze develops the concept in a way that points beyond psychosis and madness and suggests the relationship between forces, the body, and the figural.

FORCES

The body without organs, Deleuze explains, is not so much without organs as it is without organization. It has organs but it is not an *organism*, that is, a coordinated, unified, regulated whole, with senses that operate together in their reports of the outside world (i.e., touch, sight, hearing, etc. combining to assemble the discrete and fixed characteristics of objects into a recognizable and manageable environment). It is "intense, intensive," traversed by "a wave that traces on the body levels and thresholds in accordance with the variations of its amplitude" (FB 33). Deleuze likens the body without organs to the unicellular embryo of a biological entity, whose metastable distributions of energy delineate axes of movement, gradients, and zones of potential splitting without fixing or determining any one of them as the definitive locus of cellular division. The body without organ's axes, zones, and gradients are shifting oscillations of a vibratory wave flowing over a smooth ovular surface, and sensation "is like the encounter of the wave with Forces acting on the body, 'affective athleticism,' cry-sigh" (FB 34). Sensation is thus "the action of forces on the body," "the intensive fact of the body" (FB 34).

It might seem that Deleuze is here making a clear differentiation of external forces and internal sensations, but he states elsewhere that in sensation "it is the same body that gives it and that receives it" (FB 27). Hence, when the eye views an apple, the apple is not to be taken as an external force impinging on a corporeal eye. Rather, in sensation apple and eye are part of a body without organs, such that when Cézanne paints an apple with what D. H. Lawrence calls the "applyness of the apple," he paints the body.[3] The distinction finally is not between external forces and internal sensations, but between invisible forces and visible bodies, the body of sensation rendering visible the invisible forces that play through bodies. "And isn't this the genius of Cézanne, to have subordinated all the means of painting to this task: to render visible the folding force of mountains, the germinative force of the apple, the thermal force of a landscape . . . etc.?" (FB 39). The germinative force of the apple is experienced as a corporeal intensity, but that force is not a mere psychological projection any more than the apple is an extension of the human body. In sensation, there is no full differentiation of inside and outside, of human and nonhuman. As Straus indicates, sensation is pathic communication in a *Mitwelt* unfolding toward, but never arriving at, the poles of subject and object. Hence Deleuze's insistence that the germinative force is the *apple's* force, not the viewing subject's, a factual rather than a projected, phantasmagoric intensity.

Often in *A Thousand Plateaus* and elsewhere Deleuze speaks of a plane of consistency rather than a body without organs, thereby avoiding the temptation to confuse the body without organs with the commonsense notion of the human body, but in *Francis Bacon* the term is particularly useful in suggesting what Bacon is about in his rendering of human forms. The body without organs does have organs, says Deleuze, but they are *provisional* organs, temporary, shifting organs with varying functions. Whenever a force meets the oscillating wave of the body without organs, a provisional organ is determined. "An organ will thus be determined by that encounter, but a provisional organ, which lasts only while the passage of the wave and the action of the force last, and which will be displaced in order to be situated elsewhere" (FB 34). Deleuze discovers here a basic affinity between painting and hysteria, noting that nineteenth-century taxonomies of hysteria include characterizations of corporeal experiences that aptly illustrate the notion of indeterminate or provisional organs: nonorganic, shifting paralyses, hyperaestheses, anestheses; temporal anticipations or retardations in symptom formation; panic over multiple functions of an organ (the mouth as eating/breathing/drinking/vomiting apparatus); a general seizure of the body by forces in somnambulism; autoscopic phenomena in which the hysteric senses the body as being *beneath* the organism, looking in the mirror and seeing oneself as *inside* an alien head. Such hysterical provisional organs are what we see in Bacon's deformations of the human body—in the becomings-animal of a snout/mouth, wing/eyebrow, or snarl/smile, in the globular dripping of a leg, the mottled torque of a twisting back, the Sahara of a spreading forehead. Each such provisional organ is the site of a force meeting a vibratory wave, a rendering visible of an invisible force. Each is also the locus of a sensation that "envelopes a constitutive level of difference" (FB 29), a becoming that includes within itself a passage of intensity from one level to another. This synthesis of levels of intensity takes place because the body is seized by a "vital power [*puissance vitale*]" (FB 31) that overwhelms individual sense organs and traverses the entire corporeal surface. This power "is Rhythm," which "places in each sensation the levels and domains through which it passes. And this rhythm runs through a painting as it runs through a piece of music. It is diastole-systole: the world that takes hold of me in closing around me, the self [*moi*] that opens to the world and opens the world to itself" (FB 31).

What Deleuze means by rhythm is clarified through his analysis of the various forces that structure Bacon's canvases. Deleuze labels the fundamental elements of Bacon's compositions Structure, Contour, and Figure—a flat, monochromatic field (Structure), an isolating circle, ring, rectangle or cube (Contour), and an isolated form (Figure). Three kinds of movement affect these basic elements and indicate the presence of three different forces. There is a movement that passes from the monochromatic field to the figure as the field tends to roll around the isolating contour, press in on the figure, and cut it off from any narrative, "illustrational" associations. Here Bacon renders visible an invisible force of isolation (FB 42). The figure itself undergoes spasmodic movements as provisional organs emerge, becomings-animal take place, and malleable flesh writhes across bone scaffoldings. Here we see "forces of deformation, which take hold of the body and the head of the Figure, and which become visible each time that the head shakes off its face, or the body its organism" (FB 42). And then there is a movement whereby the figure attempts to escape itself, to pass out of itself through one of its organs and rejoin the monochromatic field. In Bacon's paintings of screaming popes, the spasmodic body attempts to escape itself through the screaming mouth, to empty itself out through an organ. In *Figure at a Wash Basin* (1976, Caracas Museum of Contemporary Art), a vomiting individual leans over a washbasin, as if it were attempting to pass outside of itself and pursue a line of flight through the washbasin drain. "The entire series of spasms in Bacon are of this type, love, vomit, excrement, always the body that tries to escape itself *through* one of its organs, in order to rejoin the flat field, the material structure" (FB 17). Hence the third movement passes from figure to field and indicates the presence of a "force of dissipation" (FB 42). The function of the isolating Contour is to serve as a membrane within which forces of deformation affect the figure and through which forces of isolation move from field to figure and forces of dissipation from figure to field.

Beyond the fundamental elements of Structure, Contour, and Figure, other forces are at play in Bacon's paintings. Although he frequently concentrates on individual figures, he also paints couples in various poses, always aware of the danger of introducing narrative relations between the figures rather than relations of fact.[4] In a couple, each figure has its own movements, its own rhythmic vibration, and in the matter of fact that situates the two figures vis-à-vis one another, we encounter a relation of vibration to vibration, a *resonance* between vibrations. The forces that form such resonant relations Deleuze labels "forces of coupling [*forces d'accouplement*]" (FB 55), and they are to be distinguished from the forces of isolation, deformation, and dissipation. Resonance in a sense renders two figures as one, treating the couple's relation as a single matter of fact. But there is another sense in which the rhythm that passes between the coupled figures takes on an incipient existence of its own, independent of the figures themselves. And in the relations Bacon establishes between figures in his triptychs, that autonomous existence is further accentuated.

Bacon says that he sees images in series (Sylvester 84) and hence finds the triptych an appealing form of composition. The triptych also allows him to paint multiple figures while maintaining their mutual isolation within individual canvases. Deleuze argues that in Bacon's triptychs, individual figures have different functions that may be related to the "rhythmic characters" (*personnages rhythmiques*) of Messiaen (see chapter 1), "one 'active,' with an increasing variation or amplification, another 'passive,' with a decreasing variation or elimination, and a third, finally, 'witness' " (FB 48). No rule regulates the placement of these rhythms—no privilege is granted the left, right, or central canvas, no sequence or pattern of rhythms recurs with any frequency in the triptychs—and no system allows one to assign a particular kind of figure a given rhythmic function. Figural oppositions of descent and rise, diastole and systole, naked and clothed, and augmentation and diminution may be found in Bacon's triptychs, but either pole of the opposition may take on the function of an active or a passive rhythm. The active rhythm is a "fall" (*chute*), says Deleuze, but only in the sense that it is a passage of sensation from one level to another measured against a zero degree of intensity. Hence, "In short, the fall is anything that develops (there are developments by diminution). The fall is precisely the active rhythm" (FB 55). In each triptych, then, one determines the active rhythm by locating the "fall," "that which is most living in a sensation, that in which the sensation is experienced as living" (FB 54), in opposition to which the passive rhythm takes on its function. As for the witness rhythm, it serves as a local, temporary rhythmic constant with which the active and passive rhythms may be compared. Though Bacon frequently paints figures whose apparent role is that of a witness (individuals with cameras, voyeurs, idle spectators), the witness *rhythm* is a function that may or may not coincide with that of the witness figure. The witness rhythm is generally a horizontal element—a hysterical smile, a reclining body or series of bodies—whose movement is "retrogradable," in the musical sense that it is a palindromic structure, the same backward as forward (or in spatial terms, the same from left to right as from right to left). Hence Deleuze comments of active and passive rhythms that "each is the 'retrograde' of the other, while a common and constant value appears in the witness rhythm, retrogradable in itself" (FB 54).

There is "a great mobility in the triptych, a great circulation" (FB 52) as various compositional elements assume different rhythmic functions. What is essential, however, is that in the active, passive, and witness rhythms, "It is rhythm itself that becomes sensation, that becomes the Figure" (FB 49). In the triptychs, Deleuze finds that the figures become detached from their surroundings and float in the monochromatic background surface that extends across the three canvases. The relations between figures are projected onto the flat surface and "governed [*pris en charge*] by the uniform color or the raw light" (FB 55). The relations themselves seem to emanate from and be produced by the monochromatic surface. "Such was the lesson of Rembrandt: it is light that engenders the rhythmic characters" (FB 56). The monochromatic field unites the three paintings, but it simultaneously separates the figures within them, such that "the Figures attain maximum separation in the light, in the color: a force of separation, of division, takes hold of them, very different from the preceding force of isolation" (FB 55). The background of the triptychs instills what Deleuze calls elsewhere a "disjunctive synthesis," a paralogical amalgam of the one and the many, a generative multiple/one that divides itself and distributes itself into its many constituents. Hence, in the triptychs, "The three canvases remain separated, but they are no longer isolated; the frame or edges of a canvas refer no longer to the limitative unity of each, but to the distributive unity of the three" (FB 56).

The triptychs also give us "an impression of time" (FB 49), for when the relations themselves become the subject of the canvases, it is the shape of movement itself that we sense, a pure movement extracted from and passing between the figures. In the disjunctive synthesis of the monochromatic field, however, that time loses the coordinates of the individual bodies, with their rhythmic deformations, isolating compressions and lines-of-flight dissipations. The floating time of Aion is produced, time "out of joint," the unmeasured, ecstatic time of pure becoming that we met earlier in Messiaen. "Time is no longer in the chromatism of bodies, it has passed into a monochromatic eternity. It is an immense space-time that unites all things, *but in introducing between them the distances of a Sahara, the centuries of an Aion:* the triptych and its separated panels" (FB 56).

For Lyotard, the figural is a deformation of the figurative, the "bad form" that defies recognition and ready subsumption within an organized space, thereby providing an entrance to Klee's germinative chaos and the work of the unconscious. For Deleuze, too, the figural disrupts the clichés of coded representations—what Bacon refers to as illustration—but it also makes possible "matters of fact," figures that bypass the brain and work directly on the nerves. Such matters of fact correspond to Cézanne's "sensations," whose logic Maldiney explores through the Strausian concept of a *Mitwelt* of primary sensation and the notion of a fundamental systolic-diastolic rhythm emergent from a cosmogenic chaos or abyss. Deleuze relates the *Mitwelt* of sensation not to the "lived body" but to the "body without organs" and the forces that determine "provisional organs" on its oscillating surface. Each provisional organ is a locus of deformation, a figural chaos but also a graph or diagram for the development of a canvas whose function is to harness forces. In Bacon's paintings Deleuze finds complex rhythms of movements and forces: a systolic force of isolation that passes from the background to the figure; a diastolic force of deformation that induces various "becomings"; a dissipative force whereby the figure escapes itself in a line of flight and creates a movement from figure to monochromatic ground; a coupling force that establishes a relation of fact between two figures; and a force of separation that distributes figures within a universal field of color and light in which active, passive, and witness rhythms attain an autonomous existence.

In Deleuze's characterization of the monochromatic field as a distributive unity of universal color and light one hears echoes of Maldiney's diastolic moment that disrupts the "stubborn geometry" of individual forms, that "second moment . . . of the expansive eruption of color, in the diastole of the canvas and the world, in the diastole of existence" (Maldiney 185). In this moment, according to Cézanne, "There is no longer anything but colors and in them clear light . . . that rising of the earth toward the sun, that exhalation of the depths toward love" (ibid. 185). Deleuze regards Bacon as "a great colorist" in the tradition of Cézanne,[5] and in his discussion of color, the relation of form to ground, and the position of Cézanne in the history of painting, Deleuze builds on the analyses of Maldiney in important ways, as we shall see in the next chapter.

Chapter Six

COLOR

Cézanne faults the Impressionists for capturing only a fleeting and evanescent subjective experience, whereas his desire is to create "something solid and durable as in the art of the museums" (Cézanne 121). In a similar vein, Bacon remarks that he seeks more than a mere rendering of a momentary feeling, for "the potency of the image is created partly by the possibility of its enduring. And, of course, images accumulate sensation around themselves the longer they endure" (Sylvester 58). The problem of solidity and durability is in one sense a question of form and structure. As Maldiney stresses, Cézanne recognizes not only the diastolic expansion of universal color and light but also the systolic condensation of the forms of "stubborn geometry." But it is also a question of objectivity, of providing a report of sensation that is more than subjective, a rendering of the world in which man is "absent but everywhere in the landscape," according to Cézanne, a recording of a "matter of fact," in Bacon's terms. Cézanne and Bacon pursue a figural middle course between abstraction and conventional representation, Cézanne avoiding the diaphanous fogs of Impressionism and the clichés of academic realism, Bacon rejecting what he regards as the idealized geometrical forms of abstraction and the murky confusion of abstract expressionism, as well as the ready-made images of "illustration." Both seek the truth of sensation and appearance, but the resemblance they pursue is "by non-resemblant means" (FB 75), in Deleuze's analysis. As Bacon says, he "deforms" his portraits "into appearance" (Sylvester 146), irrational, involuntary marks leading him to a more profound resemblance. "It's an illogical method of making, an illogical way of attempting to make what one hopes will be a logical outcome—in the sense that one hopes one will be able to suddenly make the thing there in a totally illogical way but that it will be totally real and, in the case of a portrait, recognizable as the person" (Sylvester 105). For Cézanne the middle course of the figural proceeds via the "motif," something that combines sensation and the solidity of a "framework" [*charpente*] (Cézanne 211); for Bacon, the graph, or diagram, opens the way to the nonrational resemblance of the matter of fact. Deleuze argues that the motif, or diagram, of the figural is what makes possible a durable sensation whereby it is possible "at the same time to render geometry concrete or sensed, and to give to sensation duration and clarity" (FB 73). How precisely does the diagram allow a sensation and a "framework" to combine?

ANALOGICAL MODULATION

One might assume that in his references to the necessity of a "framework" and the demands of "stubborn geometry" Cézanne is simply echoing his oft-quoted advice to "treat nature in terms of the cylinder, the sphere, the cone, the whole put in perspective" (FB 74). But Deleuze insists that Cézanne is misunderstood if he is seen as an advocate of abstraction (as is often the case), for there are two ways of using geometry in painting, one digital, the other analogical. The digital use proceeds via a code—in this case a limited set of simple, discrete forms used to "translate" the complex forms of nature or to serve as autonomous elements of a formal composition—whereas the analogical does not, and Cézanne's use of geometry is analogical rather than digital. To clarify this distinction, Deleuze first opposes the notions of digital and analogical languages, arguing that cries, groans, sighs, whispers, and moans can function as elements of an uncoded analogical language whose sounds lack the conventional and discrete organization of coded natural languages. In this regard, one may say in general that "painting raises colors and lines to the state of language, and that it is an analogical language" (FB 74). Animal cries, color displays, and gestures no doubt qualify as analogical languages, but we should not assume therefore

that the analogical is innate rather than acquired or that it operates via
resemblance rather than arbitrary convention. Certainly the analogical
language of painting must be learned, and there is substantial evidence
that birdsongs, mating rituals, nurturing activities, and so on are as
much acquired as innate patterns of behavior. And though codes such
as human natural languages utilize arbitrary phonemes to signify concepts, animal cries likewise are arbitrary sounds in that they bear no
resemblance to that which elicits them. What confuses the issue of resemblance is that it may be either *productive* or *produced.* It is productive
when the elements of one thing pass directly into the elements of another,
as is the case when light strikes the surface of photographic film.
Resemblance may be said to be produced, however, when "it appears
suddenly as the result of entirely different relations than those which it
is charged with reproducing: the resemblance thus arises as the brutal
product of non-resembling means" (FB 75). Cézanne's analogical use of
geometry, Deleuze argues, is nonfigurative and uncoded, and the resemblances to standard geometric forms one may find in his paintings are
not productive but simply produced via nonresembling means.

Such produced resemblances issue from the diagram, which might
seem paradoxical, given that diagrams would appear to be highly coded
entities.[1] But the diagram of painting is analogical rather than digital,
Deleuze insists, a distinction he elucidates by considering the differences between analogue and digital musical synthesizers. Analogue synthesizers, such as the Moog Synthesizer and the Buchla Electronic Music
System, basically consist of "modules" of electric circuits in which a
charge passes through oscillators that can be manipulated to vary the
frequency and amplitude of the produced sound waves. Hence, there is
a continuous, actual, and sensible presence of electronic impulses that
issues directly in a given sound. By contrast, a digital synthesizer first
codifies sound elements as digital bits of information—zeroes and ones—
then integrates this information with other digitized elements in a
homogeneous collection of data, and finally converts/translates these
digitized bits of information into actual and sensible sound.[2] One may
say, then, that analogical diagrams in painting, like analogue synthesizers, "put heterogeneous elements in immediate connection, introduce
between elements a possibility of connection that is properly unlimited,
in a field of presence or finite plane in which all moments are actual and
sensible" (FB 76).

Analogue synthesizers are said to be "modular" rather than "integrated," in that they function through independent modules (oscillators) rather than an integrated, digitized body of data (as with digital synthesizers), but Deleuze suggests that they are modular as well in that they operate via a principle of *modulation*. Deleuze takes the notion of modulation from Gilbert Simondon, who in *L'Individu et sa genèse physico-biologique* (*The Individual and Its Physico-biological Genesis*) develops the concept as a means of escaping the classical opposition of matter and form that recurs in discussions of biology from Plato to the twentieth century. The matter-form, or hylemorphic, model typically assumes the existence of a malleable matter and a shaping (ideal) form, such as one finds in brick making, in which amorphous clay is poured into a shaping mold. Simondon points out, however, that the clay, far from being passive matter upon which an active form is imposed, is in reality a metastable material in active communication with the surfaces of the mold, the clay's final form being determined by a stable internal distribution of energy reached at the end of a process of information exchange with the mold. To suggest a properly dynamic and interactive conception of physical genesis, Simondon extends the mold model to a description of the simple thermionic (or vacuum) tube known as a triode. In a triode, electrons are drawn from a negative cathode (typically a hot filament) at one end of the tube to a positive anode at the other end. Between the cathode and anode, a third electrode functions as a control grid. Variations in the voltage of the control-grid electrode regulate the flow of electrons through the tube by modifying the tube's space charge. Simondon asserts that the control grid may be seen as a mold, but one whose shape is continuously varying as its voltage increases or decreases. Unlike brick making, in which the uncasting of the brick is a separate stage in the manufacturing process, the "molding" of electrons in the triode entails a constant process of casting and uncasting. Thus the triode may be described as a "continuous temporal mold" (Simondon 41), and the process of such continuous temporal molding may be referred to as "modulation." Simondon concludes that the mold and the modulator are extreme instances of a single process in which forms are determined through the establishment of a particular regulation of energy. "To mold is to modulate in a definitive manner; to modulate is to mold in a perpetually variable and continuous manner" (Simondon 42). Thus, when Deleuze says, "*It is perhaps the notion of modulation in general (and not similitude)* which allows us to understand the nature of analogical language or the diagram" (FB 76), it is in this special sense of a "temporal, variable and continuous mold" (FB 85) that the term is to be understood.

The diagram in painting, then, is a kind of visual synthesizer, into which the figurative clichés of coded representations are fed and out of which issue resemblances produced by the nonresembling means of a temporal, variable, and continuous modulation. The diagram creates an analogical language, uncoded and affective—hence capable of conveying and bearing sensation—yet structured according to its own order, provided with a "framework" or "stubborn geometry." Deleuze identifies three dimensions of painting's analogical language: planes, colors, and bodies. In such a conception of painting—which informs the practices of Cézanne and Bacon—connections or junctures of planes replace relations of classical perspective; color relations of tonality replace relations of value based on light and shadow; and the mass and disequilibrium of the body replace figurative representations and traditional figure-ground relations. The diagram first destroys the figurative coordinates of conventional representations, but it then makes possible an invention according to an uncoded language. "So that the rupture with figurative resemblance does not propagate a catastrophe, so that a more profound resemblance may be produced, starting from the diagram, the planes must ensure their juncture; the mass of the body must integrate its disequilibrium in a deformation (neither transformation nor decomposition, but the locus of a force); and above all modulation must find its true sense and its technical formula, as law of Analogy, and must act as a continuous variable mold, which is not simply opposed to modeling in chiaroscuro but invents a new modeling through color" (FB 77).

Although Deleuze identifies three components in painting's analogical language, he deems color to be more important than planes and bodies, for the analogical "finds its highest law in the treatment of colors" (FB 78). Bacon, like Cézanne, is a "colorist" whose controlling belief is that "if you push color to its pure internal relations (warm-cold, expansion-contraction), you have everything. If the color is perfect, that is, the relations of color are developed for themselves, you have everything, form and ground, light and shadow, bright and dark [*foncé*]" (FB 89). In Bacon and Cézanne, all pictorial relations issue from "the spatializing energy of color" (FB 86), which functions via a process of modulation, or temporal, variable continuous molding. And the visual space it creates is essentially tactile, or *haptic,* rather than optical.

HAPTIC AND OPTIC

To explicate his understanding of color, Deleuze situates "colorism" and the painting of Bacon and Cézanne within a broad history that outlines the basic principles underlying Egyptian, classical Greek, Byzantine, and Gothic art. All painters rehearse the history of painting in their canvases, Deleuze claims, and in Bacon's works one can see a struggle to solve many of the problems faced by painters in the past. Those problems ultimately center on the complex relations between the hand and the eye, between the tactile and the optical—both of which are factors in visual experience. The notion of a tactile vision comes from Alois Riegl, who offers the concept as a means of differentiating Egyptian, classical Greek, and late Roman art from one another. Deleuze reads Riegl through the filter of Maldiney, who modifies Riegl's historical schema to establish optical Byzantine art as the antipode of tactile Egyptian practice, while Deleuze uses Worringer's account of the Gothic to suggest a tactile alternative to the Egyptian aesthetic. To understand Deleuze's approach to the haptic, we must now embark on a slightly circuitous route through Riegl, Maldiney, and Worringer.

Early in the twentieth century, Alois Riegl was one of the most influential art historians of Europe, whose primary concern throughout his criticism was to identify the *Kunstwollen* (often loosely translated as "will to art") that manifests itself in a unified manner across all the arts in a given age.[3] In his *Spätrömische Kunstindustrie* (*Late Roman Art Industry,* 1901), Riegl attempts to demonstrate that three distinct sets of aesthetic principles governed various plastic arts—specifically, architecture, sculpture, painting, and the decorative arts—in Egypt, classical Greece, and the late Roman empire.

Riegl sees a fundamental divide between the art of antiquity and the art of the modern world. The ancients have as their ultimate goal "the representation of external objects as clear material entities" (Riegl 21), whereas moderns (from roughly the Renaissance on) take as their aim the depiction of objects within a unified infinite space. Although we moderns tend to interpret ancient art through the eyes of a perspectival vision, and assume the existence of a single, coherent, and limitless space within which entities assume their proper relations, the ancients attempted to limit space to varying degrees in an effort to overcome basic problems inherent in perception. According to Riegl's analysis, the eye perceives the world in terms of two-dimensional colored planes; as a result, "The objects of the external world appear to us in a chaotic mixture" (ibid. 22). Since "the ancients' sense perception found external objects to be confusing and mixed" (ibid. 21), they attempted to represent as clearly as possible individually delineated objects and to emphasize their material impenetrability. Space they regarded as absence and void—hence, as the negation of the material and something that "was originally not able to become a subject for ancient artistic creation" (ibid. 21). In order to comprehend objects as independent entities, the ancients tried as far as possible to understand them without reference to subjective consciousness and experience. The simplest means of perceiving separate entities is through touch, which reveals the enclosed surface unity of objects as well as their material impenetrability. Yet touch alone only yields information about individual points, not complete surfaces. To comprehend entire objects, one must combine multiple touches through subjective consciousness and thought. Riegl finds in this basic dichotomy between objective and subjective knowledge of objects the source of a tension that played throughout ancient art. A parallel dichotomy informs vision, he argues, in that the eye initially takes in a confused image of a colored plane and only assembles the outlines of individual objects through the subjective assimilation of multiple planar perceptions. Touch is superior to vision in providing information about the material impenetrability of objects, but vision surpasses touch in informing us about the height and width of objects, since it is able to synthesize multiple perceptions more quickly than touch. A sense of depth, however, comes only through touch, since the eye sees only planes. And a knowledge of objects as three-dimensional forms requires the subjective synthesis of multiple tactile and visual experiences of the entities.

From this account of perception Riegl generates the objective/ subjective and tactile/optical oppositions that control his analysis. The latter opposition, however, is subsumed within vision, since Riegl's area of concern is visual art. Hand and eye reinforce one another in a fundamental way, since our vision of objects as impenetrable, three-dimensional entities necessarily incorporates within it knowledge gained from tactile experience. Hence Riegl speaks of a tactile or *haptic* vision (from the Greek *hapto,* to touch), in which the contributing role of touch is emphasized, and this he opposes to an *optic* vision, in which the role of touch is minimized.[4] Although the tension between objective and subjective knowledge of objects is evident throughout antiquity, the predominant effort of the ancients is to limit the subjective element and comprehend the material essence of individual objects, and thus to avoid the representation of infinite space, which, in negating material individuality and immediate sense perception, entails a high degree of subjectivity.

Riegl ascribes three phases to the development of ancient art. The first is epitomized in Egyptian art, which emphasizes the material impenetrability of entities and their relation to objective sense experience with as little reference to the mediation of subjective consciousness as possible. In painting and bas-relief sculpture this tendency is manifest in the assimilation of the figure to the tactile plane, the plane "which the eye perceives when it comes so close to the surface of an object, that all the silhouettes and, in particular all shadows which otherwise could disclose an alteration in depth, disappear" (Riegl 24). Such a haptic vision is *nahsichtig,* "near-seeing," and its concentration is on the outlines of figures, which are kept as symmetrical as possible, for "symmetry reveals to the exterior an uninterrupted tactile connection within the plane in the most convincing manner" (ibid. 25). The figure is sharply outlined but unmodeled; it stands out from the ground, yet that ground is not space but a tactile plane without depth. The composition of the figure follows from this haptic sensibility: "The head appears in profile, with the visible eye being placed to look straight ahead, the chest and the two shoulders with the arms are visible in front, while from the belly on downward begins a distortion into the profile, which is kept fully by the moving legs. This strangely contorted position can be explained in no other way than with the effort to show the entire body in as clear completeness as possible and in order to avoid as much as possible any indication of depth, which is any foreshortening of the outlines" (ibid. 59).

The second phase is represented by classical Greek art, which still attempts to render the materiality of the object, but which grants precedence to the visual over the tactile. Nonetheless, classical Greek art retains a certain connection with the tactile, and hence may be described as tactile-optical. Its perception is neither *nahsichtig* (near-seeing) nor *fern-*

sichtig (far-seeing), but *normalsichtig* (normal-seeing). Foreshortenings now appear, as do shadows, but only half shadows, which do not interrupt the tactile connection of the figure to the surface. The modeling of the figure reveals projections on the compositional plane as well as the existence of the figure as a three-dimensional entity. Figures rise from the ground in three-quarter view, their movements are more animated than Egyptian figures, and the disposition of relations between figures takes on an incipient spatial dimension. Yet the compositional principle remains essentially planar; the ground functions as a calming, tactile support for spatial movements, which tend to be assimilated within a single plane separated from, but connected to, the background plane.

The third phase is *fernsichtig*, predominantly optical, and most clearly evident in the art of late Roman antiquity. The partial delineation of a three-dimensional figure in Greek antiquity is here brought to completion, but the figure is disclosed only within a limited cubic space against a planar ground, not within an infinite space. In bas-reliefs, the figure is sharply separated from the ground, the figure undercut to create a shadowy outline around the form. The folds of drapery, facial features, and the modeling of torso and limbs also employ deep shadows that break the continuity of the plane. The composition is organized through a rhythmic dispensation of light and dark, of projected clear surface and shadowy void. Such an alternation of light and shadow is essentially visual (or "coloristic," in Riegl's terminology). The projected surfaces, however, continue to be treated in a planar manner, and the limited cubic space of the figure is superimposed against a planar ground. Finally, with the weakening of the sense of the tactile plane, late Roman art develops a compensatory emphasis on symmetry that gives it an apparent compatibility with Egyptian art.

GROUND AND FOUNDATION

In "L'Art et le pouvoir du fond" ("Art and the Power of the Ground"), Henri Maldiney offers a modified version of Riegl's history, claiming that Riegl's account of haptic and optic vision in the ancient world discloses the artistic relation between motif and ground (*fond*), which "is the aesthetic expression of the ontological relation of existence to ground" (Maldiney 173). Crucial for Maldiney is the haptic/optic distinction, which he disengages from Riegl's account of perception and interprets in terms of basic phenomenological poles. We stand in the world enveloped by space, says Maldiney, our feet on the earth and our eyes on the horizon, leaning from a *here* toward a *there,* summoned to unite earth and sky. We engage the supporting ground and enveloping horizon through the most active of our senses, touch and sight, at once grasping and possessing the world through touch and extending ourselves into the world through sight. From this opposition of touch and sight arise two different kinds of space and two different forms of seeing, one haptic, in which the motif constitutes a visual analogon of touch, the other purely optic. In haptic space, the motif is something one grasps. "It is apprehended in its individuality starting from the immobile ground, of which the motif is . . . 'the motivation.' " In optic space, by contrast, "the motif is given starting from free space and, as a result, the motif is moving and tends to make the ground move" (ibid. 194–95). Viewers face the motif and project themselves into it in haptic space, thereby possessing the object, whereas in optic space viewers inhabit the luminous space of the motif, and through the motif communicate with and become possessed by its enveloping atmosphere.

Informing this opposition of haptic and optic space is Maldiney's distinction between the systolic and diastolic moments of sensation. As we recall, Maldiney uses Straus's account of sensation to identify three basic elements of sense experience: (1) a primary generative chaos, in which world and self are indistinguishable; (2) a systolic contraction whereby objects and subject begin to take form; and (3) a diastolic expansion whereby surrounding world and self communicate and intermingle in a single *Mitwelt.*[5] Maldiney then argues that these basic moments of sensation are also the fundamental moments of aesthetic creation and reception. Although systolic and diastolic moments are mutually reinforcing and necessary, one moment may be stressed more than the other, and in haptic space it is the systolic moment that is dominant, whereas in optic space the diastolic prevails. In the systolic moment, the focus is on *taking* (*prendre*) and *keeping* (*garder*). We are exposed to the world, enveloped in a chaotic milieu from which we must detach ourselves and individual objects in order to constitute a structured environment (*Umwelt*). In grasping an object, we separate it from the chaotic surround and delineate its contours as a distinct entity, thereby converting a *there* into a *here.* Once we bring the object to ourselves, we can keep it, letting it go and subsuming it within our extended corporeal space-time schema, and thus converting its *here* into an integrated *there*. The systolic moment is thus an introjection of the world, the establishment of a coordinated here and there whereby we take and keep the object at the same time that we are taken and retained by it. In the diastolic moment, by contrast, all is light and color. We do not possess the world but are possessed by it, filled by the interplay of light and dark, appearance and disappearance, whose rhythm instills an alternation of abandon and retreat.

The relationship between the artistic motif and its ground is based on the relationship between sensation's systolic/diastolic moments and the chaotic abyss from which they arise. Maldiney relates the notion of the *fond*, or ground, of art to the concept of *Grund* in Schelling, remarking that the German *Grund* includes within it two meanings, that of a ground (*fond*) and that of a grounding (*fondement*) or process of founding (*gründen*). The generative chaos of primary sensation is the ground of experience in the first sense, and in Schelling's terms it is both an originary ground (*Urgrund*) and a groundless ground (*Ungrund*). Yet without the systolic and diastolic moments, this ground of experience would remain a formless chaos. Only as a world takes shape out of the chaotic abyss does chaos become a ground. Hence the rhythm of systole and diastole is the grounding (*fondement*) of this ground. Likewise in art, the motif is the grounding of the ground from which the motif emerges, in that the motif is created through the systolic and diastolic moments of "stubborn geometry" and expansive light. Thus Maldiney states that "the form grounds the ground [*fonde le fond*] from which it issues forth" (Maldiney 193). Of course, by form Maldiney does not mean a predetermined shape but a formative activity, a *Gestaltung* rather than a *Gestalt*, in Klee's terms, an activity whose basic constituents are the rhythms of systole and diastole. Nor does Maldiney conceive of that form as something separate from the matter out of which it is created. "Form is the rhythm of matter, the rhythmic articulation of its powers [*puissances*] and resistances which are actualized by a technique that rhythm itself instigates" (Maldiney 189). In this sense, the matter from which the motif is fashioned is the motif's ground, and the motif is the grounding of that ground. Maldiney argues that two basic senses of the ground may be identified in art, one generated from the rhythm/matter pair, the other from the opposition of object and surrounding environment. If one thinks of a work of sculpture, one may say that its form is the systolic/diastolic rhythm of the stone, and that in coming into being the form establishes the brute matter of the stone as ground, whose resistances and powers remain neutralized and amorphous until they are made manifest through the generative activity that is the statue's form. In this instance, the motif emerges as a separate entity from and against the ground. Here, the motif-ground relation emphasizes the systolic moment of individuation, the haptic taking and keeping of the object. But one may also say that the ground of the motif is the spatial world in which it appears, the landscape (in the Strausian sense) haunted and interfused by the object. In such a case, the motif appears in the ground that it grounds, irradiating the world that emerges with the emergence of the motif as self-forming form in a predominantly optic space.

Maldiney offers Egyptian art as the clearest example of the haptic relation between motif and ground, for the most part following the outlines of Riegl's analysis. The space of the artwork is structured according to the close view, as if the eye were touching the objects it traverses. That which separates the motif from the ground and at the same time unites it to the ground is the motif's contour. Always the limits of the form serve as the grounding (*fondement*) of the artwork, and the goal of all Egyptian art is to protect the object from change and becoming, from the corrupting forces of space and time and the uncertainties and confusion of variable light and shadow. Hence the emphasis on planar composition that denies the dimension of depth, as well as the symmetrical and regular forms of the contours, which in their forming activity (*Gestaltung*) avoid the unpredictable movements and variable time of organic shapes and embrace the patterns of abstract structures whose motion and time are recursive and removed from the accidents of flux and becoming. No dialogue between motif and ground is permitted, no space that might admit the world of change. The ground is suppressed and the motif itself comes to function as a ground, a stable instance of the repose of the eternal afterlife that underlies and permeates the objects of our mortal, shadowy existence.

Like Riegl, Maldiney regards classical Greek art as inhabiting a space that is a hybrid of the haptic and the optic. The Greeks admit the existence of spatial relations beyond those of the plane, but only within the limits of the contained, cubic space of the individual figure.[6] Unlike the forms of Egyptian art, which arise slightly from a flat ground, pull the ground with them, and become themselves part of a single planar ground, Greek forms commence from a foreground plane and are "chiseled out" of a cubic space receding from the near surface. Figures admit of a modeling of light and shadow, but the light is not that of a free, open space, and not that of the spectator, but the self-enclosed ambient light of the delimited cube. The object of all Greek art is the individuation of forms, and though the motif is increasingly freed from the ground, and hence brought into space, the tactile delineation of the form and its separation from unlimited, open space remain paramount concerns that prevent the space of Greek art from being purely optical.

It is only in Byzantine art that optical space becomes fully manifest in the West, according to Maldiney, although he detects definite signs of its emergence in the fourth-style murals of Herculaneum, Pompeii, and Stabiae.[7] In the mosaics and murals of such structures as Ravenna's Sant'Apollinare Nuovo, the Hagia Sophia and Karieh Djami of Constantinople, and the cathedral at Cefalù, Sicily, Maldiney finds a new relation between motif and ground, in which the ground is no longer an absolute tactile plane but an infinite, ungraspable field of light, in which "taking [*prendre*] and keeping [*garder*] are made impotent" (Maldiney 203). In such works, "it is the purely optic rhythm of light and shadow, whose phenomenal play is increasingly free of the definition of corporeal forms, which engenders spatiality" (ibid. 201). What Byzantine art discovers is "the spatializing energy of color," the "movement of space spacing itself in the irradiation of its ubiquity" (ibid. 202–3). The Cefalù Pantocrator, with its frontal view of Christ against a uniform gold background, does not lie on an absolute plane but issues from an infinite space of light and color. In Byzantine mosaics, color is nowhere localizable: the intense, saturated tint of a smalt square is echoed in the more rarefied hue of a distant marble tessera; random gold and silver tiles are placed in the figures to enhance the play of light; faces are modeled with so-called "checkerboard" patterns or through the juxtaposition of contrasting colors that create the illusion of chromatic modulation (a technique rediscovered by Chevreul in the nineteenth century and subsequently exploited by the Impressionists). Far from being flat, planar figures in their own closed realm, Byzantine figures inhabit the space in front of them that extends to and includes the viewer. As Otto Demus explains, "The image is not separated from the beholder by the 'imaginary glass pane' of the picture plane behind which an illusionistic picture begins: it opens into the real space in front, where the beholder lives and moves. His space and the space in which the holy persons exist and act are identical" (Demus 13). Byzantine figures may lack individuality and verisimilitude, as Duthuit remarks, but they "take on value only to the extent that they concretize, that they color the luminous wave that meets them: as significant as the figures represented, whether fabulous or true, is the flow which illuminates them and envelopes them, the spiritual ravishing created by the interlacing paths of light" (Duthuit 76). In Byzantine art, says Maldiney, "Color generates space before serving the elucidation of form. Space is the auto-moving con-sistence of heterogeneous moments whose isolation or tension is resolved in the diffusive unity of a radiant matter" (Maldiney 204).

Clearly, for Maldiney the optic takes precedence over the haptic. The optic "spacing of space" that Maldiney sees in Byzantine art is the aesthetic manifestation of the Strausian world of primary sensation, the landscape *Mitwelt* of an auto-moving, unfolding here/there self/horizon. Although Maldiney speaks of differences in emphasis between the ancient haptic and the modern optic sensibilities, only in the disclosure of optic space does the rhythm of systole and diastole find complete expression. The sequence of Egyptian, Greek, and Byzantine art thus represents a progressive liberation of space and light, and in Byzantine mosaics and murals we meet for the first time in the West the "colorism" that Maldiney finds most fully exploited by Cézanne in his late paintings. What allows colorism to attain a complete expression of the rhythm of Strausian sensation is that it both discloses the expansive space of a landscape *Mitwelt* and makes possible a systolic delineation of form solely through light and color. In the haptic use of color, which Maldiney labels "chromatism" or "polychromy," color illustrates the form, filling the contours of a preexisting surface shape. In colorism, by contrast, color assumes an unconditional liberty, one that in principle allows for the noncoincidence of color and form. Yet in the great works of colorism, especially in the late works of Cézanne, the free expansion of color generates form "from within" through "its own amplitude, that is, the space that irradiates its own energy" (Maldiney 191). The equilibrium between diastole and systole that Cézanne achieves is strictly optic, created through light and color alone. "On one hand, the *modulation* of color is created from a play of contractions and expansions corresponding to the cold and warm tonalities in contact with one another. On the other hand, the form is the place, itself modulating, where the horizons of colored events encounter one another. . . . Now, these conjoint moments are equally dimensions of color, which is both expansive without dissipation and concentrated without contracture" (Maldiney 191).

EXCURSUS ON THE GOTHIC LINE

As noted earlier, Deleuze argues that Bacon, like all great painters, recapitulates the history of painting in his own canvases, a history that Deleuze organizes around the opposition of the haptic and the optic. The broad structure of that history he takes from Riegl and Maldiney, differentiating first the basic characteristics of haptic Egyptian art, then those of tactile-optic classical Greek art and optic Byzantine art. But he also argues that the tactile-optic space of Greek art is continued in the traditional representational art dominant in the West from the Renaissance through the nineteenth century. For Riegl, the haptic and the optic are poles within ancient art, whose consistent goal is the suppression of the infinite space that eventually becomes the subject of perspectival representational art. For Maldiney, the optic is superior to the haptic, the optic space of Byzantine art inaugurating the progressive liberation of light and color that meets its fullest expression in Cézanne. For Deleuze, however, the haptic and the optic are both means of resisting the tactile-optic, which takes as its primary task the subordination of the hand to the eye within an organized, organic space.

Deleuze begins his historical survey by noting Bacon's echoes of elements of Egyptian art—the flat fields of background color, the emphasis on the contours of the figures, the "shallow depth" that brings figures and ground in contact within a single plane, the close proximity of the figures. Deleuze agrees with Riegl that Egyptian art is haptic, and his summary of the characteristics of this art adheres closely to Maldiney's in its emphasis on planar composition, frontality, the primacy of contour, the geometric handling of forms, and the protection of the figure from the corrupting influence of change and becoming. What Deleuze stresses in Egyptian art is the treatment of the figure as an essence, removed from the accidents of time. In this regard, Egyptian art is opposed to Modern art, which "begins when man himself no longer sees himself entirely as an essence, but rather as an accident" (FB 80). Here, then, are the *terminus ad quem* and the *terminus ad quo* of Deleuze's history—from Egyptian essence to Modern accident.

Deleuze observes that Christian art necessarily admits the accidental, since the doctrine of the incarnation requires that essence be rendered in all its mortal mutability, and it is through the incarnation that Christian art receives "a seed of tranquil atheism that will continue to nourish painting" (FB 80). But Christian art owes the admission of the accidental not to doctrine alone, but also (and above all) to the innovations of classical Greek art. Again following Maldiney, Deleuze remarks on the cubic space surrounding the classical figure, the primacy of the foreground plane, the admission of light and shadow in the modeling of forms, and the separation of the figure's cubic space from the open space of the spectator. In its rendering of the figure in depth, exposed to the variable rhythms of light and shadow, "Classical representation thus has as its object the accident" (FB 81). But in its enclosure and isolation of the figure within a controlled cubic space, it subsumes the accidental object within "an optic *organization* that makes [the object] something well-grounded (phenomenon) or a 'manifestation' of essence" (FB 81). Classical Greek art breaks with the haptic plane, but the space it creates is tactile-optic (as Riegl and Maldiney argue), and in this combination of hand and eye, accident is made subservient to an essential organization. The contour of the figure is organic rather than geometric, and hence varying and irregular, but in its isolation and enclosure it takes on an ideal, unchanging form. The figure has a tactile contour, over which play the changing effects of light and shadow, procession and recession, but the contour remains unaffected by these changes. It is as if one were looking at a stick in water that appears bent but proves straight when touched. The optic eye takes in the shifting appearances of lighting and perspective, but the haptic eye—the eye's hand—confirms that the object is identical across changing circumstances.

For a purely optic space one must turn to Byzantine art, Deleuze argues, and there one will find a means of unsettling the stability of classical organic representation. As Maldiney observes and Deleuze reiterates, Byzantine mosaics and murals take the apparition of light as their controlling principle, abandoning any reliance on tactile values. The figures issue from a field of light, their contours no longer treated as limits, but as "the result of shadow and light, of dark expanses and white surfaces" (FB 82). Forms are transformed and transfigured, converted into light. "The accident thus changes its status, and, instead of finding its laws in the 'natural' organic, it finds a spiritual assumption, a 'grace' or a 'miracle' in the independence of light (and color)" (FB 82). Classical organization gives way to "composition," which is "still organization, but in the process of disintegrating" (FB 82). The figures disintegrate, disaggregate, as they are subsumed within fields of light, and in this dissipation Deleuze finds the model for later treatments of form in terms of "an optic code" (FB 82), such as seventeenth-century chiaroscuro painting and twentieth-century abstract art.

But in addition to Byzantine art's optic disruption of classical representation, Deleuze identifies as well a haptic alternative, one first developed in Gothic art and in no way related to the haptic aesthetic of Egyptian art. Deleuze approaches Gothic art through Wilhelm Worringer, a follower of Riegl whose most influential works include *Abstraktion und Einfühlung* (*Abstraction and Empathy*) (1908) and *Formprobleme der Gotik* (*Form in Gothic*) (1912). Worringer grounds Riegl's opposition of the haptic and the optic in a fundamental distinction between abstraction and empathy, psychological principles which he sees most clearly embodied in primitive art and classical Greek art, respectively. Primitive humans are beset by a threatening, confusing universe that instills "an immense spiritual dread of space" (Worringer 1908, 15). Unable to trust visual impressions, they remain dependent on the assurances of touch. They seek tranquillity and separation from the flux of the phenomenal realm, and hence avoid whenever possible the representation of open space. Rather than projecting themselves into the world, they create in art an abstract domain of stable forms and absolute values, whose "crystalline beauty" (Riegl's phrase) is summed up in the geometric line and the haptic plane, and whose stable order is most clearly evident in ancient Egyptian art. The classical Greeks, by contrast, gain a certain mastery of the physical world through the use of reason. As a result, they can delight in the ebb and flow of existence, project themselves into the world, and discover there the beauty of organic, growing, and changing forms. They empathize with nature and enjoy themselves and their own vital movements in the art that reflects life's variable, dynamic rhythms.

In *Form in Gothic* Worringer rehearses this opposition of primitive abstraction and classical empathy in sketches titled "Primitive Man" and "Classical Man," adding a portrait of "Oriental Man" as the individual who has gone beyond rational knowledge and recognized the essentially illusory nature of reality. Having seen through the veil of Maya, Oriental Man attains to a higher abstraction. Hence, though "the art of the East, like that of primeval man, is strictly abstract and bound to the rigid, expressionless line and its correlate, the plane surface . . . in the wealth of its forms and the congruity of its solutions, it far surpasses primitive art" (Worringer 1912, 37). Yet in Worringer's estimation, Gothic art displays a sensibility that cannot be understood in terms of the primitive, classical, or Oriental models. Here we encounter abstract, geometric forms, but with no rest or tranquillity. Everywhere there is "passionate movement and vitality, a questing, restless tumult," but a movement that is "divorced from organic life," a "super-organic mode of expression" (ibid. 41).

This paradoxical nonorganic life Worringer approaches first through the ornamental Gothic line. The classical organic line traces regular, graceful patterns whose balance of movement and repose expresses our own organic vitality and harmony with life. The Gothic line initially offends our organic sensibility, but once we yield to it, we feel its ecstatic power: "Again and again the line is broken, again and again checked in the natural direction of its movement, again and again it is forcibly prevented from peacefully ending its course, again and again diverted into fresh complications of expression, so that, tempered by all these restraints, it exerts its energy of expression to the uttermost until at last, bereft of all possibilities of natural pacification, it ends in confused, spasmodic movements, breaks off unappeased into the void or flows senselessly back upon itself" (Worringer 1912, 42). The classical line seems an expression of our will, whereas the Gothic line appears to be independent of us, "to have an *expression of its own,* which is stronger than our life" (ibid. 42). The psychological basis of this opposition Worringer elucidates through the humble example of random scribbling. When we are relaxed and idly doodling, the line flows and curves according to the dictates of our will and the play of the wrist. When we are under stress or enraged, however, "the will of the wrist will certainly not be consulted: the pencil will move wildly and violently over the paper and instead of the beautiful, round, organically tempered curves, there will be a hard, angular, ceaselessly interrupted, jagged line, of the most powerful vehemence of expression" (ibid. 43).

Both the classical and the Gothic line evince repetition, but the classical line primarily exploits mirror symmetry, thereby balancing movement with moments of repose, whereas the Gothic line functions through the asymmetrical multiplication of repetitive movements. An infinite line that "stuns and compels us to helpless surrender," it leaves "a lingering impression of a formless, ceaseless activity" (Worringer 55–56). It is labyrinthine, having "neither beginning nor end and above all no centre. . . . We find no point of entrance, no point of rest" (ibid. 56). Plant and animal motifs appear in Gothic ornamentation, but they are absorbed within a maze of lines, products of a linear fantasy rather than a close observation of the organic forms of nature. When Gothic ornamentation follows a circular pattern, the movement is peripheral rather than radial. Unlike circular classical ornament, which moves outward from the center or converges on the center from without, circular Gothic ornament rotates around the edges, its forms resembling a revolving wheel or turbine engaged in an "uninterrupted, accelerating, mechanical movement" (ibid. 57).

Worringer sees Gothic art as a hybrid of abstraction and empathy, an unstable and feverish amalgam of unreconciled opposites that resembles the "exalted pathos of youth" (Worringer 1912, 81) in its yearning for transcendental liberation. Deleuze, however, regards the Gothic as a purely haptic mode that grants the hand its own active expression. Unlike Egyptian art, which regulates contours through abstract geometric forms, Gothic art embraces a dynamic geometry of jagged lines, twisting loops, and accelerating spins. Rather than delineating precise individual figures on a stable compositional plane, the Gothic line blurs the distinction between figure and ground: "In ceaselessly breaking, the line becomes more than a line, at the same time that the plane becomes less than a surface" (FB 83). The plant and animal shapes it traces deform representational images, disclosing "zones of indiscernibility of the line, in that the line is common to different animals, to man and animal, and to pure abstraction (serpent, beard, ribbon)" (FB 83). In Gothic art, the hand is liberated from the eye and given a will of its own, its movements those of a nonorganic life.

HAPTIC COLORISM

One can see why Deleuze returns frequently to Worringer's Gothic line, since it engages the themes of becoming-animal, nonorganic life, chaos, the labyrinthine fold, the asubjective will, etc.[8] And the relevance for understanding Bacon is clear—the Gothic line functions in the same manner as the diagram, a random, manual catastrophe giving rise to a figural becoming that deforms images and subsumes them within a field of nonorganic forces. But Deleuze develops the concept of the haptic beyond the Gothic line. It might seem that his opposition of Byzantine optic art and Gothic haptic art is based on the venerable contrast of color and line, but Deleuze insists that there are two uses of color, one optic and one haptic, and that if Gothic art suggests how the hand can escape the tactile-optic space of classical representation via the line, the colorism of Cézanne and especially van Gogh indicates a path of liberation for the hand via a properly haptic use of color.

Deleuze identifies two types of color relations: *"relations of value,* based on the contrast of black and white, and which define a tone as dark or light, saturated or rarified; and *relations of tonality,* based on the spectrum, on the opposition of yellow and blue, or of green and red, and which define this or that pure tone as warm or cold" (FB 84).[9] Relations of value involve relations of *light,* the brightness or darkness of colors being measurable on a gray scale ranging from white to black, whereas relations of tonality involve contrasts of hue, or *color* in the common sense of the word. Deleuze argues that relations of value entail "a purely optic function of distant vision" and relations of tonality "a properly *haptic* function" (FB 85), in that hues involve "near vision" (*vision rapprochée,* what Riegl calls *Nahsicht*), juxtaposed tones on a flat surface forming a progression and recession around a foreground "culminating point" (FB 85).[10] (Although Deleuze does not explicitly so argue, he implies that relations of tonality are essentially haptic in that warmth and coldness are basically tactile rather than visual qualities of experience.) Deleuze does recognize that value and tone are not antithetical aspects of color, and that they are often used in combination with one another. Though Byzantine mosaics, for example, tend to emphasize the play of light and dark, the modulation of gold, red, blue, and green hues is also an important element in most of these compositions.[11] Yet the principles regulating relations of value and those regulating relations of hue remain distinct. Both pertain to the eye and vision, and hence are properly visual, but the opposition of bright and dark, of light and shadow, discloses an optic space, whereas the opposition of warm and cold, of expansion and contraction, belongs to a haptic space.

Colorists are "painters who tend to substitute for relations of value relations of tonality, and to 'render' not only form, but also shadow and light, and time, through these pure relations of color" (FB 89). The tradition of colorism in painting is commonly said to extend from Titian and Veronese through Ribera, Velásquez, Rubens, and Rembrandt to Delacroix, Monet, Cézanne, Gauguin, and van Gogh—and it is in this line that Deleuze places Bacon.[12] The characteristics of colorism Deleuze identifies as "the abandonment of local tone,[13] the juxtaposition of unblended strokes, the aspiration of each color to totality through an appeal to its complementary, the passage of colors with their intermediaries or transitions, the prohibition of mixtures save to obtain a 'broken' tone, the juxtaposition of two complementaries or of two similar colors, one of which is broken and the other pure, the production of light and even time through the unlimited activity of color, clarity through color" (FB 89). Deleuze notes that Cézanne discovers a haptic use of color in his late paintings when he renders curved forms through the juxtaposition of distinct strokes arranged according to the order of the spectrum, rather than relying on the traditional techniques of shading to model such forms (in other words, techniques based on relations of value, or gradations of light and dark). This method, however, runs the danger of becoming a logical code, the fixed sequence of the spectrum invariably dictating the relations between hues.[14] A less organized haptic practice is van Gogh's use of "broken tones," which makes him "an arbitrary colorist" (as van Gogh said of himself in a letter to his brother [van Gogh 3, 6]), and it is this notion of the "broken tone" that Deleuze stresses in his discussion of Bacon's coloristic painting.

In a letter to his brother, van Gogh cites at length a passage from Charles Blanc's *Les Artistes de mon temps* (1876),[15] in which Blanc first enumerates the primary colors (red, blue, and yellow) and their complementary colors (green, orange, and violet), and then mentions the "law of simultaneous contrast" (an unacknowledged reference to Chevreul) whereby complementary colors mutually intensify one another when juxtaposed. This law Delacroix exploits in his painting, observes Blanc, while also making use of complementary colors in another way. When complementary pigments are mixed in equal proportion, they neutralize each other and create gray; when mixed unequally, however, a "broken tone" emerges, a dull, muddy version of the dominant hue. The admixture of a small amount of green to red, for instance, yields a "broken," dull red, the addition of a bit of orange to blue a "broken," muddy blue, and so forth. In the creation of broken tones, the "battle" between complementaries is "uneven, one of the two colors triumphs, and the intensity of the dominant does not preclude the harmony of the two" (Blanc 66). When two shades of the same pure hue are juxtaposed, say bright blue and dark blue, "one will obtain another effect, in which there will be a contrast through the difference in intensity"; when a pure tone and a broken tone are juxtaposed, "there will result another kind of contrast that will be tempered through the analogy" (Blanc 66). Hence, concludes Blanc, "There exist several ways, different among themselves but equally infallible, to intensify the effect of color [through the juxtaposition of complementary colors], sustain it [through the juxtaposition of differing intensities of the same pure hue], attenuate it [through the juxtaposition of pure and broken tones], or neutralize it [through the equal admixture of complementaries]" (ibid. 66).

Van Gogh quotes Blanc with clear approval and makes use of all these modes of differential contrast in his mature paintings, but in his handling of the relationship between pure and broken tones, Deleuze argues, "modulation, strictly inseparable from colorism, finds a totally new sense and function, distinct from Cézannean modulation" (FB 90). By "Cézannean modulation" Deleuze refers again to Cézanne's juxtaposition of distinct hues according to the order of the spectrum as a means of modeling curved shapes (and according to Cézanne, all shapes are essentially curved).[16] Deleuze argues that in this practice Cézanne faces two fundamental exigencies: "the exigency of a homogeneous ground and an aerial armature, perpendicular to the chromatic progression; and the exigency of a singular or specific form, which the size of the strokes seemed to put in question" (FB 90).[17] This, then, is the basic colorist problem faced by Cézanne and van Gogh alike: to create a homogeneous, structuring ground; to fashion singular, particularized forms; and to ensure the mutual communication of ground and forms through color. Cézanne's challenge in his late paintings is to solve this threefold problem while exploiting the effects of a regular sequence of spectrum tones to organize all elements of his compositions. Van Gogh takes another course, however, as on the one hand he creates background fields of bright, pure color that remain active through fine differences of saturation rather than value, the field's hue exhibiting a "passage or tendency" (FB 90) toward another hue; and on the other, he fashions volumes through one or several broken tones, whereby color is submitted to "a heating and a firing that rivals ceramics" (FB 90).[18] Thus, his response to the colorist "problem of modulation" is to instill in his canvases "the passage of bright color in the field, the passage of broken tones, and the non-indifferent relation of these two passages or movements of color" (FB 91). And in Deleuze's analysis it is along similar lines that Bacon responds to the colorist problem throughout his work.

We will recall that Deleuze identifies the three fundamental elements of Bacon's paintings as Structure, Figure, and Contour—a structuring monochrome field; one or more figural forms; and a series of surrounding and isolating rings, ovals, squares, boxes, and so on. Initially Deleuze considers these elements in terms of the invisible forces that traverse them, but his ultimate effort is to show how *"all three converge toward color, in color"* (FB 93), how "modulation, that is, relations of color," explains "at once the unity of the whole, the distribution of each element, and the manner in which each acts on the others" (FB 93).

Bacon generally situates his figures against a vivid, intense monochrome field, a single-hue expanse without variations of value (light and dark). The danger he faces is that this field will remain inert and detached from the figure. To induce movement and variation in the field, Bacon relies on "relations of proximity" (FB 94) of various sorts. In individual canvases that are not part of triptychs, he often places discrete, contrasting panels of color within the monochrome field. In the triptychs, he frequently limits the spread of the field with a contrasting monochrome contour across the base of the paintings, the lower, broad contour constituting a sort of "floor" supporting the figures and connecting the foreground and the background field. In other triptychs, Bacon simply divides the monochrome field with a horizontal white band that traverses the three canvases; occasionally, a contrasting ribbon of color arcs through the field; and in some cases, only the small contour surrounding a figure or group of figures (such as a rug or bed) interrupts the uniform expanse of the field. In all cases, the color of the field seems to shift as the eye approaches the contrasting panel, contour, band, or ribbon. Subtle variations internal to the field emerge in these "zones of proximity" near the juncture of field and contour, and as a result, undulating, imprecisely localized waves of movement begin to play across the expansive field. Hence, via these zones of proximity the field, with its rippling, diffused movements, gives rise to an unpulsed, unmeasured time, to "the eternity of the form of time" (FB 95), the time of Aion. The field also functions as a structure, or "armature," for the canvas through its zones of proximity, since these zones connect the field and the contrasting contours or bands and ensure that the various enclosing and delimiting shapes of the canvas (the floors, beds, rugs, circles, boxes, etc.) "belong to" and interact with the monochrome field.

Bacon's polychrome, heavily impasted figures, modeled in flows of broken tones, provide a sharp counterpoint to the monochrome, flat, pure tones of the field. Above all, the broken tones make palpable the *flesh* of the figures, the dominant hues of red and blue creating zones of indiscernibility between flesh and meat. The broken tones resonate with the pure tones of the monochrome field, but they also register small movements within the figure, the variegated flows of broken tones rendering visible the invisible forces that work through the figure. In this sense, the "*color-force*" of the figure stands in opposition to the "*color-structure*" of the field, while the figure's violent, localized movement as "content of time" contrasts with the field's dispersed, unpulsed movement as "form of time" (FB 96).

It would seem that in the third element of Bacon's compositions, the surrounding Contour, line must take precedence over color. But Deleuze argues that contours are determined by their relations with the nonfigural element of the monochrome field, not by their relations with the figures they contain. Because the contour is shaped within an autonomous, nonfigural element of the canvas, line does not function as the productive determinant of the contour's shape. Instead, color produces line, the contour's outer limit simply issuing from the meeting of contrasting, autonomous hues. The contours of Bacon's paintings function as membranes through which the rhythms and forces of the pure tones of the field and the broken tones of the figure communicate. They isolate entire figures, and in some cases circumscribe parts of the figure (foot, hand, head), thereby reviving the medieval use of aureoles as "reflectors" inducing a "colored pressure that assures the equilibrium of the Figure." But above all, the contours make possible a passage "from one regime of color to another" (FB 96).

ANALOGUE DIAGRAMMATIC MODULATION

Colorists believe that "if you push color to its pure internal relations (warm-cold, expansion-contraction), you have everything" (FB 89), and what Deleuze shows in this analysis of pulsating fields, broken-tone figures, and communicating contours is the specific means by which Bacon puts this belief into effect. Deleuze argues that Bacon, like Cézanne, van Gogh and other colorists, exploits a properly haptic use of color, one based on relations of tone rather than relations of value. Riegl first develops the notion of a haptic vision, but he subjugates the haptic to the exigencies of line, plane, and the exorcism of open space (most clearly exemplified in Egyptian art). Maldiney likewise subordinates haptic to optic space, arguing that Cézanne's systolic and diastolic rhythms of self-forming forms, of space spatializing itself through the expansion of pure light and color, represent a liberation from the haptic and the disclosure of a purely visual realm. Worringer's Gothic line suggests a means of revalorizing the haptic as a force of generative and creative deformation, and thus as a way of escaping the regulating and organizing control of representational, tactile-optical space. But there is another means of escaping tactile-optical space, Deleuze argues, one that is haptic yet unrelated to line, internal to the purely visual domain of color. What Maldiney regards as Cézanne's liberation from the haptic is in Deleuze's analysis a systematic exploitation of the haptic, and in van Gogh and Bacon we simply find alternative modes of developing the forces inherent in this same haptic dimension of color.

The haptic use of color is a way of seeing with the hand, yet without subordinating the hand to the eye, and in Bacon's paintings the haptic eye is made possible by the manual diagram. Bacon starts, as we all must do, with the clichéd images of figurative, narrative representation, products of a tactile-optical space in which hand and eye work together under the control of the eye. But then an involuntary movement of the hand intervenes; a random stroke, blot or swipe introduces a local catastrophe, a point of chaos that serves as a diagram of future developments. And from the manual diagram issue new relations, haptic configurations of field, figure, and contour in which the hand maintains its autonomy while inhabiting the eye.

To conclude our discussion, we must now return to the notions of colorism as modulation and painting as an analogical language. In the final chapter of *Francis Bacon*, Deleuze provides an illuminating analysis of Bacon's *Painting* (1946, Museum of Modern Art) that aptly demonstrates the relation between manual diagram and haptic color while clarifying the concept of analogue modulation. At the center of *Painting* is a seated individual (apparently male) in a black suit with yellow boutonniere. Two slender bands pass around him at the level of his feet and hips, and above his head spreads a black umbrella that shades his eyes and nose, revealing only his mouth, lower teeth, and white chin. To the left and right of his hands are two cuts of meat, and above him stretches the hanging cruciform carcass of some large butchered animal (perhaps cow, hog, or horse). The brownish-pink field covering the upper half of the canvas is broken by three slightly darker panels that resemble window shades with dangling cords. As we will recall from the previous chapter, Bacon says of this painting that initially his effort was "to make a bird alighting on a field," but that "suddenly the lines that I'd drawn suggested something totally different, and out of this suggestion arose this picture. I had no intention to do this picture; I never thought of it in that way. It was like one continuous accident mounting on top of another" (Sylvester 11). We might think, says Deleuze, that Bacon simply passes from one form to another, from an initial bird in a field to a final umbrella-shaded man in a meat locker, but such a characterization distorts the process. First, there is no direct translation of one element into another. When asked whether the bird suggested the umbrella, for example, Bacon responds that "it suddenly suggested an opening-up into another area of feeling altogether. And then I made these things, I gradually made them. So that I don't think the bird suggested the umbrella; it suddenly suggested the whole image" (ibid. 11). What corresponds to the bird, insists Deleuze, "that which is truly analogous to it, is not the umbrella-form (which would simply define a figurative analogy or an analogy of resemblance), but the series or figural whole, which constitutes the properly aesthetic analogy: the arms of the meat which rise as analogs of wings, the panels of the umbrella which fall or close, the mouth of the man like a saw-toothed beak" (FB 100). The intentional form of the bird is replaced not by another form but by "*totally different relations,* which engender the whole of a Figure as aesthetic analog of the bird (relations between arms of the meat, panels of the umbrella, mouth of the man)" (FB 100).

That which disrupts the representational form of the bird and discloses the composition's "totally different relations" is the accident diagram, which Deleuze locates in the muddy, brown-black zone below the man's right shoulder. The diagram introduces nonformal strokes and spots, "traits of birdness, of animality" (FB 100) that lie in a zone of indiscernibility between two forms, between a form-that-is-no-longer and another that does not yet exist. But if the initial form is an intentional, figurative representation, the final form is merely the product of a process of deformation, a resemblance produced through nonresembling means. The diagram deforms the bird and substitutes new relations for it, "the meat that flows, the umbrella that snaps up, the mouth that grows saw-toothed" (FB 101), inducing and distributing across the canvas "the informal forces with which the deformed parts are necessarily in relation" (FB 101). Though it is perhaps easiest to understand this process in terms of a passage from one form to another, what Deleuze's detailed analysis of field, figure and contour shows is that the forces engaged through the diagram are forces of haptic color. All the elements of the canvas—the shifting intensities of the monochrome field set in motion through zones of proximity near the background contrasting panels; the broken tones of the meat and carpet and the haptic grays of the figure resonating with the field;[19] the broad horizontal contour connecting foreground and monochrome expanse, the surrounding rings providing communication between the contorted rhythms of the figure and the undulating rhythms of the field—all issue from the diagram.

The diagram is a modulator, a machine into which figurative forms are fed and out of which emerge haptic color relations. Like the control grid of a triode tube, it provides a continuous and variable temporal molding and unmolding of elements. It functions both in the process of creation and in the final created set of relations.[20] The diagram guides the construction of the painting, yet it also remains in the completed painting, a specific zone of the canvas that continues to interact with the other elements of the composition once the artwork is fully constituted. Its modulation generates haptic color relations, but these relations are themselves modulations, continuous and variable movements—oscillations, perturbations, flows, twists, spasms, jolts—that issue forth from interacting hues and result in the forms of the completed canvas, not as objects to be represented, but as products of a self-forming process whereby color in its systolic and diastolic unfolding "spatializes space," spreads into monochrome fields, fills out figures, communicates across contour membranes.

The diagram generates analogues of figurative representations, but only as produced resemblances, the figurative bird that precedes *Painting* finding analogues in various relations, processes and movements, such as the flow and spread of the meat, the grasping contraction of the umbrella, the denticulation of the mouth. Painting here functions as an analogue language, both in the sense that it produces resemblances by nonresembling means, and in the sense that it operates like animal cries, howls, moans, or sighs—uncoded affective responses to external (or internal) situations that the responses register but do not resemble. The haptic color relations of *Painting* thus are analogical responses to the figurative bird, so many color-cries occasioned by the bird, but one might say as well that the haptic rhythms and movements of hues are analogues of the *process of metamorphosis* whereby a becoming-bird passes into a becoming-meat/umbrella/mouth. The paint renders visible the forces inherent in sensation, in the systolic-diastolic *Mitwelt* between fusional chaos and differentiated subjects/objects. At the same time, the paint gives structure to sensation, yet without submitting it to a code. Thus, the color analogues of the process of becoming render at once what Cézanne calls "sensation" and the "stubborn geometry" of particularized forms. In Bacon's terminology, they render "the brutality of fact," the solid, objective, durable evidence of a specific configuration of forces that registers directly on the nerves without passing through the brain.

Painters never face a blank canvas, for the world comes to them already organized and structured through networks of visual clichés. The problem for painters is to undo those clichés, not simply because they are tired and boring, but because they are *facialized*, permeated by power relations that operate in conjunction with the mixed semiotic of the despotic-passional regime of signs. The human face serves as a substance of expression for linguistic forms of expression, each speech act resonating with an accompanying facial expression that reinforces relations of power. An abstract machine of signification and subjectification coordinates the interaction of linguistic signs and facial expressions, the combination of words and smiles/frowns/grimaces enforcing binary oppositions that encode world and self according to dominant patterns of social practice. But facialization extends beyond the face per se to include the body and surrounding world. The abstract machine of faciality converts the face into a structuring grid that interacts with signs without resembling them. That same abstract machine similarly grids the body and landscape, not by making them resemble the face, but by establishing a corresponding complex network of corporeal gestures, postures, and attitudes and surrounding "looks," atmospheres, spatial densities, orientations, and vectoral regularities. And that complex network functions in conjunction with the face and linguistic signs as a disciplinary social machine.

The goal of painting is to counter the clichés of facialization, to deterritorialize the face-landscape, and in so doing to render visible the invisible forces that play through bodies and the world. The facialized universe is one of stable forms and fixed shapes, rational coordinates and coherent narratives. To deterritorialize this universe is to submit its "good forms" and commonsense structures to the metamorphic forces of what Lyotard calls the figural and Maldiney the systolic and diastolic rhythms of a spatializing space. For Bacon, this deterritorialization proceeds through the diagram, a manual catastrophe that introduces a limited site of chaos through which a composition of figures, contours, and fields may arise. The diagram functions as a modulator of forces, a temporally varying mold that pilots and orients the construction of each painting. The resulting configuration of figures, contours, and fields, renders visible various forces—the vibratory forces of isolation, deformation, and dissipation that affect individual figures; the resonating forces of coupling that relate two or more figures to one another; and the forces of separation that space and divide the triptychs. The triptychs harness forces and thereby convey the "brutality of fact," allowing sensation to bypass the brain and register directly on the nerves. The triptychs embody sensation, but in a compound, heterogeneous, and dispersed "body without organs" that includes all the triptych's compositional elements and that cannot be subsumed within any experience of the "lived body." Bacon's figures, contours, and fields give solidity and specificity to sensation and forces, yet not through the exploitation of line—even Worringer's haptic, Gothic line—but through the manipulation of color. By making use of the haptic quality of broken tones, Bacon counters the dominant conventions of classical representation and its hybrid, tactile-optic perspectival space. By setting in resonance the broken tones of the figures and the vibrating monochrome fields, and by generating membranous contours through the dilation and contraction of interacting zones of color, Bacon develops a haptic colorism that treats all the forces of figure, field, and contour as forces of color.

Deleuze's approach to painting is Modernist in its emphasis on the disruption of conventions and the deformation of good form. In his study of Bacon, he articulates the case for a specific kind of Modernism, a "figuralism" that rejects conventional representation but without embracing either geometric abstraction or abstract expressionism. Yet there are signs that his views and Bacon's are not identical and that he finds value in paintings from diverse periods and cultures. In *What Is Philosophy?* he praises a wide range of Modern painters of various tendencies for their success in embodying sensation. He finds in Giotto and El Greco a mad, pagan carnality, and in various colorists, from Veronese, Velásquez, and Rembrandt to Delacroix, Cézanne, and van Gogh a laudable resistance to the dominance of classical line. The haptic space of Egyptian art and the optical space of Byzantine art he sees as means of escaping the classical system's coordination and mutual subordination of hand and eye. Deleuze nowhere offers a systematic history of painting, but if such a history were to be constructed it would no doubt focus on "transverse" relations, diagonal lines of mutation specific to individual painters' cultural circumstances. Every painter confronts a different set of problems, a different catalogue of visual clichés, a different collection of aesthetic conventions, a different network of facialized bodies and landscapes within a given regime of signs. Every painter invents means of undoing those clichés, conventions, and facializations, working within the parameters of a particular historical situation. The means vary with the situation, but always with the goal of finding a transverse line of flight, a line of development that admits into painting the metamorphic forces of becoming and sensation.

Part III

THE ARTS

Chapter Seven

SENSATION AND THE
PLANE OF COMPOSITION

Although Deleuze writes copiously about literature and cinema, those arts play a relatively minor role in his discussions of the collective domain of the arts as a whole. His treatments of music and painting, by contrast, are much less extensive, and yet they are central to his aesthetic theory, and especially to his articulation of both the relationship between philosophy and the arts and the relationship of the various arts to one another. Painting reveals the aesthetic dimension of sensation. Music makes evident the connection between artistic sensation and creation in the natural world. And it is as modes of thought that these arts, and the arts in general, form their relationship with philosophy.

At several points in his writings, Deleuze comments briefly on philosophy's relationship to the arts and the arts' relationship to one another, but it is only in *What Is Philosophy?* (1991), Deleuze's last collaborative effort with Guattari, that these topics are addressed at length. In many regards *What Is Philosophy?* provides a synthetic summation of Deleuze's and Deleuze-Guattari's various treatments of the arts, yet the work also extends their thought in several challenging ways, chief of which for our purposes is in their demarcation of the spheres of activity of philosophers and artists. In *A Thousand Plateaus*, Deleuze and Guattari approach artistic and philosophical creation alike in terms of the construction of planes of consistency, but in *What Is Philosophy?* one of their central concerns is to differentiate between philosophy and the arts, and to do so by distinguishing between a philosophical plane of immanence and an artistic plane of composition. The philosophical plane of immanence they identify as that of the virtual and the pure event, and the artistic plane of composition as that of the possible and sensation. Given the insistent presence of the concepts of the virtual and the event in nearly all of Deleuze's and Deleuze-Guattari's analyses of the arts, such a configuration is puzzling. Solving that puzzle, however, is central to understanding Deleuze and Guattari's sense of philosophy and the arts as complementary modes of thought, and it is on the basis of this understanding that one may determine how Deleuze conceives the specificity of each of the arts and their relative affinities with one another and with philosophy.

SENSATION

In *What Is Philosophy?* Deleuze and Guattari define the work of art as "*a block of sensations, that is, a compound [un composé] of percepts and affects*" (QP 154; 164). In *Francis Bacon,* as we have seen, Deleuze develops at length the notion of sensation, both as Cézanne uses the term and as it may be applied to Bacon's paintings. Here, Deleuze and Guattari divide sensation into two components, percepts and affects. Percepts are not perceptions, and affects are not affections (i.e., feelings), for percepts are "independent of a state of those who undergo them" (QP 154; 164), and affects do not arise from subjects but instead pass through them. The percept we met earlier in Cézanne's paradox of "man absent, but everywhere in the landscape" (Maldiney 185). As Cézanne remarked to Gasquet, "At this moment I am one with my canvas [i.e., the world to be painted]. We are an iridescent chaos. I come before my motif, I lose myself there. . . . We germinate" (ibid. 150). The percept, then, "is the landscape before man, in the absence of man" (QP 159; 169). The affect is the "becoming-other" with which we are now familiar, here characterized primarily in terms of "becoming-animal." Hence, "*affects are precisely these non-human becomings of man,* just as percepts (including the city) are *the nonhuman landscapes of nature*" (QP 160; 169). In painting, Cézanne's landscapes of "iridescent chaos" are percepts, Bacon's portraits of heads-becoming-animal are instances of affects. In music, Messiaen's "melodic landscapes" and bird-becomings are examples respectively of percepts and affects. Thus, in all the arts, the goal "is to wrest the percept from perceptions of objects and from states of a perceiving subject, to wrest the affect from affections as passage from one state to another. To extract a block of sensations, a pure being of sensation" (QP 158; 167). When percepts and affects are successfully wrested from human perceptions and affections, "one is not in the world, one becomes with the world, one becomes in contemplating it. All is vision, becoming. One becomes universe. Becomings animal, vegetable, molecular, becoming zero" (QP 160; 169).

In their treatments of music and painting in *A Thousand Plateaus*, Deleuze and Guattari stress the concept of force, characterizing painting's goal as a rendering visible of invisible forces, and music's aim as a rendering audible of inaudible forces; likewise, in *Francis Bacon* Deleuze says that "there is a community of the arts, a common problem . . . of harnessing forces" (FB 39). In *What Is Philosophy?* Deleuze and Guattari reiterate these themes and integrate the concepts of sensation and force, noting that "there is a full complementarity between the grip [*étreinte*] of forces as percepts and becomings as affects" (QP 173; 182). Is this not "the definition of the percept itself," they ask, "to render perceptible [*sensible*] the imperceptible [*insensibles*] forces that populate the world, and that affect us, make us become?" (QP 172; 182). In a "becoming universe," cosmic forces impinge on artists, inducing affects, or becomings, which themselves are compositions of forces—a simple "vibration," or passage of force from one level of corporeal intensity to another; an "embrace [*étreinte*] or clinch [*corps-à-corps*, literally "body-to-body"]" in which forces resonate with one another; or a "withdrawal, division, distension" (QP 159; 168) whereby forces separate and spread out.[1] And as the artists become other, they pass into things, they become "absent, but everywhere in the landscape," at which point they are able to render palpable in the work of art the impalpable forces of the world.

Besides linking sensations and forces, Deleuze and Guattari also treat sensations in terms of the refrain, identifying "the refrain in its entirety" as "the being of sensation" (QP 175; 184). In their discussion of the refrain they rehearse the arguments of plateau 11 of *A Thousand Plateaus* (which we examined in chapters 1 and 3), stressing the role of forces in the passage of the refrain from milieus through territories and into the cosmos. Art "begins perhaps with the animal, at least with the animal that fashions a territory" (QP 174; 183). Its various territorial refrains, such as the stagemaker's song, overturned leaves, and ruffled neck feathers, are "blocks of sensations in the territory, colors, postures and sounds, which sketch out a total work of art" (QP 174–75; 184). The animal's refrains circumscribe a space, but that space also issues forth into the cosmos along a line of flight. Hence, the refrains enable a general movement from "endo-sensation to exo-sensation," in that "the territory does not merely isolate and join, but it opens onto cosmic forces that arise from the inside or come from the outside, and it renders perceptible their effect on the inhabitant" (QP 176; 185–86).

Though *What Is Philosophy?*'s treatment of art reads at times like a free variation on familiar themes—sensation, forces, refrains, among others—Deleuze and Guattari's primary purpose is less to recapitulate and synthesize previous positions than to explore a relatively new concern, that of the being of art. Percepts and affects are "*beings* that have validity in themselves and exceed any lived experience [*tout vécu*]," and the work of art is "a being of sensation, and nothing else: it exists in itself" (QP 155; 164). Two issues immediately arise from these formulations, and both are questions of embodiment: What is the relationship between sensations and physical bodies, human and otherwise, and what is the relationship between the artwork and the matter in which it is realized (paint, sound, words, etc.)? One means of approaching these issues is to consider the concept of the "house" (QP 169; 179), which Deleuze and Guattari introduce while discussing the phenomenological concept of the "flesh."

After asserting that sensations "incarnate the event" (QP 167; 176), Deleuze and Guattari ask whether Merleau-Ponty's notion of the "flesh" might explain such incarnation, as some phenomenologists claim. In *The Visible and the Invisible,* Merleau-Ponty describes the "flesh" as "a new type of being, a being by porosity, pregnancy, or generality, and he before whom the horizon opens is caught up, included within it. His body and the distances participate in one same corporeity or visibility in general, which reigns between them and it, and even beyond the horizon, beneath his skin, unto the depths of being" (Merleau-Ponty 149). A preconceptual intertwining of the "flesh of the body" and the "flesh of the world" makes possible a communication of embodied self and embodied world, and this "intercorporeity" (Merleau-Ponty 141) is rendered perceptible in works of art.

Noting the strange sensual piety of this essentially religious model of incarnation, Deleuze and Guattari make the somewhat bizarre proposal that the house rather than the flesh be seen as the intermediary between inner and outer worlds. The flesh is "too tender" (QP 169; 179), they claim, too malleable when engaged in a becoming-other; it requires a scaffolding for its support, an "armature" to which the clay of the flesh may adhere. The house is "the armature" (QP 169; 179), the framework inhabited by the malleable flesh. The house is defined by its "sections [*pans*]," its walls, floor, ceiling, roof, "that is, the fragments of diversely oriented planes that give the flesh its armature" (QP 170; 179). The house's planes orient the body in space (up, down, left, right, foreground, background, etc.), but also form part of a "house-territory system" (QP 174; 183). The floor delimits and founds a territorial habitat, the walls separate inside and outside, the roof "envelops the singularity of the place" (QP 177; 187). The house "frames" the world, each side of the paradigmatic cube-house serving as a picture frame or cinematic frame that carves out a chunk of space, but the house also has windows and doors, frames that allow a communication between inside and outside. The house in this sense is a filter that affords a passage of forces into and out of the habitat. It is a porous, selective membrane through which the inhabitant and the cosmos interact. Deleuze and Guattari conclude, then, that "the being of sensation is not the flesh, but the compound [*le composé*] of non-human forces of the cosmos, of non-human becomings of man, and the ambiguous house that exchanges and adjusts them, makes them swirl around like winds. The flesh is only the photographic developing solution [*le révélateur*] that disappears in that which it develops [*révèle*]: the compound [*le composé*] of sensation" (QP 173; 183).

Deleuze and Guattari's basic point, of course, is that Merleau-Ponty's concept of the flesh as aesthetic mediation between outside and inside ties the work of art too closely to the *corps vécu*, whereas the concept of the house emphasizes the non-human dimension of the aesthetic. But the figure of the house suggests as well something of the artwork's relation to human experience. In one sense, the house may be seen as the paradigmatic material artwork. Art in this regard is a functioning part of our inhabiting of the world, one of the ways whereby we build a territorial home for ourselves, structure and orient our bodies, frame and delimit space, but also a means whereby we communicate with the outside, the artwork serving as a filtering membrane that permits an interchange and circulation of forces across its surface. Yet we must not push this reading too far. The "house" is a figure for the material artwork as an entity, but it also is a figure for the structuring, modulating, and shifting configuration of forces within the artwork. "The work of art is a being of sensation" (QP 155; 164), and the being of sensation is the *compound,* or *composite,* of percepts ("non-human forces of the cosmos"), affects ("non-human becomings of man"), *and* house (in the second sense of the term, as configuring structure of forces). This suggests that though the artwork as material artifact ("house" in the first sense of the term) is in relation with other material bodies and the physical world, and hence not isolated and self-contained, the artwork as "being of sensation" is distinct from the material artifact, just as percepts and affects are distinct from the perceptions and affections experienced by human beings.

This point Deleuze and Guattari emphasize especially in their description of the artwork as "monument" (QP 155; 164).[2] The artwork as monument does not so much commemorate as conserve. The successful artwork has a certain solidity, a viability or self-sufficiency, as if it were able to stand on its own. Its solidity, viability, or "monumentality" has nothing to do with its physical size, but arises from the block of sensations that it conserves. The smile of a young boy captured in a portrait is conserved in the painting. The smile is distinct from the artist who painted it, the boy who served as its model, and finally from the boy himself figured in the painting. The smile as monumental, enduring moment conserves *itself* in the painting, and it is perpetually reactivated and recommenced at each viewing. In a way, it depends for its continued existence on the material survival of the paint and canvas, but the smile is finally distinct from the matter in which it is embodied. The smile itself has an unspecified, free-floating existence, and even if the material of paint and canvas "were to endure only a few seconds, it would give the sensation the power of existing and of conserving itself in itself, *in the eternity that coexists with that short duration*" (QP 157; 166).

The material of the artwork, however, does have a necessary relation to the self-conserving sensation it embodies. The formation of the artwork takes place on a "plane of composition." That plane Deleuze and Guattari subdivide into a "technical plane of composition," which concerns the material of the artwork, and an "aesthetic plane of composition" (QP 181; 192), which concerns sensations. Though artists have developed limitless means of engaging the two planes, Deleuze and Guattari propose two basic poles in their interrelation. In the first, "*the sensation realizes itself in the material*" (QP 182; 193), that is, sensation adapts itself to a well-formed, organized, and regulated matter. In painting, this is the mode of representational, perspectival art, in which sensations are, as it were, projected onto a material surface that already contains within it the spatial schemata that structure its figures. In music, traditional tonal compositions exemplify this mode, sensations seeping into the conventionally structured sonic material. In literature, it is the mode of mimetic fiction and standard style, in which words and representations are imbued with sensation without themselves becoming markedly strange or deformed. In the second case, "*it is instead the material that passes into the sensation*" (QP 182; 193). Rather than sensation being projected onto a calm material surface, the material rises up into a metamorphic plane of forces. In painting, the paint itself—its thickness, saturation, texture, etc.—articulates forces; in music, variegated timbres, microintervals, and fluctuating rhythms make up a malleable sonic force-matter; in literature, mutant sounds, syntactic patterns, and semantic elements submit to a continuously varying modulation of forces. Yet what is essential is that in both cases matter becomes *expressive* in the artwork. There is finally "only a single plane, in the sense that art involves no other plane than that of aesthetic composition: the technical plane in fact is necessarily covered over [i.e., when the sensation realizes itself in the material] or absorbed by [i.e., when the material passes into the sensation] the aesthetic plane of composition" (QP 185; 195-96).

"Composition, composition is the sole definition of art" (QP 181; 191), and "everything (including technique) takes place between the compounds [*les composés*] of sensations and the aesthetic plane of composition" (QP 185; 196). Sensations are percepts and affects, "beings" extracted from the perceptions and affections of everyday corporeal experience, which then become the compositional elements, the *composés,* that the artist shapes on an aesthetic plane of composition and renders perceptible through materials that have been rendered expressive. When the artist succeeds, he or she not only creates sensations within the artwork, but also "gives them to us and make us become with them; [the artist] takes us up into the compound [*le composé*]" (QP 166; 175). The plane of composition is an "infinite field of forces" (QP 178; 188), the artwork a territorial house opening onto the cosmos, a monument erected on a plane that constitutes a "universe" (QP 185; 196). And when we become with the artwork, we, too, open to the cosmos and "become universe." "Perhaps this is the proper sphere of art, to pass through the finite in order to rediscover, to give back the infinite" (QP 186; 197). What we have, then, is a circuit of embodiments and dis-embodiments, a passage of sensations through bodies—first extracted from bodily perceptions and affections, then rendered perceptible in the expressive matter of the artwork, then engaged by embodied audiences swept up into the artwork, and then extended into an infinite field of forces. Though this blending of bodies and sensations, of people, art-works, and cosmos, may sound like sheer mysticism, it is based on a coherent theory of nature as creation. How artists are able to render matter expressive is something of a mystery, but less so is the sense in which matter itself is expressive. The key is to understand the plane of composition as both an aesthetic plane of artistic creation and a ma-terial plane of physico-biological creation.[3] To do so, however, we must first situate the arts' plane of composition in relation to philosophy's plane of immanence.

PLANE OF IMMANENCE, PLANE OF COMPOSITION

In *A Thousand Plateaus*'s plateau 10, "Becoming-Intense, Becoming-Animal, Becoming Imperceptible...," Deleuze and Guattari propose a Spinozist description of the "plane of consistency of Nature" (MP 311; 254) in terms of speeds and affects. The elements of this plane of consis-tency have neither form nor function (unlike atoms, which have definite form), yet they are not indefinitely divisible; they are "the infinitely small ultimate parts of an actual infinity" (MP 310; 254), distinguished solely by the relative speeds of their movements and by their affects (i.e., their powers of affecting and being affected by other particles). This plane is a "plane of immanence or univocity," in that it is a single plane of the whole of nature in which "the One expresses in a single and same sense all of the multiple, Being expresses in a single and same sense all that dif-fers" (MP 311; 254). It is also a "plane of composition" on which each body is "a composition of speeds and affects" (MP 315; 258), formed through "a natural play of haecceities, degrees, intensities, events, acci-dents" (MP 310; 253). It is a virtual plane, "like an immense abstract Machine, abstract yet real and individual, whose pieces are the diverse assemblages or individuals, each of which groups an infinity of particles under an infinity of more or less composite [*composés*] relations" (MP

(MP 322; 263). This virtual plane is actualized in the formed entities and
stable functions of a "plane of organization and development" (MP 326;
266). The plane of consistency, in short, is "the plane of Nature" (MP
315; 258), a "pure plane of immanence, of univocity, of composition"
(MP 312; 255), a virtual plane of events that is actualized in a plane of
organization and development.

What Is Philosophy?, one might say, is an effort to describe philosophy
in terms of this Spinozist model. If the whole of Nature is composed
of a plane of consistency's speeds and affects in process of actualization, where might one situate philosophy, and where locate its related
spheres of activity, the sciences and the arts? Deleuze and Guattari's strategy is to divide *A Thousand Plateaus*'s Spinozist plane of consistency/
immanence/composition in two, and thereby differentiate between a philosophical plane of immanence and an artistic plane of composition,
each with its special kind of becoming, and to assign the sciences a complex position within the actual on a "plane of reference" (QP 112; 118).
To each plane corresponds a specific object of creation—the philosophical concept, the artistic sensation, and the scientific functive—and to each
a peculiar kind of agent—the conceptual persona (*personnage conceptuel*),
the aesthetic figure, and the partial observer. The sciences' plane of reference, functives, and partial observer are of less concern to us here than
philosophy's plane of immanence, concepts, and conceptual personae
and their relation to the arts' plane of composition, sensations, and aesthetic figures. We already have some sense of what the artistic domain is
like, but the philosophical sphere of concepts, the plane of immanence,
and the conceptual persona requires some elaboration.

Philosophy is the creation of concepts, and concepts are events.
"Always to disengage an event from things and from beings, this is the
task of philosophy when it creates concepts, entities" (QP 36; 33). The
concept is "an incorporeal," "a pure Event, a haecceity, an entity" (QP 26;
21). Each concept has three basic characteristics: its components connect
it to other concepts; its components have an inner consistency, or adhe-
sion, created by zones of indiscernibility in which one component shades
into another; and the concept is "in a state of *overflight* [*survol*] in relation
to its components" (QP 26; 20). Deleuze and Guattari offer as an example the concept of the Cartesian cogito, which they illustrate with a simple diagram (see below). Its components are "to doubt," "to think," and

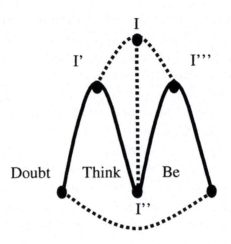

"to be," and its full articulation is the perpetual event of "I, the one who doubts, am the I who thinks, therefore I am, i.e., I am a thing that thinks." A series of "I"'s marks the three processes of doubting (I'), thinking (I"), and being (I"'); a zone of indiscernibility between I' and I", and another between I" and I"', give the concept endo-consistency; and the unifying "I" is like an aleatory point passing at an infinite speed through the points I, I', I" and I"'. Each component is capable of extending the concept toward other concepts, doubt to different kinds of doubt (perceptual, scientific, obsessional), thought to various modes of thought (sensing, imagining, having ideas), being to diverse types of being (infinite being, a finite thinking being, extended being). In the passage of the concept toward diverse types of being the concept reaches its limits, in that the cogito is not an infinite being; a "bridge" then extends from the concept of the cogito to the concept of God, a mobile bridge that also functions as a crossroads for movement toward yet other concepts.

The notion of "overflight," or *survol,* requires special attention. The word *survol* designates the act of flying over the ground in an airplane, and by extension, the act of rapidly scanning a page with the eyes. Deleuze and Guattari take the idea of *survol* as developed here from Raymond Ruyer, who identifies this "overflight" with the primary consciousness of all living forms. As we saw in chapter 3, Ruyer distinguishes aggregates such as heaps of sand, clouds, and human crowds from living forms, which are self-shaping, self-sustaining, self-enjoying entities. Such self-forming forms extend from subatomic particles through molecules to the entire range of complex multicellular organisms, and the thematic unity of each living form's self-forming activity constitutes a primary consciousness. To get at the nature of this consciousness, Ruyer considers the example of a human being seated at a table and looking at that table's checkerboard surface. Often, he notes, analysts of perception reason that if a two-dimensional surface requires a third dimension to be perceived as a surface (i.e., an eye must be above the surface of a table looking down on it in order to see it as a flat square), the three-dimensional perception of a human observer requires an additional dimension for its description, a second observer standing behind and above our seated observer (and by implication, a third observer behind the second, and so on in an infinite regress). Ruyer agrees that the *representation* of a dimension requires an additional dimension or at least an additional, external, perspective—that a photograph of a table surface requires a camera above the surface, and a photograph of the camera-photographing-the-surface requires a second camera behind and above the first—but this has nothing to do with the consciousness of our seated observer. For the observer, the table top is "a surface grasped in all its details, without a third dimension. It is an 'absolute surface,' which is not relative to any point of view external to itself, which knows itself without observing itself" (Ruyer 1952, 98). It is a surface with only one side, that grasped by the perceiving consciousness. The individual squares of its checkerboard surface are distinct and separate, yet they are not totally detached. They are grasped in "an absolute unity which is nevertheless not a fusion or confusion" (ibid. 99). The observing "I" is present at all places on the surface at the same time; it is in "absolute overflight," in a "non-dimensional overflight" across the surface. In a geometric space, distances on a plane vary, point B being closer to point A than a faraway point C, but in an absolute surface all points are co-present. The absolute surface is "trans-spatial," and its distances defy the limits of physical space-time, the "I"'s "overflight," as it were, passing at an infinite speed over all points of the surface at the same time. For Ruyer, these characteristics of human consciousness are those of all living forms. Every self-forming form, as ongoing self-shaping, self-sustaining, and self-enjoying activity, is a theme of development in infinite "overflight" across its own absolute surface.

If we return to the diagram of the Cartesian cogito, we can say that the points and paths are like Ruyer's checkerboard tablecloth, and that the cohesion, or consistency, that holds the concept together is the "overflight" of a ubiquitous aleatory point. "The concept is defined by *the inseparability of a finite number of heterogeneous components traversed by a point in absolute overflight, at infinite speed*" (QP 26; 21). Concepts are " 'absolute surfaces or volumes,' forms that have no other object than the inseparability of distinct variations" (QP 26; 21). With the notion of "overflight," then, Deleuze and Guattari describe the "togetherness" of the concept's components without resorting to talk of "unity," and they indicate the virtual nature of the concept, which is outside physical space-time in a "trans-spatial" dimension of infinite speeds (or put another way, in a dimension of events, whose free-floating time is that of the *infinitive*). We shall see shortly what bearing the concept's overflight has on the overflight that Ruyer regards as evident in all living forms.

The creation of concepts takes place on a plane of immanence, a "horizon of events," an "absolute horizon" (QP 39; 36). The plane of immanence is "not a concept that is thought or thinkable, but the image of thought" (QP 39; 36–37), the "pre-philosophical" condition that makes thought possible. In *Difference and Repetition*, Deleuze outlines traditional philosophy's dogmatic "image of thought," with its presuppositions of good sense, common sense, and a natural inclination of thought toward truth, and calls for an "imageless thought," but here Deleuze and Guattari propose that all thought entails an "image of thought," that is, a sense of what it means to think, to make use of thought, and to situate oneself within thought. What counts as thinking? What lies outside legitimate consideration—dreams, visions, error, intoxication, misperception, stupidity? How does one go about thinking—winnowing wheat from chaff, unfolding signs, following preexisting paths? In a 1988 interview, Deleuze clarifies that the image of thought is not "method, but something more profound, always presupposed, a system of coordinates, of dynamisms, of orientations" (PP 202; 148), and he offers as examples of images of thought the three he describes in *The Logic of Sense* (series 18), Plato's ascension to the heights of Ideas, Nietzsche's Empedoclean descent into the depths of roiling matter, and Carroll's glide along the surfaces of words and bodies. And he adds that in *A Thousand Plateaus*, "The rhizome is the image of thought that spreads out below that of trees" (PP 204; 149).

The creation of concepts presupposes a plane of immanence, but also a *personnage conceptuel*, a conceptual "persona," or "character" (as a character, *personnage*, in a novel or drama), who is "the becoming or the subject of a philosophy, who counts for the philosopher" (QP 63; 64). When engaged in genuine thought, "I am no longer myself, but an aptitude of thought for finding itself and spreading across a plane that passes through me at several places" (QP 62; 64). Nietzsche's Zarathustra is perhaps the most obvious example of a conceptual persona, but Deleuze and Guattari argue that every philosophy is articulated under the guise of a conceptual persona. Nicholas of Cusa thinks in the guise of the *ignorans* or *idiota* (Latin: unlearned person, layman), and Descartes in another version of the *idiota,* the simple man of sound judgment, who is given the name "Eudoxe" in *The Search for Truth by Natural Light.* Kierkegaard's conceptual persona is yet another version of the "idiot," in this case the fool or madman who refuses to accept the impossible.[4] The conceptual persona and the plane of immanence presuppose one another, the persona in one sense *preceding* the plane, plunging into chaos to determine the coordinates of a particular planar slice of that chaos, but at the same time *following* the plane, putting various concepts in relation with one another on the plane. Concepts do not arise directly from the plane, but "the conceptual persona is needed in order to create them on the plane, just as [the conceptual persona] is needed in order to trace the plane itself" (QP 73; 75–76).

Philosophy, then, is the invention of concepts on a plane of immanence. The plane of immanence provides the basic orientation of thought, and the concepts take shape within that plane as aleatory points in overflight above an absolute surface. Through the conceptual persona, thought at once opens up a given plane of immanence and follows along that plane, putting concepts in relation to one another.

Philosophy, the sciences, and the arts are all means of confronting chaos. Chaos itself is unthinkable, immeasurable, and unworkable, a perpetually metamorphosing play of shifting evanescences and dissolutions that has no consistency. Chaos "chaotizes," and common sense, received truth, orthodox opinion, good form, and so on are among the means whereby humans protect themselves from chaos. Philosophy, science, and art must struggle against chaos, concede Deleuze and Guattari, but only in order to use chaos in a common battle against the protective shield of *doxa,* the "already thought and perceived," which is comfortably recognizable and comprehensible. Philosophy plunges into chaos and cuts out a slice, a plane of immanence that retains the infinite speed of chaos but with a consistency that permits a creation of interconnected concepts, each concept being "a chaoid state par excellence" (QP 196; 208). Science slows the infinite speed of chaotic elements, establishes limits, selects variables, and demarcates coordinates on an actual plane of reference, but always with an affinity for chaos and the infinite. Asymptotic functions, differential relations, catastrophic folds, strange attractors, are only a few of the ways in which science tends toward the chaotic and forms a "referenced chaos that becomes Nature" (QP 194; 206). And art, too, commences in chaos, with Cézanne's "iridescent chaos" out of which the painting arises, or Klee's chaotic gray point that leaps out of itself and generates a self-forming line, but only in order to wrest sensations from bodies, in order to form a "chaosmos," a composition of chaoid sensations that render chaos perceptible and make possible a passage through the finite to the infinite.

In distinguishing the philosophical concept from the scientific functive, Deleuze and Guattari make it clear that the concept is virtual, whereas the functive is actual. The virtual is actualized in bodies, states of things, perceptions, and affections, and these actual entities are the subject of scientific investigation. But immanent within the actual is the virtual, something extra that exceeds the actualizations of every occurrence, both something left over, perpetually in reserve, and something still about to occur, an "infinite awaiting that is already infinitely past, awaiting and reserve" (QP 149; 158). The virtual, in its actualization, or "effectuation," impinges on commonsense experience as a chaotic force, inducing disequilibrium and a becoming-other; and philosophy disengages the virtual from the actual in a movement of "counter-effectuation." What it disengages is not a chaotic virtual, but "the virtual become consistent, an entity that forms itself on a plane of immanence that cuts a slice of chaos. This is what we call the Event" (QP 147; 156). Philosophy and science, then, have qualitatively different objects of concern, one virtual, the other actual, and every effort to integrate the two only compromises and confuses each activity. But if philosophy's plane of immanence is virtual and science's plane of reference is actual, where does the aesthetic plane of composition fit in?

VIRTUAL AND POSSIBLE

In *A Thousand Plateaus*, the Spinozistic plane of consistency is a plane of becoming, labeled indifferently a "plane of immanence" or a "plane of composition." In *What Is Philosophy?* Deleuze and Guattari state that *becoming* is common to the arts and philosophy, but that aesthetic becoming is "the act through which something or someone ceaselessly becomes-other," whereas conceptual becoming is "the act through which the common event itself escapes that which is" (QP 168; 177). Art's becoming "is alterity engaged in a matter of expression"; philosophy's becoming is "heterogeneity grasped in an absolute form" (QP 168; 174). The work of art does not actualize the event, but "incorporates or incarnates it: [the work of art] gives it a body, a life, a universe" (QP 168; 174). The concept, by contrast, disengages the pure event from bodies. Art's "plane of composition," we might say, is one of embodied becoming, philosophy's "plane of immanence" one of disembodied becoming. Artworks create universes that "are neither virtual nor actual; they are possible, the possible as aesthetic category ('the possible, or I'll suffocate'), the existence of the possible, whereas events are the reality of the virtual, forms of a Nature-thought that fly over [*survolent*] all possible universes" (QP 168; 177-78).

In labeling art's universe "possible," Deleuze and Guattari are in one sense simply reiterating the common argument that art creates imaginary worlds, alternative universes of the "as if." In another sense, they are emphasizing the hope of art, the promise of something genuinely new, the possibility of escaping the intolerable and living otherwise ("the possible, or I'll suffocate"). But the possible is also the realm of signs. Deleuze and Guattari open *What Is Philosophy?* by considering the concept of *l'Autrui*, "the Other Person," a concept Deleuze first examines in an essay on Michel Tournier's *Friday* (LS 350-72; 301-21) and then develops in *Difference and Repetition* (DR 333-35; 259-61). If I see another person's screaming face, but I do not see what is causing the scream (Bacon's screaming pope, for instance), the face expresses a possible world. Until I discover the source of the scream, the screaming face remains a sign of some unspecified possible universe. In this regard, "The Other Person is first of all this existence of a possible world" (QP 22; 17). The face as sign, in Deleuze's sense of the term, is an embodied difference, an entity that enfolds something unknown and requires unfolding in order to be deciphered. The face's possible world "is not real, or at least not yet, but still it exists nonetheless: it is an expressed [*un exprimé*] that exists only in its expression" (QP 22; 17).

Art's possible worlds are not virtual in the same sense that philosophy's plane of immanence is virtual, but they do arise from and participate in the virtual. In *Difference and Repetition*, Deleuze says that genuine thought only begins with an external violence to thought, a jolt that forces thought out of its ordinary habits. That jolt is a fundamental encounter, a disequilibrium or deregulation of the senses "that can only be sensed" (DR 182; 139). All thought, then, begins in sense experience, in the becoming-other of the senses. That becoming-other is the sign of the passage of the virtual into the actual. It takes place, one might say in a first approximation, along the surface of the virtual's entry into the actual. If we think of a biological embryo, we can say that its self-forming form, its overall theme of development, is initially everywhere present, in "overflight," as a virtual difference (not a unity, not a preexisting blueprint, but a problem to be unfolded). As the embryo's single cell divides into two cells, a process of individuation takes place along its dividing surface. Two individuated entities are created, but the *process* of individuation, the *passage* of the virtual self-forming form into the two formed entities, precedes the entities, always along the surface of the soon-to-be-entities in formation. We may differentiate, then, between the virtual as something distinct in itself, as the self-forming form in overflight grasped independently of its actualization, and the virtual as self-forming form engaged in a process of individuation. If we extrapolate generally, we may say that the production of the actual is everywhere a becoming actual of the virtual, a process of individuation along a surface of becoming. Sense experience registers this passage of the virtual into the actual as chaos, as a jolt of disequilibrium, a becoming-other. The virtual is actualized, but it remains immanent within the actual, something left over, in reserve and still to come. Philosophy disengages the virtual from bodies and countereffects it as Event, as a virtual that has been given consistency. Art seizes the becoming-other of the virtual's passage into the actual, wrests it from organized bodily perceptions and affections, and then renders it perceptible in artworks.

This surface of passage between the virtual and the actual, this site of chaotic effectuation and chaoid countereffectuation, is the realm of sensation. Deleuze and Guattari elaborate on this realm and its relationship to the virtual in their concluding remarks on philosophy, science, and art as modes of thought. The three domains are the daughters of chaos, "the Chaoids," and each is equally a form of thought and a form of creation (QP 196; 208). That which thinks in all three is the brain, which they define as *"the junction* (not the unity) *of the three planes"* (QP 196; 208) of immanence, reference and composition. The *brain* thinks, not the human being, who is merely "a cerebral crystallization" (QP 198; 210). "Philosophy, art, science are not the mental objects of an objectifed brain, but the three aspects under which the brain becomes subject, Thought-brain, the three planes, the rafts on which the brain plunges into and confronts chaos" (QP 198; 210). This brain-subject is first of all a "superject" (a term taken from Whitehead), an "I conceive" in absolute overflight. It is a *"form in itself"* (QP 198; 210) with all the characteristics of the self-forming form described by Ruyer—a self-surveying overflight, at infinite speed, of an absolute surface with a single side and no supplemental dimensions (QP 198; 210). This superject is not itself a concept, but the faculty of forming concepts, "the mind/spirit [*esprit*] itself" (QP 198; 211). At the same moment that the brain becomes superject, the concept, plane of immanence, and conceptual persona come into being. The brain is also an "I function" of scientific knowledge, an "eject" that extracts selected elements from the actual—limits, constants, variables, and so forth—while tracing a plane of reference. Finally, the brain is an "I feel [*je sens*]," a *"soul [âme]* or *force"* (QP 199; 211), an "inject" (QP 200; 212), a subject that is not in overflight above things (*super*ject), like the subject of philosophy; nor "ejected" at an objective distance from things, like the subject of the sciences; but in the midst of things, interfused with them, *in*jected.

The inject is the "I feel" of sensation, and it is no less a mode of thought than the "I conceive" of the superject. The inject of sensation conserves, contracts, composes, and contemplates. Here, Deleuze and Guattari make use of a line of reasoning that Deleuze first touches on in his early book on Hume, *Empiricism and Subjectivity* (1953), and then develops in *Difference and Repetition*. One of Hume's great insights, according to Deleuze, is that the conception of cause-and-effect relations presupposes a passive synthesis of time. For Hume, all ideas derive from impressions, and there can be no direct sensate impression that generates the idea of causality. Object A may follow object B any number of times, but if A vanishes when B appears, the two remain separate and unrelated events. Hume reasons that we do have a genuine idea of causality, and that it arises from an inner impression, an "impression of reflexion" (Hume 165) whereby the understanding establishes the connection between A and B. But in Deleuze's reading of Hume, there is an intermediary moment between the unrelated succession of A and B and the understanding's active reflection on A and B. Something happens in the mind (specifically, in the imagination): A is retained, or conserved, such that it is brought into coexistence with B. This retention, or conservation, takes place through no *action* of the mind, but automatically, *in* the mind, as in a container; here, a *passive* synthesis brings together one moment with a succeeding moment. Such a retention of A into B makes possible the idea of causality, but it also is the foundation of all habits, which presuppose a primary retention of a past into a present and toward a future.

In *Difference and Repetition*, Deleuze expands on Hume's analysis, arguing that the passive syntheses of perception lead directly to the passive syntheses of organic processes, to the "primary sensibility that we *are*" (DR 99; 73). Every organism is "the sum of its retentions, contractions and expectations" (DR 99; 73), its past retained in its genetic makeup and its future projected from its present in the form of need. On the ground of these fundamental contractions and expectations arise the active syntheses of such higher-order functions as memory, instinct, and learning. Every organism's contact with its environment also involves retentions and contractions, its absorption of heat, light, water, nutrients, and so on being so many contractions of elements within its ongoing self-formation. The organism's various contractions Deleuze characterizes as Humean habits, retentions that take place in a "soul," which does not actively synthesize elements but simply contemplates that which is contracted within it. For every contraction there is a contemplative soul, for which reason one must "attribute a soul to the heart, to the muscles, to the nerves, to the cells, but a contemplative soul whose only role is to contract a habit" (DR 101; 74). What we commonly call habits, the sensori-motor habits we develop as active creatures, presuppose "the primary habits that we are, the thousands of passive syntheses that organically compose us. Simultaneously, it is in contracting that we are habits, but it is through contemplation that we contract" (DR 101; 74). In this sense, Deleuze regards the thesis of Samuel Butler's *Life and Habit* as basically correct: all life is habit. And likewise, Plotinus's vision in the Third Ennead's Eighth Tractate: all of Nature is contemplation.

In *What Is Philosophy?* Deleuze and Guattari make similar points, describing the "I feel" brain's sensation in terms contraction, habit, and contemplation. Sensation is fundamentally a conservation or retention of vibrations, a contraction of vibrations that takes places in a contemplative soul, not through an action, but "a pure passion, a contemplation that conserves the preceding in the following" (QP 199; 212). The realm of actualized bodies, of mechanistic physical actions and reactions, is distinct from that of sensation, which constitutes a "plane of composition, where sensation is formed in contracting that which composes it, and in composing itself with other sensations that it contracts in turn. Sensation is pure contemplation, for it is through contemplation that one contracts, contemplating oneself to the extent that one contemplates the elements from which one arises. To contemplate is to create, the mystery of passive creation, sensation" (QP 200; 212). The flower, as sensing soul, absorbs water and sunlight; it conserves vibration after vibration of the stream of photons and water molecules it is absorbing; it contracts the light stream by contemplating that stream, and likewise contracts the water stream; it brings together the two contracted streams, composes them into a block of sensations, and then contemplatively contracts that composition; finally, it senses itself in beatific self-enjoyment, as if it were smelling the scent it exudes.

It might seem that sensation in this account is merely a behavioristic *reception* of stimuli, but sensation entails creation, "the mystery of passive creation," and the "soul" of sensation is *"soul* or *force"* (QP 199; 211), albeit a force "that does not act" (QP 201; 213), a force "in retreat" (QP 199; 211). In what sense is sensation "passive creation," and the contemplative soul "a force that does not act"? Deleuze and Guattari assert that "in the final analysis, the same ultimate elements and the same force in retreat constitute a single plane of composition bearing all the varieties of the Universe" (QP 201; 213), and they cite Ruyer's vitalism as a philosophy of nature that posits such a force that does not act.[5] At first glance Ruyer seems to assert the opposite, for he stresses that self-forming forms are "essentially active and dynamic" (Ruyer 1952, 104), processes of forming activity rather than static states or completed forms. Yet in his view the dynamism of self-forming forms is different from that of the standard physics of mechanistically interacting solid bodies. The absolute overflight of a self-forming form involves a connecting or joining of elements, a process of relating parts within a single field without fusing them into an amorphous "one" or simply collecting them as aggregates, part-against-part (a simple though too static example of this nonfusing connection being that of the individual squares of the checkerboard table top grasped by an observing consciousness). The primary form of every connection is that of absolute overflight, but that form, Ruyer stresses, is "also essentially a force of connection [*une force de liaison*]" (ibid. 113). Ruyer takes as the fundamental connection of self-forming form the molecular bond, which cannot be construed in the terms of a classical physics of solid bodies and contiguous part-to-part relations. The atoms that bond are not stable, shaped things, but activities whose forms are "virtual and dependent on forces of composition" (Ruyer 1958, 58), a carbon atom, for example, being not so much a solid tetrahedral pyramid as a quadruple orientation of possible syntheses. The electrons of a bond are not localizable or assignable to a given atom, but constitute a zone of indiscernibility between atoms; a bonding of two atoms is something like a continuous self-structuring of two regions of electronic density in ongoing vibratory resonance (though finally the exchange of electrons in a bond "is not representable, but a fundamental fact" [Ruyer 1952, 220]). The absolute overflight of a *form* and its activity as a *force* of connection or bonding are one and the same, a single process of self-forming form, and from molecules to macromolecules, viruses, bacteria, and multicellular organisms, the same molecular "temporalized structuring activity" (Ruyer 1958, 63) prevails. In this sense, an elephant is "a macro-microscopic being" (Ruyer 1952, 113), which is "more 'microscopic' than a soap bubble" (ibid. 227), in that the soap bubble is a static form composed of an aggregate of elements, whereas the elephant is a self-forming form comprising multiple self-forming forms (molecules, macromolecules, organs, etc.) within a single ongoing activity.

The force of classical physics is a force of macroscopic entities and molar aggregates, whereas the force of self-forming forms is molecular, the bonding between atoms representing a different mode of force, not different in nature but different in quantity and spatio-temporal manifestation. For Ruyer, "all force is mental in origin [*d'origine spirituelle*]" (Ruyer 1952, 225), in that self-forming form, in Ruyer's definition, *is* consciousness, and the molecular force of self-forming forms is primary, whereas the force of classical physics is only "a macroscopic result" (ibid. 226). In his view, then, a self-forming form in absolute overflight is a virtual in process of actualization, and as process it is essentially *une force de liaison*, a force of connection or bonding, which from the perspective of macroscopic bodies and classical physics is minuscule in quantity and mysterious in its functioning, and perhaps in this sense "a force that does not act." It is the force of all living things (which include all self-forming forms, whether organic or inorganic), and hence a force of creation: a force of composition that operates through bonding and connection. Like Ruyer, Deleuze and Guattari see the fundamental process of creation in nature as a continuous actualization of the virtual, and they regard the absolute overflight of the virtual as entailing a creative force of composition through which the virtual becomes actual. But they distinguish between the *form* and the *force* of the virtual, between an *esprit* in overflight and a *soul* that conserves, arguing that the connections and bondings through which self-forming forms build, grow, and take shape presuppose a passive synthesis, a contraction of a past into a present within a conserving, contemplating soul. Every self-forming form in this regard is necessarily a sensing form, in that its self-forming activity presupposes a retentive contraction of past into present, and that contraction is sensation.

Ruyer's effort is to establish the energetic continuity between molecular forces of self-forming forms and molar forces of aggregates (the forces are different in mode, not in nature), whereas Deleuze and Guattari wish to differentiate a virtual dimension of force that is immanent within the virtual's actualization. The virtual's actualization takes place in actual bodies as a dynamic process of individuation, a process that may be described in terms of active, physical forces, but immanent within that process is a virtual connecting, or bonding, through a process of retentive, contracting, self-conserving sensation. Immanent within the active forces of bodies in formation, then, is a passive force of the virtual. Put another way, the actualization of the virtual must be described twice, once in terms of actual bodies and the standard physics of material forces, and a second time in terms of the passive syntheses of retentive contractions that make up the condition of possibility of all bondings and connections. The actualization of the virtual is a single process, but the passage of the virtual into the actual does not exhaust the virtual; the virtual remains immanent within the actual, an excess always in reserve, and that virtual immanent within the actual is manifest as sensation.

To return to the example of the embryo: as the embryo's cells divide, it forms increasingly complex configurations of multiplying cells. Its morphogenesis proceeds through an internal process of splitting into more and more cells, but the process requires as well the continual incorporation of external nutrients within the internal process (and if one considers morphogenesis to extend throughout the organism's life, as Ruyer insists we must, its absorption of nutrients at various stages of its life history—in the case of humans, in the womb, in infancy, and through adulthood—must be viewed as part of a single process of growth and development). The internal multiplication of cells and external absorption of nutrients may be seen as so many bondings and connections, and those processes of internal individuation and external incorporation of nutrients may be described in terms of actual physical bodies and kinetic forces. But the processes may also be described in terms of a virtual self-forming form, in absolute overflight, differentiating itself through various internal and external connections. The form, when considered in its "dynamic" and "kinetic" becoming (the words are imprecise but unavoidable), is force, a force of connection whereby the form unfolds and constructs itself. That connecting force, however, is a passive force of retention, contraction, and conservation, not an active force. The unfolding of the virtual self-forming form is a process of actualization, each discrete state of the embryo an actual manifestation of the form, and the kinetic emergence of those actual states involves actual, physical forces. But immanent within them is the force of the virtual form itself, a purely passive, receptive force of sensation that doubles actual forces and remains within them as a perpetual reserve.

The plane of immanence is the domain of philosophy, the plane of composition, that of the arts, but both are finally planes of nature, planes of the actualization of virtual self-forming forms. The plane of immanence is that of every living form in absolute overflight, the plane of composition that of every living form in its process of ongoing embodiment. Philosophy and the arts, then, are activities that arise from and are connected to the general processes of the natural world. This is no reductive view of human action as "mere" animal behavior or physico-mechanical process. Philosophy is a highly specialized mode of engaging the plane of immanence, perhaps one that takes place only in human beings. Yet philosophy's invention of concepts ultimately is but one version of a general process of absolute overflight characteristic of all living forms. It is for this reason that Deleuze and Guattari speak of events as "forms of a Nature-thought that fly over [*survolent*] all possible universes" (QP 168; 177–78). Likewise, the arts are quite specialized activities (although Deleuze and Guattari do see some animals as artists). The specialized function of the human arts, like the specialized function of philosophy, may be seen as a form of deterritorialization whereby an activity becomes increasingly autonomous, but finally the arts, like philosophy, remain part of a general process of natural creation. It is in this sense that art's plane is "a plane of composition of Being" (QP 179; 189) and its object, that of engaging life in an "enterprise of co-creation" (QP 164; 173).

Philosophy's domain is virtual; art's domain is possible—but finally this opposition of virtual and possible is not absolute, for the possible is the embodied virtual, the event as "alterity engaged in an expressive matter" (QP 168; 177).[6] The world of art is a world of signs, a world of immanent, virtual forces within bodies. Its universe is that of an expressive matter that renders sensations palpable. The being of sensation is the being of the virtual as retentive, contractive, self-conserving, contemplative force immanent within the actual. Philosophy "countereffects" the virtual, "disengages an event from things and beings" (QP 33; 31), but both "art and even philosophy can apprehend [the event]" (QP 149; 158), and above all, "It is art . . . that can seize the event" (PP 218; 160).

Conclusion

Deleuze describes the problem common to the arts in various ways—as the harnessing of forces, as the tracing of lines, as the embodiment of sensation. Yet each art has its particular concerns, processes, and capacities, which cannot be transferred or translated from that art to another. For this reason Deleuze and Guattari say that "in no way do we believe in a system of the fine arts," and that "art seems to us a false concept, solely nominal" (MP 369; 300–301). What, then, are the domains specific to music and painting? In what manner and in what matter does each art render perceptible percepts and affects? How might we frame Deleuze's various conceptualizations of music and painting in terms of the embodiment of sensation?

SPECIFIC DOMAINS

If each art embodies sensation, music does so in a highly pliable and almost "incorporeal" matter. As Deleuze remarks in *Francis Bacon*, music indeed "deeply traverses our bodies, and puts an ear in our belly, in our lungs, etc.," but ultimately it "rids bodies of their inertia, of the materiality of their presence. It *disincarnates* bodies" (FB 38). In turn, through the manipulation of its sonic matter, it "gives the most mental [*spirituelles*] entities a disincarnated, dematerialized body" (FB 38). In *A Thousand*

Plateaus, Deleuze and Guattari frame this power of disincarnation as a high quotient of deterritorialization. Music engages human bodies most fundamentally as a deterritorialization of the voice, and in comparison with painting, which deterritorializes the face, "music has a deterritorializing force that is much greater, much more intense and collective at the same time, and the voice a power of being deterritorialized that is also much greater" (MP 371; 302). Yet in another sense, music is perhaps the most material of the arts, the most elemental and cosmic, for its specific object is the deterritorialization of the refrain, which is manifest throughout the world of living forms. The refrain's coexisting movements are those of the point of stability, the surrounding circle, and the line of flight. Milieus are formed out of the rhythmic interactions of various components, each a point of stability emergent from a chaotic background. A territory arises when a milieu component is extracted from the milieu as an expressive quality and possessive property. Through this action, a territorial space is circumscribed; the territory's inhabitant asserts its possession of the space; and the component expresses the entirety of the territorial configuration of interconnected rhythmic elements. Within the territory as well is a line of flight, an opening to the outside. And it is via this line that other, nonterritorial, forms of social organization issue, along with increasing numbers of deterritorialized rhythmic components. Human musicians continue nature's ubiquitous deterritorialization of rhythmic elements, fashioning rhythmic characters and melodic landscapes from sonic materials, their deterritorialization of refrains proceeding through diverse becomings, such as the elaborate and extended becoming-bird of Messiaen.

From milieus through territories to cosmic lines of flight, the rhythms of interacting components form interrelated refrains, which musicians engage through becomings, extract from the world, and then render perceptible in a sonic material that captures forces. In Western art music, the Classical age is marked by refrains that wrest order from chaos, each composition the musical counterpart of a milieu constructed of components in harmonic and contrapuntal accord. Romantic composers exploit territorial motifs, various mythic, regional, national, and ethnic elements inspiring works that seek a new relation between the earth and the people. The Romantics convert discretely sectional and relatively symmetrical Classical forms into a great form in continuous development, while treating sound as a moving matter in continuous variation, thereby intensifying the deterritorializing tendencies within Classical music. Modern composers extend this deterritorializing movement, attempting through lines of flight to harness cosmic forces that range from the molecular (for example, Varèse's sonic "crystallizations" and "ionizations") to the geological and sidereal (Messiaen's *From the Canyons to the Stars*). Through such cosmic refrains, modern composers render perceptible duration itself, capturing in sonic matter what Messiaen describes as "the endlessly long time of the stars, the very long time of the mountains, the middling one of the human being, the short one of insects, the very short one of atoms (not to mention the time-scales inherent in ourselves—the physiological, the psychological)" (Rößler 40).

Music, then, makes perceptible the most elemental forces, but in such a way that our corporeal experience of these forces tends to "disincarnate" and "dematerialize" our bodies. Painting, by contrast, "discovers the material reality of the body, with its system of lines-colors and its polyvalent organ, the eye" (FB 38). Painting, one might say, is the most carnal of the arts, the art that most directly engages percepts and affects as they arise in human bodies. It is for this reason that painting reveals most clearly the "logic of sensation," the affective dimension of art that allows an aesthetic material, as Bacon says, to bypass the brain and come across "directly onto the nervous system" (Sylvester 18). In Bacon's works we have clear visual evidence of the becoming-animal of human figures. We see the vibratory forces at play in the body's metamorphoses and in the diastolic and systolic rhythms that pass between figure and ground; we see the forces of coupling that conjoin two figures in a "matter of fact"; and we see the forces of separation that situate figures within intense, self-spacing monochrome fields. Ultimately, the force of a fluctuating time is revealed in Bacon's triptychs, but that ethereal force remains enmeshed in the human body's becoming.

The carnal dimension of painting is evident not simply in Bacon's treatment of figures, but in his handling of color as well. In formal terms, the play of forces in Bacon's paintings issues from the diagram, a point of chaos within the canvas that functions as a modulator through which the composition's structuring relations arise. Yet Bacon is above all a great colorist, and his effort finally is to make color the generative element from which the canvases' diagrams, figures, fields, and forces arise. All great painters repeat the history of painting, says Deleuze, and

in Bacon we can see the tactile shallow depth of Egyptian painting and the composite haptic-optic space of classical Greek art, as well as the projective space and optic play of light of Byzantine mosaics. But most important is Bacon's use of Cézanne's modulations of contrasting tones and van Gogh's broken tones, for in these practices Bacon exploits a properly haptic dimension of color. It is this tactile, palpable, sensual use of color that most patently reveals art's ability to embody sensation, to harness forces within a material, sensate world that remains close to our own corporeal existence.

The same corporeality is evident in painting's deterritorialization of the face and landscape. Music deterritorializes the human voice, but only as one means of reaching the basic goal of deterritorializing the refrain, the refrain having no privileged relation to the human body. Painting, by contrast, has as its fundamental aim the deterritorialization of the effects of facialization, through which the human face extends its encoding powers to the human body and beyond to the world at large. In the despotic-passional regime of signs, an abstract machine of faciality turns the face into a white wall-black hole system of signification and subjectification, a set of gestural expressions that combine with linguistic signs to enforce power relations. A coordinated disciplinary organization facializes the entire body, and a general facialized gridding spreads to structure the landscape surrounding the body. Painting in this regard has close ties with language and its intertwined institutions and practices, and through these ties painting assumes its political function of inventing a people by undoing the fixed codes and static grids that structure the world in conventional configurations. All the arts have the vocation of inventing a people-to-come (music's effort being evident in the invention of the "Dividual," as in Berio's *Coro*), but painting's invention of a people proceeds directly through the human body, via the "probe heads" that metamorphose faces, and thereby make possible a larger deformation of facialized bodies and facialized landscapes.

We may say, then, that sound, the material of music, has the capacity of disincarnating human bodies and granting sensations an abstract, "dematerialized body." Painting's material, the paint on the canvas, has the power of rendering visible the sensations that traverse the human body and connect it to the world. And each art in its specific fashion seeks the invention of a people through the creation of new ways of perceiving and feeling.

In *What Is Philosophy?* Deleuze and Guattari insist that no hierarchy governs relations among philosophy, science, and the arts. Each is a separate sphere with its own problems and objects of analysis. Yet each also has its own relation to what it is not. *"Philosophy needs a non-philosophy that comprehends it, it needs a non-philosophical comprehension, just as art needs non-art, and science non-science"* (QP 205–6; 218). Each sphere "is in an essential relation with the No that concerns it" (QP 205; 218). One might assume that science and the arts function equally as the nonphilosophy with which philosophy is concerned, and that nonart and nonscience are similarly constituted. Deleuze and Guattari do not elaborate on this point, but in scattered texts published shortly before *What Is Philosophy?*, Deleuze suggests that there is a special affinity between philosophy and the nonphilosophy of the arts, and that this affinity resides in the internal relation of the philosophical concept to art's affects and percepts. In a 1988 interview, Deleuze explains that his books on painting and cinema must be seen as books of philosophy, for "the concept, I believe, includes two other dimensions, those of the percept and the affect" (PP 187; 137). In a 1989 preface to a special issue of *Lendemains* devoted to his books on Spinoza, Deleuze notes that Spinoza is a great stylist who creates movement in the concept, yet the concept, Deleuze adds, "does not move solely within itself (philosophical comprehension), it also moves in things and in us: it inspires in us new *percepts* and new *affects*, which constitute the non-philosophical comprehension of philosophy itself" (PP 223; 164). Deleuze observes further, "Style in philosophy strains toward these three poles, the concept, or new ways of thinking, the percept or new ways of seeing and hearing, the affect or new ways of feeling. They are the philosophical trinity, philosophy as opera: all three are needed to *create movement [faire le mouvement]*" (PP 224; 164–65). Percepts and affects, it would seem, are at once inside and outside concepts, dimensions *of* concepts yet *non*philosophical dimensions, constituents of "the non-philosophical comprehension of philosophy itself." What this suggests is that affects and percepts are the surface or membrane between philosophy and the arts, between new ways of thinking and new ways of perceiving and feeling, yet a surface proper to philosophy itself. In *What Is Philosophy?* Deleuze and Guattari wish to distinguish philosophy from the arts and hence emphasize the difference between thinking in concepts and thinking in percepts and affects, but in one of Deleuze's last essays, *Critique et clinique*'s concluding essay, "Spinoza and the Three 'Ethics,' " Deleuze implies that a properly philosophical thought in percepts and affects is also possible. In Spinoza's *Ethics,* Deleuze argues, the definitions, axioms, propositions, and so on exemplify thought through concepts, but the scholia represent a thought in affects, and part 5 a pure thought in percepts, as if "signs and concepts vanished, and things began to write by themselves and for themselves" (CC 186; 150), as if thought proceeded "no longer through signs or affects, nor concepts, but Essences or Singularities, Percepts" (CC 183; 148), direct visions of things.

The arts have a privileged relation to philosophy, for "the affect, the percept and the concept are three inseparable powers [*puissances*], which go from art to philosophy and vice versa" (PP 187; 137). Deleuze's studies of the arts engage powers that are at once inside and outside philosophy, and each art has a different affinity with the formation and movement of concepts in his thought. Deleuze, of course, is a writer of books, and as such shares with novelists, poets, and dramatists the vocation of creating in the medium of language. He often approaches literary writers as philosophers, and some of the philosophers he values most are commonly regarded as more literary than philosophical figures. Frequently, Deleuze speaks simply of "writing" when discussing literature, and much of what he says about writing seems applicable both to literature and to philosophy—especially the creative writer's problem of "boring holes in language," as Beckett puts it, a problem Deleuze himself addresses, in that much of his work is an effort to articulate the ineffable, to talk about those things that lie beyond words or along their surface. Even when Deleuze and Guattari insist in *What Is Philosophy?* that philosophy and art are different enterprises, they must concede that in some philosophers the line between philosophical and literary writing is difficult to discern. This is especially true of the distinction between philosophy's "conceptual personae" and art's "aesthetic figures." Conceptual personae, such as Nicholas of Cusa's *idiota*, Descartes' Eudoxe, Kierkegaard's knight of faith or Nietzsche's Zarathustra, are "powers [*puissances*] of concepts," unlike aesthetic figures, which are "powers of affects and percepts," yet Deleuze and Guattari observe that "the two entities often pass into one another, in a becoming that carries them both into an intensity that co-determines them" (QP 64; 66). Art's plane of composition and philosophy's plane of immanence "can slide into one another" (QP 65; 66), and there are philosophers and creative writers who are capable of moving back and forth between domains. They do not synthesize art and philosophy, but they straddle the two, like "acrobats torn apart in a perpetual show of strength" (QP 65; 67). Nietzsche's Zarathustra is at times a conceptual persona and at others an aesthetic figure; likewise, Mallarmé's Igitur by turns fulfills each of these functions. And through the oscillation of their characters' functions Nietzsche and Mallarmé are able to combine the powers of concepts and affects-percepts within a single work.

Nietzsche, of course, is the exception rather than the rule, an unconventional philosopher who deliberately blurs the distinction between philosophy and literature. Yet even the most unliterary of philosophers can engage the powers of affects and percepts at the level of style, and it is in style, finally, that Deleuze finds the fundamental affinity between philosophy and literature, as well as the arts of music and painting. Literary style is a matter of stuttering in one's own language, of making words and syntax stammer. And many philosophers are also great stylists, Deleuze claims. "Style is a process of putting language in variation, a modulation, and a straining of the whole of language toward an outside," and "style in philosophy is the movement of the concept" (PP 192; 140). For Deleuze, style is above all "a matter of syntax" (PP 223; 164), and in philosophy "syntax" involves the line of development of an argument, the passage from one point to another, the "movement of the concept." Spinoza's definitions, axioms, and demonstrations unfold at a calm and even pace, but his scholia are discontinuous, violent eruptions, and in part 5 the line of proof takes "fulgurating shortcuts, functions through ellipses, implications and contractions, proceeds through piercing, rending flashes" (PP 225; 165). In Foucault, concepts at times assume "rhythmic values," at others they become "contrapuntal, as in the curious dialogues with himself with which he closes some of his books" (PP 138; 101). His syntax gathers together "the mirrorings, the scintillations of the visible, but it also twists like a whip, folds and unfolds, or cracks to the rhythms of the phrases" (PP 138; 101). It is at the level of style that literature and philosophy come closest to one another, both literary and philosophical writers putting syntax in variation, each in their own way making language strain toward an outside.

It is also at this level that philosophy and music converge, the syntactic line of an argument resembling a melodic line, each line tracing a creative line of movement. Philosophy has a fundamental affinity with music, Deleuze remarks in a late interview: "It seems certain to me that philosophy is a veritable song that is not a song of the voice, and that it has the same sense of movement as music" (PP 222; 163). As one can see from Deleuze's characterizations of the styles of Spinoza and Foucault, the movement of concepts is an affectively charged movement, one whose dynamism has the same elemental yet abstract emotional force as music. Thus, when philosophers succeed in creating movement through concepts, we encounter "philosophy as opera" (PP 224; 165), a voiceless song that "has the same sense of movement as music" (PP 222; 163). At such moments, a new way of thinking functions simultaneously as a new way of feeling.

But Deleuze says that style in philosophy strains toward *three* poles, toward new ways of *perceiving* as well as new ways of thinking and feeling. And though Deleuze speaks of percepts as "new ways of seeing and hearing" (PP 224; 165), it is evident that for him new perception is above all a matter of vision. Foucault's syntax gathers together "the mirrorings, the scintillations of the visible" (PP 138; 101). Spinoza's style in part 5 presents essences as "pure figures of light" (CC 184; 148). The movement of the concept involves not simply the shape of an argument, but the straining of words toward that which is beyond words, and though there is much that is beyond words, for Deleuze the visible seems to hold a particular fascination. To think differently is to *see* differently, and in his works on painting, Deleuze attempts to create concepts that are adequate to visible creations that defy commonsense assimilation and categorization—to those "visibilities" that render palpable Bacon's "brutality of fact." In these studies, arresting visual images are the object of analysis, hence they constitute that which stimulates the generation and movement of thought. But the thought thereby engendered evokes its own images, the idiosyncratic "visions" of paintings that are the product of Deleuze's unique way of seeing and that he seeks to render visible through his texts. In this evocation of visions, Deleuze's writings on the visual image are thus paradigmatic of philosophy's general aim of inventing new ways of seeing—ways of seeing that form the outer limit of new ways of thinking.

Philosophy and the arts are modes of thought, the one a thought in concepts, the other a thought in percepts and affects. Thought in concepts extracts the virtual event from the actual and gives it the consistency of a self-forming form in absolute overflight. Thought in percepts and affects disengages the virtual from corporeal experience and then embodies it in materials that render perceptible the imperceptible. Each of the arts shapes a material with specific characteristics and capabilities, sounds, colors, words, and moving images embodying sensations in discrete yet interrelated ways. The arts disclose the possible, philosophy the virtual, but ultimately both engage the becoming of the virtual in its passage into the actual. Philosophical thought in concepts and artistic thought in percepts and affects are two manifestations of the virtual, as *form in overflight* and as *passive force*. And though highly specialized activities, both are constituent elements of a general process of natural creation. Philosophers and artists think differently, yet there is a passage of powers between philosophy and the arts that forms a special bond between the two spheres. Concepts are not the same as percepts and affects, but the three constitute the "philosophical trinity" necessary for the creation of movement within philosophical thought. A writing proper to philosophy induces a syntactic metamorphosis of language; a voiceless music emerges in the affective rhythms of lines of argument; and an imagistic vision demarcates the outside of moving concepts. Philosophy does not need the arts, any more than the arts need philosophy, but the elements of the arts exist within philosophy, in the percepts and affects that animate philosophical concepts. Deleuze's thought on the arts constitutes only one dimension of his philosophy, but it is a privileged dimension that reveals philosophy's proper function as a creative, perceptive, and affective mode of thought.

Notes

CHAPTER ONE

1. For an overview of the development of these ideas, see Spitzer.

2. A useful and reliable introduction to the Pythagoreans may be found in W. K. C. Guthrie's *A History of Greek Philosophy, Vol. 1, The Earlier Presocratics and the Pythagoreans*, pp. 146–340. See also Lippman, 1–44.

3. Guthrie notes that Pythagoras "was traditionally supposed to have been the first to apply the name *kosmos* to the world, in recognition of the order which it displayed" (Guthrie 208). It is also worth observing that the Pythagoreans may have been the first to use the word *philosophia* in its modern sense, that of "using the powers of reason and observation in order to gain understanding" (ibid. 205).

4. See Guthrie, "Time and the Unlimited," appendix, pp. 336–40. No specific name is given to the time of the Unlimited, but Guthrie clearly establishes that the Pythagoreans, Plato, and Aristotle were able to distinguish between mere succession and *chronos*, or measured time, and so could "speak without absurdity of a time before time existed" (Guthrie 338).

5. See Say, pp. 1–24, and De Bruyne. On Boethius, see Chadwick, especially pp. 78–101.

6. The Bergsonian concept of the "open whole" is implicit throughout *A Thousand Plateaus*, but only explicitly developed in Deleuze's *Cinema 1* (IM 9–22; 1–11). For a discussion of the Bergsonian open whole in Deleuze's cinema theory, see Bogue, *Deleuze on Cinema*, chapter 1.

7. For detailed descriptions of the stagemaker, see Marshall, 154–64, and Gilliard 273–81.

8. Particularly useful treatments of Messiaen's music are Robert Sherlaw Johnson's *Messiaen* and Paul Griffiths's *Olivier Messiaen and the Music of Time*. Also of interest are the books on Messiaen by Halbreich, Périer, and Nichols.

9. "Conférence de Bruxelles," 1958, cited by Johnson, p. 32. Compare this passage with Deleuze's remarks on rhythm and meter in *Difference and Repetition* (33; 21): "But a duration only exists in being determined by a tonic accent, controlled by intensities. One is mistaken about the function of accents if one says that they are reproduced at regular intervals. On the contrary, tonic and intensive values act by creating inequalities, incommensurabilities, in metrically equal durations or spaces. They create remarkable points, privileged instants that always mark a polyrhythm."

10. One must mention as well the extensive use in Messiaen's music of ancient Greek meters and the Hindu "deçî-tâlas" ("rhythms from the different regions") of Sharngadeva. See Samuel, pp. 33–49, and Johnson, pp. 32–39. Johnson provides a table of the 120 deçî-tâlas in an appendix, pp. 194–98.

11. Deleuze treats the concept of Aion at great length in *The Logic of Sense*, especially LS 122–32; 100–108 and LS 190–97; 162–68. For a discussion of Aion and Stoic thought, see Bogue, *Deleuze and Guattari*, pp. 67–71.

12. In his extended analysis of the structure and form of the *Catalogue*, Johnson concludes that the "remarkable coherence which undoubtedly exists in these pieces" is to be found in the interplay of musical "groups" organized around "a continuum of varying characteristics which will vary according to the parameter chosen," with no single unifying principle necessarily holding the groups together (Johnson 137–39). In Deleuze-Guattari's terms, the problem Johnson is addressing is that of sonic blocks, lines of continuous variation and the "consistency" that holds the heterogeneous elements of a machinic assemblage together.

CHAPTER TWO

1. The concept of "becoming-woman" has aroused some controversy among feminist theorists. Deleuze and Guattari assert that "if all becomings are already molecular, including becoming-woman, it must also be said that all becomings begin and pass through becoming-woman. It is the key to the other becomings" (MP 340; 277). Yet they also assert that "the woman as molar entity *must also become-woman*" (MP 338; 275). Some see in this position a denial of the specificity of feminist concerns and a subversion of effective political action. For thoughtful discussions of the possible use of this concept in feminism, see Braidotti, Griggers, Grosz, and the collection of essays edited by Buchanan and Colebrook, *Deleuze and Feminist Theory* (especially Colebrook's helpful introduction).

2. This judgment, it should be noted, is much more commonly applied by critics to Wagner than to Verdi. Consider, for instance, Dent's comments: "The fundamental difference between Verdi and Wagner lay in their mental outlook on opera. Wagner was always more interested in the orchestra than in the singers; he imagined his characters as emerging from the orchestra, created, as one might say, by the imagination of the orchestra, which was the real expression of his own imagination. . . . Verdi's conception of opera was the exact opposite of this" (Dent 92). Deleuze and

Guattari are aware of this reading of Verdi: "It has often been said that [Verdi's] opera remains lyrical and vocal, despite his destruction of the bel canto, and despite the importance of the orchestration in his final works; still the voices are instrumentalized and they make singular gains in tessitura or in extension (the production of the Verdi-baritone, of the Verdi-soprano)." They insist, however, that "it is nonetheless not a matter of a given composer, certainly not Verdi, nor of this or that genre, but of the most general movement affecting music, a slow mutation of the musical machine. If the voice rediscovers a binary distribution of the sexes, it is in relation to the binary groupings of instruments in the orchestration" (MP 378; 308).

3. Deleuze and Guattari make use here of the distinction drawn by the linguist Louis Hjelmslev between *matter,* the unorganized material from which a semiotic system may be constructed; *form,* which shapes that matter; and *substance,* or the matter once it has been formed. Hjelmslev likens matter to an undifferentiated surface upon which the shadow of a net is cast. The grid work pattern of the net delineates a form, and each of the squares of matter demarcated by the grid is a unit of substance.

4. Deleuze and Guattari make frequent reference to a charming book by Marcel Moré, *Le Dieu Mozart et le monde des oiseaux,* in which he details at some length the use of birdsong motifs in Mozart's oeuvre, including *The Magic Flute.* Moré also discusses Paul Klee's fascination with Mozart, as well as what Moré regards as Messiaen's misunderstanding of Mozart and misuse of birdsong in his own music.

5. Klee's comment appears at the conclusion of his remarks prepared for a lecture in 1924 and published as *Paul Klee: Über die moderne Kunst (Paul Klee: On Modern Art).* He says that "sometimes I dream of a work of really great breadth," but "this, I fear, will remain a dream, but it is a good thing even now to bear the possibility occasionally in mind. . . . We must go on seeking it! We have found parts, but not the whole! We still lack the ultimate power, for: the people are not with us [*Uns trägt kein Volk*]. But we seek a people" (Klee 1948, 54–55).

6. Varèse's rhythmic practices are obviously quite similar to those of Messiaen, what Carter identifies as Varèse's addition or subtraction of notes resembling Messiaen's "added values" and Varèse's distortion of inner cell relationships echoing Messiaen's use of "rhythmic characters." Such similarities are understandable, since for many years Messiaen regularly led his students through Varèse's scores, and during the 1940s and early 1950s he was largely responsible for keeping Varèse from sinking into total obscurity in France. Carter observes, however, that though Varèse and Messiaen use similar rhythmic techniques, Varèse consistently creates a sense of forward drive, whereas Messiaen does not (Van Solkema 77). Messiaen's effort is to create a circular, timeless time, and hence he deliberately avoids a sense of forward drive. It is perhaps for this reason that no clear counterpart to Messiaen's "nonretrogradable rhythms" exists in Varèse. Yet in Varèse's thought on rhythm one finds a certain compatibility with Messiaen's reflections on the topic, despite Vivier's claims that Varèse and Messiaen "are opposed to each other on this subject with the exclusive lucidity of contemporary creators" (Vivier 90). For Varèse, the basis of rhythm is "the immobile charged with its power [*puissance*]" (Vivier 90). A

stretched string, when plucked, must necessarily pass through its initial position of rest in order to continue to vibrate. Hence, Varèse sees rhythm as an element of stability and cohesion. "It has little to do with cadence, which is the regular succession of tempos and accents. For example, rhythm in my works gives rise to reciprocal and simultaneous effects between independent elements that intervene in foreseeable but irregular lapses of time. This, moreover, corresponds to the conception of rhythm in physics and philosophy, that is, a succession of alternate states, opposed or correlative" (Vivier 90). It would seem that Varèse's commitment to the forward drive of rhythm is at least partially tempered by this conception of rhythm as source of stability and cohesion.

CHAPTER THREE

1. For a succinct summary of the relationship between deterritorialization/reterritorialization and decoding/recoding, see Holland 1996. For an account of the expanded role of deterritorialization/reterritorialization in *A Thousand Plateaus*, see Holland 1991.

2. Consider, for example, Eibl-Eibesfeldt's typical textbook definition of territory: "Ethologically a territory is defined as a space in which one animal or a group generally dominates others, which in turn may become dominant elsewhere (E. O. Willis, 1967). Domination can be achieved by diverse means, for example by fighting threat, territorial songs, and olfactory marking. By these means the territory owners usually banish those that do not belong to the group or any conspecific if it is solitary" (340).

3. This work has not yet been translated into English. My references will be to the French translation, which Deleuze and Guattari cite in *A Thousand Plateaus*. Throughout the French translation, *Bedeutung* is rendered as *signification*, which I shall translate as "meaning." The difficulties of dealing with the German terms *Bedeutung* and *Sinn*, the French *sens, signification*, and *signifiance*, and the English *sense, meaning*, and *signification*, are well known, and of course of great concern in translating Deleuze's *Logique du sens*. They are of less moment here, however, since von Uexküll uses *Bedeutung* in a fairly straightforward fashion and does not follow Frege and others in distinguishing between *Sinn* and *Bedeutung*. The French edition also contains a translation of von Uexküll's 1934 *Streifzüge durch die Umwelten von Tieren und Menschen*, translated as *Mondes animaux et monde humain*. Most of my remarks will be restricted to *Théorie de la signification*, but I shall make brief reference to *Mondes animaux et monde humain* in summarizing von Uexküll's views on territoriality.

4. See especially DR 279; 216, AO 340; 286, PL 137–139; 102–103, QP 198; 210. On the importance of Ruyer and Whitehead in the thought of Deleuze and Guattari, see the final chapter of Éric Alliez's *La Signature du monde*, 67–104.

5. A helpful introduction to the work of Maturana and Varela and other recent developments in biology is Capra's *The Web of Life*, especially pp. 174–75, 264–74.

6. Lynn Margulis and Dorion Sagan especially have stressed the importance of cooperative values in evolution. See also Goodwin (179–81) and Capra (232–63).

7. Deleuze and Guattari also make use of a geological vocabulary of strata, substrata, epistrata, and peristrata to describe physical and biological systems in plateau 2 of *A Thousand Plateaus*. For a brief presentation of this material, see Bogue, *Deleuze and Guattari*, pp. 125–30.

8. In their analysis of the strata of creation, Deleuze and Guattari remark, "It is difficult to explain the system of the strata without seeming to introduce a kind of cosmic or even spiritual evolution from one to the other, as if they were ordered in stages and ascended in degrees of perfection. Not at all. The different figures of content and expression are not stages. . . . Above all, there is no lesser, no higher or lower, organization" (MP 89; 69).

CHAPTER FOUR

1. The hole should be conceived of as a part of a topologically continuous surface. The idea is that the white wall–black hole system of the abstract machine of faciality creates a "flattened," reduced reality lacking the multidimensional complexity of a heterogeneously interconnected realm. It is a kind of surface, but one with holes corresponding to the black-hole component of the abstract machine. The holes, however, are one with the surface, and hence do not introduce an additional dimension or depth.

2. "In the literature on the face, the text of Sartre on the gaze and that of Lacan on the mirror make the mistake of relying on a form of subjectivity, of humanity reflected in a phenomenological field, or split in a structural field. *But the gaze is only second in relation to eyes without a gaze, to the black hole of faciality. The mirror is only second in relation to the blank wall of faciality*" (MP 210; 171).

CHAPTER FIVE

1. Like Maldiney, Deleuze makes use of Guillaume's theory of verb tenses and his concept of "implicated time," most notably in *Difference and Repetition* (DR 265; 205) and *A Thousand Plateaus* (MP 431; 349). In his studies of the temporal system of verbs, Guillaume distinguishes between explicated and implicated time. He notes that tenses involve the location of events within an objective time frame (past, present, future) that exists outside the events. This time frame involves explicated time, or what one commentator on Guillaume proposes to call "Universe Time" (Hewson 26). Aspect, by contrast, involves time relations that are internal to the event. The prospective aspect of "I will sing," the progressive aspect of "I am singing," and the retrospective aspect of "I have sung" are all situated in relation to a present "I sing," but the same aspects may be located in relation to a past "I sang" (prospective: "I would sing"; progressive: "I was singing"; retrospective: "I had sung"). The time relations of aspect are "implicated," or enfolded within the event (hence Hewson's designation "Event Time"), and in themselves are independent of the temporal coordinates of explicated time.

2. Deleuze identifies three approaches to the diagram in modern painting: abstraction, "which reduces to the minimum the abyss or chaos" (FB 67), thereby replacing the diagram with a code; abstract expressionism, in which "the abyss or chaos is deployed to the maximum" (FB 68), the diagram taking over the entire canvas (as in

the paintings of Jackson Pollock or Morris Louis); and the figural, the middle course adopted by Bacon. Bacon says that the image he paints is "a kind of tightrope walk between what is called figurative painting and abstraction" (Sylvester 12). He finds abstraction too cerebral and too subjective, and abstract expressionism too "sloppy" (ibid. 94). "I really like highly disciplined painting although I don't use highly disciplined methods of constructing it" (ibid. 92). "I want a very ordered image but I want it to come about by chance" (ibid. 56).

3. Cézanne objects to the ephemeral, insubstantial nature of Impressionist painting and insists on the need for a solidity to sensation, a certain endurance and weight. Hence, remarks Deleuze, "the lesson of Cézanne beyond the impressionists: Sensation is not in the 'free' play or disincarnation of light and color (impressions), but instead it is in the body, even if it's the body of an apple" (FB 27).

4. "Of course, so many of the greatest paintings have been done with a number of figures on a canvas, and of course every painter longs to do that. But, as the thing's in such a terribly complicated stage now, the story that is already being told between one figure and another begins to cancel out the possibilities of what can be done with the paint on its own. And this is a very great difficulty. But at any moment somebody will come along and be able to put a number of figures on a canvas" (Sylvester 23).

5. The notion of "colorism," of course, may be traced at least back to the last quarter of the seventeenth century, when a debate flourished over the primacy of line or color. The debate was revised in the nineteenth century when "a Neo-Classical faction championed the intellectual and austere qualities of line while the more progressive group (chiefly artists of the Romantic persuasion) exploited the sensuous and emotive possibilities of color" (Mras 119). Notable among the Romantic colorists was Delacroix (see Mras 119–23). The question of what precisely colorism entails will concern us in the next chapter.

CHAPTER SIX

1. Deleuze acknowledges Peirce as a source for his conceptualization of the diagram, noting that though Peirce distinguishes between icons based on relations of similarity and symbols based on relations of conventional rules, he recognizes that conventional symbols require iconic elements to establish isomorphic relations and icons transcend relations of similitude to include diagrammatic elements. Nonetheless, Peirce "reduces the diagram to a similitude of relations" (FB 75), and Deleuze's interest is in developing the concept of an analogical diagram.

2. See Manning 119–22 for a characterization of early analogue synthesizers and 213–88 for a brief history of the development of digital synthesizers. Deleuze also remarks that in digital synthesizers timbral modifications are effected through filters via addition, a given timbre being built up through the cumulative addition of codified units, whereas analogue synthesizers modify timbre through subtractive filters that eliminate a given band of frequencies. Deleuze relates the subtractive mode of analogue filters to the intensive fall of sensation in Bacon's painting.

3. For general discussions of Riegl's work, see Schapiro (301–03), Pächt, and Zerner. On the concept of *Kunstwollen,* see especially Pächt 190 and Zerner 180–81.

As several commentators have noted, Riegl uses the term *Kunstwollen* in a loose manner, suggesting at times that it refers to a common set of conventions and practices, at others to a *Weltanschauung* or ideal *Zeitgeist*. Pächt remarks that "the ambiguity of this term which yet has galvanized art-historical thinking for half a century was a stumbling-block to all efforts to arrive at an agreed interpretation, and naturally also an obstacle to a satisfactory translation. Shall we say artistic will, form-will, or as Gombrich suggests will-to-form? All these translations fail to take into account that Riegl did not say *Kunstwille*, but *Kunstwollen*, which literally translated would mean: 'that which wills art'. An additional difficulty is that the term most certainly changed its meaning for Riegl himself as new problems arose" (Pächt 190). In *Cinema 2: The Time-Image*, Deleuze perhaps alludes to Riegl's *Kunstwollen* (as well as Nietzsche's *Wille zur Macht*) when he speaks of a *"volonté d'art,"* or "will-to-art," that guides modern film directors in their cinematic innovations (IT 347; 266).

4. Zerner notes that "the tactile-optical alternative is taken over, of course, from Hildebrand's influential *Problem of Form*, and rests on a theory of perception which, as Sedlmayr pointed out, had already become obsolete during Riegl's lifetime" (Zerner 180). In *The Problem of Form in Painting and Sculpture* (1893), Adolf Hildebrand argues that the principles governing the construction of forms "must come from our perception of space. The artist's activity consists, then, in further developing such of his faculties as provide him with spatial perception, namely his faculties of sight and touch. These two different means of perceiving the same phenomenon not only have separate existence in our faculties for sight and touch, but are united in the eye. . . . An artistic talent consists in having these two functions precisely and harmoniously related. To set forth the consequences of this relation has been my chief object in this work" (Hildebrand 14). Hildebrand posits two modes of seeing an object: a purely visual *Fernbild* or "distance picture," and a "mixed visual-kinesthetic" view of the object at close hand. The object seen from afar may be taken in at a single glance, whereas the nearer view requires movement of the eye and head and a synthesis of multiple images of the same object. As one comes within reach of the object, touch and sight reinforce each other as the object's contours are felt and seen; hence, it is kinesthetic vision that combines the visual and the tactile in a single kind of seeing. The artist's problem is to combine the *Fernbild* and kinesthetic vision in a unified artistic form, which goes beyond the object's mere visual appearance (its "perceptual form") as grasped from a particular angle in a single situation and represents its "actual form," which is "independent of the object's changing appearances" (Hildebrand 36).

Although Riegl adopts both the optical-tactile and the "distance picture"–"near picture" oppositions, he makes a very different use of them than does Hildebrand. Riegl's effort is to differentiate various historical periods and their aesthetics through this opposition, whereas Hildebrand seeks fundamental principles for a universal artistic practice. It should be noted that Hildebrand's concept of a tactile, kinesthetic vision need not be rejected simply because his theory of perception is faulty. Riegl's notion of the haptic, finally, is primarily a phenomenological and aesthetic concept.

5. Although Maldiney speaks frequently of a sequence of moments (first the systolic, then the diastolic moment), he also indicates that the two are parallel

(Maldiney 190). Hence, one should regard the sequence as merely a convenient pedagogical fiction and consider the two "moments" as simultaneous processes.

6. Maldiney attributes this view to Riegl, who does say that "the great achievement of Greek art was the emancipation of space relations," and that Greek art "eventually reached the recognition of a kind of space which was cubically enclosed in all three dimensions, but not the one of free space" (Riegl 61). Yet Riegl asserts repeatedly that the development of a cubic space for the figure occurs in late Roman antiquity. Maldiney is less interested than Riegl in the distinction between classical Greek and late Roman art, however, and it would seem that he is simply assimilating Greek and Roman art within a single broad category which he opposes to Byzantine art.

7. In his reading of Riegl, Maldiney regards the optic, *fernsichtig* style of late Roman antiquity as merely the last phase of the dissolution of the classical Greek tactile-optic space. Maldiney subsumes Riegl's opposition of the ancient suppression of infinite space to the modern depiction of infinite space within the haptic/optic opposition. Maldiney finds suggestions within Riegl's work, reinforced by comments of Riegl's follower Wilhelm Worringer, that Byzantine art indeed represents for Riegl the fulfillment of an unlimited, optic space. In the introduction to *Spätrömische Kunstindustrie*, Riegl does briefly contrast Byzantine and late Roman mosaics, saying that "the gold ground of the Byzantine mosaic, which generally excludes the background and is a seeming regression, is no longer a ground plane but an ideal spatial ground which the people of the west subsequently were able to populate with real objects and to expand toward infinite depth. Antiquity knew unity and infinity only on the plane. Modern art, however, searches for both in deep space; late Roman art stands exactly in between because it has separated the individual figure from the plane and thus overcome the fiction of a level ground which gives birth to everything. Yet still following antiquity it recognizes space as an enclosed individual (cubic) shape and not yet as an infinite free space" (Riegl 12–13). Clearly, Maldiney is right that Riegl grants Byzantine art a pivotal role in the development of modern infinite space, but it is less certain that Riegl's haptic/optic distinction is synonymous with the distinction between the ancient plane and modern space.

8. See MP 614–24; 492–99, QP 172–73; 182–83, PP 95; 67. Deleuze and Guattari treat Riegl, Maldiney, and Worringer in their discussion of smooth and striated space in *A Thousand Plateaus*, arguing that Riegl, Maldiney, and Worringer all associate the haptic with Egyptian art, and hence with an imperial regime, thereby betraying the essentially nomadic nature of the haptic. Worringer's Gothic line is haptic and nomadic, they argue, and must be opposed to the Egyptian line, which subordinates the hand to the eye within a striated space (what Deleuze refers to in FB as a tactile-optic space). Worringer betrays his own discovery in not recognizing the Gothic line's disruption of striated space.

9. Color theorists generally identify three dimensions of color: value, hue, and saturation. Deleuze appears to include saturation within the category of value in this passage, but later he speaks of saturation as a means of modulating hue without relating it to value: "Now, if initially modulation could still be obtained through

differences of value (as in [Bacon's] 'Three Figures at the Base of a Crucifixion' of 1944), it appears soon that it must consist solely of internal variations of intensity or saturation, and that these variations themselves change according to relations of vicinity of this or that zone of the flat background" (FB 94).

10. Deleuze may well have in mind Gowing's analysis of Cézanne's schematic modeling of forms according to sequences of juxtaposed hues organized around a culminating point: "Cézanne pursued his discovery that colors placed in order one against another carried an inherent suggestion of changes of plane. The series of colors, always in the order of the spectrum and always placed at regular intervals along it, mounted toward a culminating point; beyond that point, where it was repeated in the opposite order in the watercolors of the nineties, it gave a sense both of melodic response and of the continuous curvature of the surface. Cézanne was quite explicit about this; 'the contrast and connection of colors,' he told Bernard, '—there you have the secret of drawing and modeling' " (Gowing 59).

11. Deleuze cites Maldiney (241–46), who in turn comments on Grabar's analyses. That Byzantine art stresses value over hue is confirmed by James's recent study of light and color in Byzantine mosaics and painting. She argues that the modern stress on hue distorts the Byzantine sense of color, and that qualities of brightness, intensity, texture, and reflectivity were much more important for their sense of color than for our own. The color vocabulary of Greek antiquity, which was adopted by Byzantine commentators on art, was vague in regard to hue, and color differentiations often make more sense if interpreted in terms of gray-scale gradations from bright to dark. Representations of rainbows in Byzantine art, she shows, confirm this emphasis of value over hue (James 91–109).

12. *The Adeline Art Dictionary,* for example, in the entry "colorist" identifies as colorists Titian, Veronese, Ribera, Velásquez, Rubens, Rembrandt, Delacroix, and the Pre-Raphaelites.

13. The venerable concept of "local tone," or "local color," enunciated frequently in Renaissance commentaries on painting, presumes that objects have inherent, "true" colors, and that shifts in color created by contextual variables—effects of light and shadow, contiguity to contrasting colors, etc.—are secondary modifications of those true colors. An object's "local color" is its true color, which Renaissance painters were frequently encouraged to render in their works. Of course, colorists would deny that such a thing as "local color" exists at all.

14. Gowing stresses the rational side of Cézanne's enterprise, observing that Cézanne's effort is to develop a "logic of *organized* sensation," one that involves both immediate sense experience and the operations of abstract thought. The spectral sequence does not occur in nature in the modeling of observed objects, but the optical effect of that sequence, discovered through logical analysis, renders natural effects in a mode that corresponds to sense experience. "When one of [Cézanne's] visitors was puzzled to find him painting a grey wall green, he explained that a sense of color was developed not only by work but by reasoning. In fact the need was both emotional and intellectual" (Gowing 57–58). Hence Cézanne's vision, in the words of his friend Emile Bernard, "was much more in his brain than in his eye" (ibid. 59).

15. The English edition of *The Complete Letters of Vincent van Gogh* mistakenly identifies the passage from Blanc's *Les Artistes de mon temps* (pp. 64–66) as "the French pages by Delacroix." Van Gogh interpolates Blanc's footnote reference to Blanc's own *Grammaire des arts du dessin: architecture, sculpture, peinture*, 3rd. edition, in a parenthetic aside midway through the passage, "(*See* his *Grammaire des art de* [sic] *dessin*, 3rd ed. Renouard.)," but in such a way that the casual reader would assume that the *Grammaire des arts du dessin* is by Delacroix (since Blanc is nowhere mentioned by name, and the immediate antecedent for "his" in "his *Grammaire*" is Delacroix). It should be noted that one of the striking passages Deleuze cites as van Gogh's is actually by Blanc: "When the complementary colors are produced in equal strength, that is to say in the same degree of vividness and brightness, their juxtaposition will raise them both to an intensity so violent that human eyes will scarcely be able to bear the sight of it" (Blanc 65; van Gogh 2, 365). Conversely, what appears to be the concluding sentence of the passage attributed by the van Gogh correspondence editors to Delacroix (and cited by Deleuze) does not occur in *Les Artistes de mon temps*: "In order to intensify and to harmonize the effect of his colors he used the contrast of the complementary and the concord of the analogous colors at the same time; or in other terms, the repetition of a vivid tint by the same broken tone" (van Gogh 2, 366). It would seem that this sentence is van Gogh's own summary comment on Blanc's passage, and that the "he" van Gogh is referring to is Delacroix.

16. Modulation is an important term for Cézanne. Among the "opinions" of Cézanne published by Emile Bernard (with Cézanne's permission) in 1904, the following are particularly noteworthy in this regard: "To read nature is to see it, as if through a veil, in terms of an interpretation in patches of color following one another according to a law of harmony. These major hues are thus analyzed through modulations. Painting is classifying one's sensations of color." "One should not say modeling, one should say *modulation*." "There is no such thing as line or modeling, there are only contrasts." "The contrast and connection of colors—there you have the secret of drawing and modeling" (Cézanne 36). Gowing convincingly argues that Cézanne's famous remark about the primacy of sphere, cylinder, and cone in nature simply reflects his observation that the visual field is essentially curved rather than flat, and that the "modeling" of objects in painting consists above all in the rendering of curved surfaces. Cézanne's discovery that spectral sequences of color create movements of recession and procession allowed him to model curved surfaces through a modulated sequence of discrete strokes. As Gowing notes, when Cézanne speaks of modulation "it is difficult to know how many of the associations of the word *moduler* were intended. Perhaps all of them. The meaning of tempering, the employing of a standard measure, and the musical analogy itself may all have played some part" (Gowing 59). The musical analogy, as I understand it, is that of modulation as a movement that entails a transposition from one key to another. In this sense, the colors of the spectrum (red–orange–yellow–green–blue–violet) would correspond to the twelve notes of the musical chromatic scale, the initial hue of a particular sequence (e.g., red or yellow) to the tonic of a given key, the relationship between two sequences that commence with

different initial hues representing a transposition of keys (e.g., sequence 1: red–orange–yellow–green; sequence 2: yellow–green–blue–violet).

17. Gowing observes that Cézanne's sequences of color patches that follow the order of the spectrum "imply not only volumes but axes, armatures at right angles to the chromatic progressions which state the rounded surfaces of forms" (Gowing 66). In many of the late paintings, the color patches "create an invisible upright scaffolding around which the hues fan out like a peacock's tail" (Gowing 66–67). Deleuze relates this question of scaffolding or armature to the general problem of the ground as structuring force and its relation to individual forms. Cézanne's method raises problems in the delineation of forms, since "there is an optimum size for the units that touch off the sense of color interval. The patches must be large enough to remain perceptible in their own right—which prevents them from particularizing specific objects" (Gowing 67).

18. Deleuze offers as an example of this practice van Gogh's 1888 *Portrait of Joseph Roulin* (Museum of Fine Arts, Boston). In a letter to Emile Bernard (early August 1888), van Gogh says of this painting, "I have just done a portrait of a postman. . . . A blue, nearly white background on the white canvas, all the broken tones in the face— yellows, greens, violets, pinks, reds" (van Gogh 3, 510). One might suggest as additional examples van Gogh's *Portrait of Joseph Roulin* (collection of Mr. And Mrs. Walter B. Ford II), *Portrait of Patience Escalier* (private collection), *Self-Portrait* (1888, Fogg Art Museum, Harvard University), and *Portrait of Joseph Roulin* (Art Museum, Winterthur).

19. Bacon's use of broken tones to render his figures is not as clearly illustrated in his 1946 *Painting* as in his later works, particularly the triptychs of the 1960s and 1970s. The man of *Painting* is painted mostly in black, gray and brown. But Deleuze points out that the colorist gray differs fundamentally from the gray based on relations of value. The colorist gray is produced by the blending of equal amounts of complementary colors, red-green grays, blue-yellow grays, purple-orange grays, not through the mixture of black and white. And colorists insist that for them black and white are colors that have a function unrelated to relations of value. As van Gogh writes Emile Bernard in 1888, "Suffice it to say that black and white are also colors, for in many cases they can be looked upon as colors, for their simultaneous contrast is as striking as that of green and red, for instance" (van Gogh 3, 490).

20. As Bacon remarks, the accident that led him from a bird's landing in a field to the 1946 *Painting* was "one continuous accident mounting on top of another," something he "gradually made," but the accident also "suddenly suggested the whole image." As Deleuze comments, the diagram suggests both a *series,* a compositional sequence or process, and a *whole* (*ensemble*), a configuration of relations.

CHAPTER SEVEN

1. This taxonomy of sensations, of course, is a reprise of Deleuze's classification of forces in Bacon's paintings—forces of deformation, forces of coupling, forces of separation (see chapter 5).

2. I suspect that Deleuze and Guattari may have recalled Maldiney's Heideggerian meditation on the monument in developing this concept (Maldiney 174–82). The

monument is *Denkmal,* both sign (*denken* = to think) and body (*Mal* = mark; *malen* = to paint). The monolith is the simplest and most ancient of monuments, and the prototype of all artworks, a surging forth of a self-forming form. In Maldiney's analysis, nature itself forms monuments, the Matterhorn being a self-forming form that surges forth from a chaotic un-foundation (*Ungrund*), and in forming itself through a founding rhythm establishes its surrounding landscape as its foundation (*Grund*). These themes are of course central to Maldiney's treatment of Cézanne and to Deleuze's discussion of Bacon (see chapter 5).

3. It must be admitted that Deleuze and Guattari's treatment of the relationship between artistic and physico-biological creation is rather cryptic. What follows is thus a somewhat speculative reconstruction of their argument. In a 1988 interview, Deleuze said that he and Guattari planned to resume their collective enterprise and produce "a sort of philosophy of Nature" (PP 212; 155). No doubt many of the ensuing points would have been clarified had Deleuze and Guattari completed such a work.

4. It is important not to mistake Deleuze and Guattari's discussion of the conceptual persona of the "idiot" for a treatment of the motif of the "idiot" in its current vernacular sense. On Nicholas's use of the terms *ignorans* and *idiota* (evident in the titles of his *De Docta Ignorantia, Idiota de Sapientia, Idiota de Mente, and Idiota de Staticis Experimentis*) see Gandillac, especially 63–66; on the figure of Descartes's "Eudoxe," see Alquié's commentary in Descartes, vol. 2, p. 1108; on Kierkegaard and the impossible, see Shestov's essay "Kierkegaard and Dostoyevsky," in *Kierkegaard and the Existential Philosophy,* 1–28.

5. Deleuze and Guattari's reference to Ruyer appears in the observation that "vitalism has always had two possible interpretations: that of an Idea that acts, but that is not, that hence acts solely from the point of view of an external cerebral knowledge (from Kant to Claude Bernard); or that of a force that is, but that does not act, hence that is a pure internal Sensing [*Sentir*] (from Leibniz to Ruyer)" (QP 201; 213). Deleuze and Guattari here seem to be making use of chapter 18 of Ruyer's *Néo-finalisme,* in which Ruyer criticizes Kant, Claude Bernard, and various "organicists" for explaining biological morphogenesis in terms of a directing vital "idea" that is separated from physical force. Ruyer argues that vital and physical force are one, though the microscopic manifestation of force at the level of molecular bondings "is indissociable from a true form, from a veritable domain of overflight" (Ruyer 1952; 221), and such microscopic forces differ in quantity and mode of relation from macroscopic forces. As will become evident, only in a loose sense do I see Ruyer as positing a "force that does not act." Deleuze discusses the Leibnizian notion of a force that does not act in chapter 8 of *The Fold,* concluding that "the soul is the principle of life through its presence and not through its action. *Force is presence and not action*" (LP 162; 119). For an excellent discussion of the relation of Ruyer's thought to *What Is Philosophy?,* see Bains.

6. Deleuze and Guattari offer little clarification of this issue in *What Is Philosophy?,* but I find broad confirmation of this reading in Deleuze's presentation of the Leibnizian virtual and possible in *The Fold.* Deleuze argues that for Leibniz the

virtual is *actualized* in monads, whereas the possible is *realized* in bodies: "The world is a virtuality which is actualized in the monads, or souls, but also a possibility that must be realized in matter, or bodies" (LP 140; 104). Deleuze diagrams this relationship with a wavy line that splits into two divergent arrowed lines:

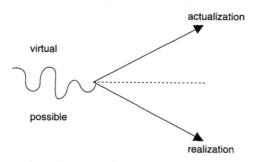

This Leibnizian scheme is by no means directly applicable to *What Is Philosophy?* (Deleuze and Guattari make no parallel distinction between actualization and realization, nor do they advocate a straightforward Leibnizian monadism), but I believe Deleuze and Guattari make use of the Leibnizian notion of the possible in part to suggest a similar affinity both between the virtual and the possible and between the possible and bodies.

Works Cited

The Adeline Art Dictionary. Trans. Hugo G. Beigel. 1891. Reprint, New York: Frederick Ungar, 1966.

Alliez, Eric. *La Signature du monde, ou qu'est-ce que la philosophie de Deleuze et Guattari.* Paris: Cerf, 1993.

Altum, Bernard. *Der Vogel und sein Leben.* 1868. Reprint, New York: Arno, 1978.

Ansell Pearson, Keith. *Germinal Life: The Difference and Repetition of Deleuze.* London: Routledge, 1999.

Bains, Paul. "Subjectless Subjectivities." *Canadian Review of Comparative Literature* 24 (September 1997): 511–28.

Barraqué, Jean. *Debussy.* Paris: Seuil, 1962.

Beckett, Samuel. *Three Novels by Samuel Beckett: Molloy, Malone Dies, The Unnamable.* New York: Grove Press, 1965.

Bensmaïa, Réda. "The Kafka Effect." Trans. Terry Cochran. In Gilles Deleuze and Félix Guattari, *Kafka: Toward a Minor Literature,* ix–xxi. Minneapolis: University of Minnesota Press, 1986.

———. "On the Concept of Minor Literature: From Kafka to Kateb Yacine." In *Gilles Deleuze and the Theater of Philosophy,* ed. Constantin V. Boundas and Dorothea Olkowski, 213–28. New York: Routledge, 1994.

———. "Traduire ou 'blanchir' la langue: Amour bilingue d'Abdelkebir Khatibi." *Hors Cadre* 3 (Spring 1985): 187–206.

———. "Les Transformateurs-Deleuze ou le cinéma comme automate spirituel." *Quaderni di Cinema / Studio* 7–8 (July–December 1992): 103–16.

Berio, Luciano. *Two Interviews: With Rossana Dalmonte and Bálint András Varga.* Trans. and ed. David Osmond-Smith. New York: Marion Boyars, 1985.

Blanc, Charles. *Les Artistes de mon temps.* Paris: Firmin-Didot, 1876.

———. *Grammaire des arts du dessin: architecture, sculpture, peinture.* 3rd ed. Paris: Renouard, 1876.

Bogue, Ronald. *Deleuze and Guattari.* London: Routledge, 1989.

———. *Deleuze on Cinema.* New York: Routledge, 2003.

Bomford, David. "The History of Colour in Art." In *Colour: Art and Science,* ed. Trevor Lamb and Janine Bourriau, 7-30. Cambridge: Cambridge University Press, 1995.

Boulez, Pierre. *Notes of an Apprenticeship.* Trans. Herbert Weinstock. New York: Knopf, 1968.

Boundas, Constantin V. "Deleuze-Bergson: An Ontology of the Virtual." In *Deleuze: A Critical Reader,* ed. Paul Patton, 81-106. London: Blackwell, 1996.

Braidotti, Rosi. "Discontinuing Becomings: Deleuze on Becoming-Woman in Philosophy." *Journal of the British Society for Phenomenology* 24 (January 1993): 44-55.

Brelet, Gisèle. "Béla Bartók." In *Histoire de la musique,* ed. Alexis Roland-Manuel, vol. 2, 1036-74. Paris: Gallimard, 1963.

Buchanan, Ian. *Deleuzism: A Metacommentary.* Durham, N.C.: Duke University Press, 2000.

Buchanan, Ian, and Claire Colebrook, Eds. *Deleuze and Feminist Theory.* Edinburgh: Edinburgh University Press, 2000.

Butler, Samuel. *Life and Habit.* 1877. Reprint, London: Jonathan Cape, 1923.

Buydens, Mireille. *Sahara: L'Esthétique de Gilles Deleuze.* Paris: Vrin, 1990.

Capra, Fritjof. *The Web of Life: A New Scientific Understanding of Living Systems.* New York: Anchor, 1996.

Cézanne, Paul. *Conversations avec Cézanne.* Ed. P. M. Doran. Paris: Macula, 1978.

Chadwick, Henry. *Boethius: The Consolations of Music, Logic, Theology, and Philosophy.* Oxford: Clarendon, 1981.

Colebrook, Claire. *Gilles Deleuze.* London: Routledge, 2001.

Colombat, André. *Deleuze et la littérature.* New York: Peter Lang, 1990.

De Bruyne, Edgar. *The Esthetics of the Middle Ages.* Trans. Eileen B. Hennessy. New York: Frederick Ungar, 1969.

De Franciscis, Alfonso. *La Pittura di Pompei.* Milan: Jaca, 1991, plate 170, Villa c. D. Di Arianna (Antiquarium).

Demus, Otto. *Byzantine Mosaic Decoration: Aspects of Monumental Art in Byzantium.* Boston: Boston Book and Art Shop, 1955.

Dent, Edward J. *Opera.* Harmondsworth, U.K.: Penguin, 1940.

Duthuit, Georges. *Le Feu des signes.* Geneva: Skira, 1962.

Eibl-Eibesfeldt, Irenäus. *Ethology: The Biology of Behavior.* Trans. Erich Klinghammer. 2nd ed. New York: Holt, Rinehart & Winston, 1975.

Eisenstein, Sergei. *Film Form and Film Sense.* Trans. Jay Leyda. New York: Meridian Books, 1957.

Fernandez, Dominique. *La Rose des Tudors.* Paris: Julliard, 1976.

Gandillac, Maurice Patronnier de. *La Philosophie de Nicolas de Cues.* Paris: Aubier, 1941.

Gilliard, E. Thomas. *Birds of Paradise and Bower Birds.* London: Weidenfeld & Nicolson, 1969.

Gogh, Vincent van. *The Complete Letters of Vincent van Gogh.* (No translator indicated.) 3 vols. Boston: Bulfinch Press, 1991.

Goléa, Antoine. *Rencontres avec Olivier Messiaen.* Paris: Julliard, 1960.

Goodchild, Philip. *Deleuze and Guattari: An Introduction to the Politics of Desire.* Thousand Oaks, Calif.: Sage, 1996.

——. *Gilles Deleuze and the Question of Philosophy.* Madison, N.J.: Fairleigh Dickinson University Press, 1996.

Goodwin, Brian. *How the Leopard Changed Its Spots: The Evolution of Complexity.* New York: Touchstone, 1994.

Gowing, Lawrence. "The Logic of Organized Sensations." In *Cézanne: The Late Work,* ed. William Rubin, 55-71. New York: Museum of Modern Art, 1977.

Grabar, André. *Byzantine Painting.* Trans. Stuart Gilbert. Geneva: Skira, 1953.

Griffiths, Paul. *Olivier Messiaen and the Music of Time.* Ithaca: Cornell University Press, 1985.

Griggers, Camilla. *Becoming-Woman.* Minneapolis: University of Minnesota Press, 1997.

Grosz, Elizabeth. "A Thousand Tiny Sexes: Feminism and Rhizomatics." In *Gilles Deleuze and the Theater of Philosophy,* ed. Constantin V. Boundas and Dorothea Olkowski, 187-210. New York: Routledge, 1994.

Grout, Donald Jay. *A History of Western Music.* New York: Norton, 1960.

Guthrie, W. K. C. *A History of Greek Philosophy. Vol. 1, The Earlier Presocratics and the Pythagoreans.* Cambridge: Cambridge University Press, 1962.

Halbreich, Harry. *Olivier Messiaen.* Paris: Fayard, 1980.

Hardt, Michael. *Gilles Deleuze: An Apprenticeship in Philosophy.* Minneapolis: University of Minnesota Press, 1993.

Hartshorne, Charles. "The Relation of Bird Song to Music." *Ibis* 100 (1958): 421–45.

Hewson, John. *The Cognitive System of the French Verb.* Philadelphia: John Benjamins, 1997.

Hildebrand, Adolf. *The Problem of Form in Painting and Sculpture.* Trans. Max Meyer and Robert Morris Ogden. 2nd ed. 1893. Reprint, New York: G. E. Stechert, 1932.

Hinde, R. A. "The Biological Significance of the Territories of Birds." *Ibis* 98 (1956): 340–69.

Holland, Eugene W. *Deleuze and Guattari's Anti-Oedipus: Introduction to Schizoanalysis.* London: Routledge, 1999.

——. "Deterritorializing 'Deterritorialization'—From the *Anti-Oedipus* to *A Thousand Plateaus.*" *SubStance* 66 (1991): 55–65.

——. "Schizoanalysis and Baudelaire: Some Illustrations of Decoding at Work." In *Deleuze: A Critical Reader,* ed. Paul Patton, 240–56. London: Blackwell, 1996.

Howard, Henry Eliot. *Territory in Bird Life.* 1920. Reprint, London: Collins, 1948.

Hume, David. *A Treatise of Human Nature.* Ed. L. A. Selby-Bigge. Oxford: Clarendon, 1988.

James, Liz. *Light and Colour in Byzantine Art.* Oxford: Clarendon, 1996.

Jeffers, Jennifer M. "The Image of Thought: Achromatics in O'Keeffe and Beckett." *Mosaic* 29 (1996): 59–78.

Johnson, Robert Sherlaw. *Messiaen.* Berkeley: University of California Press, 1975.

Kennedy, Barbara M. *Deleuze and Cinema: The Aesthetics of Sensation.* Edinburgh: Edinburgh University Press, 2000.

Klee, Paul. *Notebooks.* Ed. Jürg Spiller. Vol. 1. Trans. Ralph Manheim. New York: Wittenborn Art Books, 1961.

——. *Paul Klee: On Modern Art.* Trans. Paul Findlay. London: Faber & Faber, 1948.

Lambert, Gregg. *The Non-Philosophy of Gilles Deleuze.* London: Continuum Books, 2002.

Leroi-Gourhan, André. *Le Geste et la parole.* Vol. 1, *Technique et langage.* Paris: Albin Michel, 1964.

Lippman, Edward A. *Musical Thought in Ancient Greece.* 1964. New York: Da Capo Press, 1975.

Lizot, Jacques. *Le Cercle des feux.* Paris: Seuil, 1976.

Lorenz, Konrad. *On Aggression.* Trans. Marjorie Kerr Wilson. New York: Harcourt, Brace & World, 1966.

Lyotard, Jean-François. *Discours, figure.* Paris: Klincksieck, 1971.

Maldiney, Henri. *Regard Parole Espace.* Lausanne: Editions l'Age d'Homme, 1973.

Manning, Peter. *Electronic and Computer Music.* 2nd ed. Oxford: Clarendon, 1993.

Margulis, Lynn, and Dorion Sagan. *Microcosmos.* New York: Summit, 1986.

Marshall, A. J. *Bower-Birds: Their Displays and Breeding Cycles.* Oxford: Clarendon, 1954.

Massumi, Brian. *A User's Guide to Capitalism and Schizophrenia: Deviations from Deleuze and Guattari.* Cambridge, Mass.: MIT Press, 1992.

Maturana, Humberto, and Francisco J. Varela. *Autopoiesis and Cognition.* Dordrecht, Netherlands: D. Reidel, 1980.

——. *The Tree of Knowledge: The Biological Roots of Human Understanding.* Boston: Shambhala, 1987.

May, Todd. *Reconsidering Difference: Nancy, Derrida, Levinas, and Deleuze.* University Park, Pa.: Pennsylvania State University Press, 1997.

Mayr, Ernst. "Bernard Altum and the Territory Theory." *Proceedings of the Linnaean Society, New York* 45–46 (1935): 24–30.

McClary, Susan. "The Politics of Silence and Sound." Afterword to *Noise: The Political Economy of Music*, by Jacques Attali. Trans. Brian Massumi, 149–60. Minneapolis: University of Minnesota Press, 1985.

Merleau-Ponty, Maurice. *The Visible and the Invisible*. Trans. Alphonso Lingis. Evanston, Ill.: Northwestern University Press, 1968.

Messiaen, Olivier. *The Technique of My Musical Language*. Trans. John Satterfield. 2 vols. Paris: Alphonse Leduc, 1956.

Moffat, C. B. "The Spring Rivalry of Birds." *Irish Naturalist* 12 (1903): 152–66.

Moré, Marcel. *Le Dieu Mozart et le monde des oiseaux*. Paris: Gallimard, 1971.

Mras, George P. *Eugène Delacroix's Theory of Art*. Princeton, N.J.: Princeton University Press, 1966.

Nichols, Roger. *Messiaen*. London: Oxford University Press, 1975.

Noble, G. K. "The Role of Dominance on the Social Life of Birds." *Auk* 56 (1939): 263–73.

Olkowski, Dorothea. *Gilles Deleuze and the Ruin of Representation*. Berkeley: University of California Press, 1999.

Osmond-Smith, David. *Berio*. Oxford: Oxford University Press, 1991.

Ouellette, Fernand. *Edgard Varèse*. Trans. Derek Coltman. New York: Orion Press, 1968.

Oyama, Susan. *The Ontogeny of Information: Developmental Systems and Evolution*. Cambridge, U.K.: Cambridge University Press, 1985.

Pächt, Otto. "Art Historians and Art Critics—VI: Alois Riegl." *Burlington Magazine* 105 (April 1963): 188–93.

Paris, Jean. *L'Espace et le regard*. Paris: Seuil, 1965.

Patton, Paul. *Deleuze and the Political: Thinking the Political*. London: Routledge, 2000.

Périer, Alain. *Messiaen*. Paris: Seuil, 1979.

Plotinus. *The Enneads*. Trans. Stephen MacKenna, 4th ed. New York: Pantheon, 1969.

Rajchman, John. *The Deleuze Connections*. Cambridge, Mass.: MIT Press, 2000.

Riegl, Alois. *Late Roman Art Industry*. Trans. Rolf Winkes. Rome: Giorgio Bretschneider, 1985.

Riley, Bridget. "Colour for the Painter." In *Colour: Art and Science*, ed. Trevor Lamb and Janine Bourriau, 31–64. Cambridge, U.K.: Cambridge University Press, 1995.

Rodowick, D. N. *Gilles Deleuze's Time Machine*. Durham, N.C.: Duke University Press, 1997.

Rößler, Almut. *Contributions to the Spiritual World of Olivier Messiaen*. Trans. Barbara Dagg and Nancy Poland. Duisburg, Germany: Gilles & Francke, 1986.

Russell, James A. and José Miguel Fernández-Dols, eds. *The Psychology of Facial Expression*. Cambridge, U.K.: Cambridge University Press, 1997.

Ruyer, Raymond. *La Conscience et le corps*. Paris: Presses Universitaires de France, 1937.

——. *Eléments de psycho-biologie*. Paris: Presses Universitaires de France, 1946.

——. *La Genèse des formes vivantes*. Paris: Flammarion, 1958.

——. *Néo-finalisme*. Paris: Presses Universitaires de France, 1952.

Samuel, Claude. *Conversations with Olivier Messiaen*. Trans. Felix Aprahamian. London: Steiner & Bell, 1976.

Sartori, Claudio, "Giuseppe Verdi." In *Histoire de la musique*, ed. Roland Manuel, vol. 2, 620–56. Paris: Gallimard, 1963.

Sartre, Jean-Paul. *Being and Nothingness*. Trans. Hazel E. Barnes. New York: Philosophical Library, 1956.

Say, Albert. *Music in the Medieval World*. 2nd ed. Englewood Cliffs, N.J.: Prentice-Hall, 1975.

Schapiro, Meyer. "Style." In *Anthropology Today*, ed. A. L. Kroeber, 287–312. Chicago: University of Chicago Press, 1953.

Shestov, Lev. *Kierkegaard and the Existential Philosophy*. Trans. Elinor Hewitt. Athens, Ohio: Ohio University Press, 1969.

Simondon, Gilbert. *L'Individu et sa genèse physico-biologique*. Paris: Press Universitaires de France, 1964.

Smith, Daniel W. " 'A Life of Pure Immanence': Deleuze's 'Critique et Clinique' Project." In *Gilles Deleuze, Essays Critical and Clinical*, trans. Daniel W. Smith and Michael A. Greco. Minneapolis: University of Minnesota Press, 1997.

——. "Deleuze's Theory of Sensation: Overcoming the Kantian Duality." In *Deleuze: A Critical Reader*, ed. Paul Patton, 29-56. London: Blackwell, 1996.

Spitzer, Leo. *Classical and Christian Ideas of World Harmony*. Ed. Anna Granville Hatcher. Baltimore: Johns Hopkins University Press, 1963.

Stewart, Andrew. *Greek Sculpture: An Exploration*. New Haven, Conn.: Yale University Press, 1990, vol. 2, plate 61, Funerary monument erected by Amphalkes to Dermys and Kittylos, from Tanagra (Boeotia), ca. 600-575, limestone, ht. 1.47 m., Athens.

Stivale, Charles J. *The Two-Fold Thought of Deleuze and Guattari: Intersections and Animations*. New York: Guilford, 1998.

Stokes, Allen W., Ed. *Territory*. Stroudsburg, Pa.: Dowden, Hutchinson & Ross, 1974.

Straus, Erwin. *The Primary World of Senses: A Vindication of Sensory Experience*. Trans. Jacob Needleman. 2nd ed. New York: Free Press, 1963.

Sylvester, David. *The Brutality of Fact: Interviews with Francis Bacon*. 3rd ed., expanded. New York: Thames & Hudson, 1987.

Thorpe, W. H. *Bird-Song: The Biology of Vocal Communication and Expression in Birds*. Cambridge, U.K.: Cambridge University Press, 1961.

Uexküll, Jakob von. *Mondes animaux et monde humain, suivi de Théorie de la signification*. Trans. Phillippe Muller. Paris: Gonthier, 1956.

Van Solkema, Sherman, Ed. *The New Worlds of Edgard Varèse: A Symposium*. Institute for Studies in American Music Monographs number 11. New York: ISAM, 1979.

Varela, Francisco J., Evan Thompson, and Eleanor Rosch. *The Embodied Mind: Cognitive Science and Human Experience*. Cambridge, Mass.: MIT Press, 1991.

Virilio, Paul, *L'Insécurité du territoire*. Paris: Stock, 1977.

Vivier, Odile, *Varèse*. Paris: Seuil, 1973.

Wilden, Anthony. *System and Structure: Essays in Communication and Exchange*. London: Tavistock, 1972.

Worringer, Wilhelm. *Abstraction and Empathy: A Contribution to the Psychology of Style*. Trans. Michael Bullock. 1908. Reprint, New York: International Universities Press, 1953.

Worringer, Wilhelm. *Form in Gothic*. Trans. Sir Herbert Read. 1912. Reprint, London: Alec Tiranti, 1957.

Zerner, Henri. "Alois Riegl: Art, Value, and Historicism." *Daedalus* 105 (Winter 1976): 177-88.

Zourabichvili, François. *Deleuze: une philosophie de l'évènement*. Paris: Presses Universitaires de France, 1994.

Index

absolute surface, 173, 175. *See also* overflight (*survol*)

abstract machine: of faciality, 90–95, 105, 158, 190; of the plane of consistency, 170

abstraction and empathy (Worringer), 147

actual, the. *See* virtual, the

added values, 26. *See also* Messiaen

affects. *See* percepts and affects

aggression and territoriality, 56–57

aion and chronos, 16, 28, 34, 91, 129, 153, 171, 198n. 11

Alliez, Eric, 200n. 4

Altum, Bernard, 56

analogical: geometry, 132–33; languages, 132–33, 135, 155, 158; modulation, 134–36, 155

analogue versus digital synthesizers, 133–34, 202n. 2

Artaud, Antonin, 124

Attali, Jacques, 13

autopoiesis, 66–67. *See also* Maturana, Humberto; Varela, Francisco

Bacon, Francis: and broken tones, 154, 190, 207n. 19; and face/head 106, 111–12; and the diagram, 123–24, 149, 155–57, 189, 207n. 20; and fact, 112, 122–23, 130–31, 158–60, 189, 194; and the figural, 131–32, 201–02n. 2; and the history of painting,

145, 190; and illustration, 121–22, 131; and provisional organs, 126; and the possible, 177; and rhythmic characters, 128–29; and sensation, 112, 121–22, 124–25, 164, 189, 202n. 2; as colorist, 130, 135–36, 151, 189; forces in, 127–30, 189, 207n. 1, 207–08n. 2; on multiple figures in painting, 202n. 4; *Painting* (1946), 122–23, 155–56, 207n. 19–20; Structure, Contour and Figure in, 126–27, 153

Bartók, Béla, 48–50

Baugin, Lubin, 99

Beckett, Samuel, 71–72, 75

becoming, 23, 29–30, 34–35, 43, 75, 164–67, 170–71, 176–77: becoming-animal, 29, 34–35, 75, 110–12, 126–27, 149, 164–65; becoming-child, 34–36, 75, 109; becoming-woman, 33–36, 75, 109, 198n. 1

Beethoven, Ludwig von, 38

Bergson, Henri, 197n. 6

Berio, Luciano, 50–52, 190

Bernard, Claude, 208n. 5

black hole (faciality), 89–92, 103, 107, 190, 201n. 1–2. *See also* white wall (faciality)

Blanc, Charles, 151–52, 206n. 15

body without organs, 124–26, 130, 159

Boethius, 16, 197n. 5

Boulez, Pierre, 34, 38, 121

Bonnard, Pierre, 103

217

Lightning Source UK Ltd.
Milton Keynes UK
UKOW06f0103261017

311638UK00005B/553/P

9 780415 966085